The Marxist Theory of Party: Classics, Innovations and the Communist Party of China

Wu Meihua
Translated by Wang Qin

CANut

Originally published as Marxist Theories of Party and Party Building in 2007
by China Renmin University Press.

Original Chinese Edition Copyright © 2007 by Wu Meihua
ISBN: 978-7-300-07617-1

The Marxist Theory of Party: Classics, Innovations and the Communist Party
of China
ISBN: 978-3-942575-01-0

Published by
Canut International Publishers
Yorck Street. 66
10965 Kreuzberg
Berlin-Germany

Canut International Publishers
12a Guernsey Road E11
London 4BJ–England-U.K.

URL: http//www.canut.us
E-Mail: canut@aol.com

Acknowledgements

Over the years, Marxist Theories of Party and Party Building has been a basic course for students at the Department of the History of the Communist Party of China at Renmin University of China. We have compiled this book as a reference book for young scholars and for those interested in the subject. When compiling this book, we have sorted out the theoretical history, explained basic principles and also tried to discuss several realistic problems. We would like to note thankfully that we have benefited from other teaching materials and academic monographs and included abundant research results from other writers. We have earnestly tried to make the book theoretically and realistically as good as possible and forward-looking.

Professor Wu Meihua (doctorial advisor and Doctor of Law) was the chief compiler responsible for compiling the Introduction and Chapters 1, 4, 5, 8 and 12 and editing the whole book. Associate Professor Yang Deshan (doctorial advisor and Doctor of Law) compiled Chapters 2, 3, 6 and 10. Associate Professor Wang Haijun (graduate tutor and Doctor of Law) compiled Chapters 7, 9, and 11.

Here, we would like to extend our sincere gratitude to Acquiring Editor Guo Xiaoming and Editor-in-Charge Fu Aixia from China Renmin University Press, who gave us a lot of help and worked hard to get the book published.

We would appreciate any criticism or suggestions for inaccuracies and omissions that may possibly appear in this book.

Compilers
March 2007

Publisher's Note

This book is from Chinese academy, which studies the most delicate subject of politics—party theory—rarely studied as part of the academy. Marxist parties pursuing power for a new society have a long history since 1847 and have encountered many changes since then. Today, the societal and political conditions in some regions have radically changed, presenting new challenges for Marxist parties. Inner-party or extra-party coalitions with progressive left-wing forces are full in debate and impose new trials on them. And as the argument on the disintegration of proletariat spreads wider, Marx's emphasis of "education of the educators" poses urgency again and adds to the topicality of Marxist party building theories.

After radical changes in Soviet Union and Eastern Europe, it has been proved true that the Marxist party is a key link in building the desired socialist society—the emancipation of the proletariat and humans transcending capitalist society.

Often, many defects of post-capitalist societies were attributed to ruling Marxist parties, their rigid structures, bureaucratization, over-centralization and false interpretation of Marx's relevant ideas. Grave policy mistakes or loss of belief were also considered as part of structural degeneration and distorted class links.

This book offers a realistic approach to the problems in the history of Marxist parties; the historical development of ideas on Marxist party. The book was written by scholars from Renmin University of China, debating problems with their societal and historical environment; suggesting courageous trials, innovations, institutionalization, transparency, inner-party democracy, empowerment of members and supervision from outside the Marxist party. And this book is unique as it studies the concept of the ruling Marxist party more comprehensively, and delves into the less debated parts of the party building theory: party's work style and ideological line concepts.

Readers may find abundant concrete and up-to-date material in this book about the CPC's party building practice and also its recent theoretical and practical course, which has the largest membership in the globe.

Cem Kizilcec
Berlin, November 2010

Introduction

Marxist Theory of Party Building and Academy

Marxist Theory of Party Building is an important part of Marxism. Regarding its theoretical system, it falls into the category of scientific socialism, one of the three components of Marxism. As for its disciplinary position it belongs to the studies of political parties in political science studies. This book tries to explore and establish this theory as an academic discipline and strives to promote the theoretical research and innovate Marxist views in this sphere.

We suggest, Marxist Theory of Party Building as a science should study how the proletarian parties came into being, developed, built themselves and how they have achieved ruling power. Obviously its study object will be proletarian parties, a special type among all the political parties. The term "party" has deep roots in human civilization and was introduced into English language from Latin etymology "pars" whose original meaning is "part." It also means "partner," "troop" and "gathering" and one of its derived meanings is "social or political organization." In ancient Chinese classics, there was only the word "*dang*" (party), rather than "*zhengdang*" (political party). In Chinese, "*dang*" refers to a local grassroots organization, or relatives and friends, or some faction inside the ruling class. In Zhou

Dynasty (1046-256 BC), five tribes or five hundred households constituted a party. In the Spring and Autumn and Warring States periods (770-221 BC), there were such expressions as "*pengdang*" (clique) and "*dangren*" (partisan). And people called low-class mass organizations "*huidang*" (secret society) such as Tiandihui (Heaven and Earth Society), Hongmenhui (Hong Society), Dadaohui (Big Sword Society) and Gelaohui (Society of Brothers). Certainly the above were quite different from contemporary political parties.

There are different theories and definitions about "political parties". Edmund Burke defined a political party as "a body of men united to promote—by their joint endeavors—the national interest of a country, and associated around some particular principles in which they all agree." Another definition assumes that a political party is a political group organized to support candidates for government posts so as to control government bodies. Among abundant definitions given, a part of them indeed seem quite vogue.

A common academic definition could be proposed as follows: A political party is a political organization established by the most conscious elements of a social class, stratum or group who profess the same political doctrine and make coordinated actions for the same interests to ensure the control over the political power and finally realize that doctrine.

A political party is a political organization, but quite different from normal political organizations, because it is stricter and tighter. It is part of the political superstructure, but different from bodies of state power, because a party itself is not an entity of power. It is a social organization, but since it has a definite political goal, it is quite different from other common social groupings.

A political party carries out its activities concentrating on state political power. As a special social and political organization, a political party possesses four distinctive features: Firstly, a political party advocates a political doctrine to express its stand to the society. Secondly, it has a definite goal on which it can base and plan a series of concrete tasks and policies. Thirdly, a party has a sound and stable group of dedicated and respected leaders who generally form a collective. There are also one or two outstanding individuals at the core of this collective who are bound to shoulder the responsibility for leading the whole party. Fourthly, it maintains certain forms of organizations and rules to organize its members and integrate the whole party.

Political parties are not products of natural evolution and will not last forever. They are a kind of historical phenomenon as well as products of social and economic development and class struggle which have emerged at a certain phase in history. Scientifically, political parties have appeared with the occurrence of commodity economy and ideas of freedom and democracy, especially with the establishment of parliaments challenging autocracy. The world's earliest parties had appeared in British parliament, the "Mother of All Parliaments". In the 1670s, the Whig Party and Tory Party were born in the English Bourgeois Revolution with different views debating and wrestling on who would succeed the British throne. In the 1830s, the Whig Party which represented the interests of the industrial bourgeoisie was renamed as Liberal Party, while the Tory Party representing the new noble was renamed Conservative Party. After 150 years of development, they gradually evolved into two major capitalist parties in Britain. In the 19th century, many other political parties appeared and were built in other countries. Statistics show that today there are about 5,000 political parties around the world.

Political parties can be categorized according to different criteria. By origin, they can be divided into endogenous and exogenous parties. By class foundation, they can be divided into proletarian and bourgeois parties. By their social foundation and pattern of their constitutions, they can also be divided into cadre and mass parties. By their position in state politics, they can be divided into ruling and opposition parties. By legal status, they can be divided into lawful and unlawful parties. By the number of seats in the parliament, they can be divided into the majority and minority. By their activity scope, they can be divided into regional, national and international parties. By organizational structure, they can be divided into big and small parties, or tightly- and loosely-organized parties. By the attitude towards capitalism, they can be divided into three types: upholding, improving and opposing capitalism. By their political attitude, parties are divided into the left-wing, the middle and the right-wing. Recently we observe that various political forces are regrouping and reshaping in the contemporary world arena, thus political parties with diversified ideologies are developing and especially nationalist, religious and green-type parties are expanding their ranks.

Proletarian parties appeared after bourgeois parties. At times when the working class was still at the stage of class-in-itself, workers took part in struggles as followers of the bourgeois party. In the mid-18th century, the expansion of working class and dynamic labor movement provided the class foundation; while the establishment of Marxist theory provided the ideological basis for the establishment of proletarian parties. These two components interwoven and have jointly generated the proletarian parties. In June 1847, Karl Marx and Friedrich Engels founded the Communist League, the first international proletarian party in the world under the direction of scientific socialism (today known as communism). In August 1869, Social Democratic Workers' Party of Germany (also known as the Eisenacher group) was founded, the first proletarian party independently founded in a nation state. Later, independent proletarian parties successively came into being in European countries and the United States. After the World War II, proletarian parties reached their prime; the number of proletarian parties around the world exceeded 180 with a membership of nearly 100 million. After drastic changes in Eastern Europe and the disintegration of the Soviet Union, Communist parties suffered serious setbacks in some countries and their members worldwide dropped to 60 million, marking a trough in the history of communism. Since the 1990s, several Communist parties were dissolved, some have changed their nature, while some reorganized themselves and sought a new path of development under adverse general situation. At present, 127 parties in 100 countries retain their original Communist names or persist in their Marxist nature. Among them, 29 are in Asia, 55 in Europe, 8 in Africa, 3 in Oceania, and 32 in the Americas. The membership of these Communist parties exceeds 80 million. And 30 Communist parties respectively have members over 10,000, while 25 are ruling parties or parties already participating in state affairs. Over a century, although the world situation has changed a lot, proletarian parties have always been the major force in reforming the world and Marxist Theory of Party Building, as theoretical guidance for proletarian parties, still maintains its enduring vitality.

What Kind of Party to Build and How to Build It?

Marxist Theory of Party Building as an academic discipline has an independent scientific system embodying three major laws.

First is the law governing the appearance and evolution of proletarian parties: Why did the proletariat establish a party? What basic conditions were required for the establishment of proletarian parties? What kind of party should be built? The proletarian parties were inevitable for the proletariat to assume a leading role and fulfill its historical mission. It was an important sign marking that the proletariat progressed from a class-in-itself to a class-for-itself. The founding of a proletarian party needs two basic conditions: class foundation and a sound theoretical basis. In this sense, the proletarian party was a product of Marxism in combination with labor movement. The proletariat aimed to establish a Marxist party with a broad mass basis that would always stand in the forefront of the times.

Second is the law governing the self-building of proletarian parties: How does a proletarian party maintain its purity, advanced and vanguard nature? This question covers three aspects: how to form a scientific judgment of its historical direction; how to improve the party ideologically, politically, organizationally, its working style, and institutional pattern; and how to fulfill the party's historical mission.

For a mature communist party, ideological development covers: what ideology the Party adopts as its guidance; what ideological line it adheres to; how to develop its theories and bring forth new contents and innovate its theoretical system; and how to improve Party members' theoretical conduct through education against various non-proletarian ideologies.

Political development refers to: what program and political line the

Party formulates and implements and how to ensure they are implemented successfully.

Organizational development means: what organizational principle the Party persists in; and how to build a strong membership, strengthen the ranks of its cadres and improve organizations at all party levels, especially at the grassroots level, thus guaranteeing Party's vitality.

The improvement of working style is to carry forward the Party's fine traditions and good style of work, resist and overcome improper practices inside the Party, punish and prevent corruption, and maintain close ties with the masses.

Institutional improvement includes: how the Party adheres to and improves the system of democratic centralism and formulates and improves specific systems related to it, hence developing a sound mechanism for its operation.

The above five aspects are closely interwoven with each other and make up an integrated grand system of Party building.

Third is the law enabling proletarian parties to uphold their leadership: How does a proletarian party uphold its leadership? How to give correct direction and guidance to the people in emancipating themselves and consciously struggling for their own interests? How to improve the party's leadership and governance capability? The CPC has undertaken the role and responsibilities of an educator, organizer and leader throughout all the consecutive stages: revolution, country construction and reform. Leadership in party activities is realized through political, ideological and organizational forms. Political leadership refers to the leadership in political principles, direction and major decision-making. Ideological leadership means the leadership in guiding ideology, ideological line and ideological work. Organizational leadership implies that the Party unites and leads the people to fulfill its mission with the aid of Party organizations at all levels as political cores and its militant bastions, with the aid of Party cadres as mainstay and through an exemplary and vanguard role of all Party members. We should mention that: particularly after the Party assumes state power, the environment, status and conditions for its governance encounter revolutionary changes and the range of its activities expand greatly. Only by constantly improving its style of leadership and governance, can the ruling Party consolidate its leadership status.

The above three laws are logically connected; they systematically expound and explore the issues of "what kind of a Party to build and how to build it."

Proletariat and Aspects of Party Building

The concept of Party building refers particularly to the building of proletarian parties. In a broad sense, it includes Marxist Theory of Party Building and related practices; in a narrow sense, it refers to the former. Marxist Theory of Party Building covers its historical aspect and its principles in development. The history of Marxist Theory of Party Building mainly explains—in diachronic dimension—the historical background and the context in which this theory was established and developed and how its principles were put into practice by proletarian parties in different periods in different countries and it is a specialized history of ideology, an important branch of the history of Marxism. The study on principles of Marxist Theory of Party Building explores the principles and their interrelations in a synchronic dimension, focusing on theoretical achievements and studies how these principles are applied under current conditions. The practices of Party building includes the realities, activities and work of the Party, such as its organs of power, organs of leadership, members, cadres, primary organizations, decision-making procedures, inner-Party supervision, discipline measures, measures for promoting Party building, and basic experiences of Party building.

Thus we can see that Party building combines both theory and practice; it is a theory arising from practice and developing in practice, and a practice under the guidance of Marxist Theory of Party Building as well. For the purpose of standardization and accuracy and to distinguish it from other party theories, we suggest the term "Marxist Theories of Party and Party Building" to cover the content on the theory and practice of building proletarian parties.

Marxist Theories of Party and Party Building came into being in the same step with emergence of proletarian parties. Recently in Chinese academy it has been separated from scientific socialism as an independent subject. In regard to Party building, the CPC suffered serious setbacks in the Cultural Revolution period. Afterwards CPC has met with new problems of Party building since the reform and opening-up policy was set, and had to face new challenges in the volatile world situation. All these have made Marxists pay more attention to Party building, an issue closely related to the destiny of the Party, the state and the people. Practice demands for theoretical innovation while theory develops in practice. Marxists engaged with theoretical work on Party building and those directly related with Party affairs have undertaken that challenge: study brand new conditions and try to solve brand new problems. During those in-depth studies a rather complete system of study subjects along with some sub-branches have emerged, such as Studies on Party Constitution, Studies on Party Style, Science of Leadership, Studies on Publicity—replacing old terming propaganda—and Studies on Organizational Work. With such developments, it was inevitable that Marxist Theories of Party and Party Building became an independent academic discipline. Today, this long-standing but young subject is on the upswing.

Party Building Studies: King of Kings in Academy

Marxist Theories of Party and Party Building are interrelated with proximate subjects or disciplines while having distinctions from them.

Party and Politics: Politics is a science about social and political phenomena in social development and reveals the law governing social and political development which is mainly centered around state power. Its core is the relationship between political parties and power in contemporary human society. Political parties have many things in common—winning allies, fighting against enemies—in appearance, existence and demise; but their relations always change with social and historical conditions and altering class relations. For this reason, political parties cannot be studied alone in isolation, and the study on proletarian parties certainly involves politics.

Political science also studies in a broad sense the law governing the appearance, evolution, building and functioning of various types of political parties, but on the other hand Party building as an independent discipline focuses on the self-building of proletarian parties and how to give play to the role of their leadership.

Party and Scientific Socialism: Scientific Socialism is a science about the law governing how socialism will replace capitalism as a trend, the law governing the establishment and development of socialist society, and strategies and policies with which the proletariat and its party lead the people to realize socialism through various struggles. In China it includes general principles of scientific socialism and the theory of building socialism with Chinese characteristics. The party is the leading force in realizing socialism and communism, and its nature, guiding ideology, historical mission and its many more issues are all closely related to Scientific Socialism. Without Scientific Socialism, the basic questions about Party building cannot be studied. However, Scientific Socialism offers a comprehensive study of classes, political parties, states, revolutions, strategies, polities, etc. Study on proletarian parties make up only a part of scientific socialism as a fundamental condition for realizing socialism and communism. Thus Scientific Socialism alone cannot expound —in a systematic and in-depth manner—the laws governing the self-building of proletarian parties or elucidate the methods for sound leadership tasks.

Inter-relations with CPC history and history of New China in the contemporary era: The CPC history is a discipline about how the CPC came into being, developed and has realized its leadership. The history of New China is a science about the history of the People's Republic of China, coverings its politics, economy, culture, society, military affairs and diplomacy. The two and Marxist Theories of Party and Party Building are all about the CPC and their activities; they all cover the CPC history from aspects of appearance, development to expansion, the CPC guidelines and politics, and basic experience of Party building. However, the CPC history covers every period and every aspect of the CPC history. The history of New China is much wider, and Party building is only part of this discipline.

To summarize, Marxist Theories of Party and Party Building and inter-related proximate subjects are to an extent overlapping in their contents, but they are different in the range and depth of the study of Party theories.

The world today is a world of political parties and politics. Political parties came into being and have developed with the aim of seizing state power, thus a political party ascending to power is the supreme form of politics, and a common form of contemporary politics. According to Aristotle, politics is the most important among all the social sciences, and is the "king of sciences." In politics, the issue of political parties is at the core, so to express its significance, I may simply suggest: the study of political parties is "king of kings".

History and practice tell us once and again that the key to grasp the merits of Chinese development lies in her Communist Party. In contemporary China, all the theoretical and practical issues facing communists can be summarized in two compactly formulated questions: firstly, what is socialism and how to build it; secondly, what kind of Party shall be built and how to build it. The two issues are related and promote each other; they are integrated in the great practice of building socialism with Chinese characteristics. Answers to the two topics are set as the two basic tasks of the Marxists in China: first is the building of a moderately prosperous and a harmonious socialist society in all respects in nearly four decades, and this presents an answer to the first question; second is the new great project of propelling and innovating Party building in all respects to cope with the second issue. If unable to answer the first question correctly, Marxists could lose sight and will be disoriented in Party building task; if unable to answer the second question correctly, China's Marxists will not ensure the building of socialism. All that the China's Marxists have done over 50 years since they have assumed power is actually a process of exploring, evaluating and re-evaluating and answering these two questions; and all their experiences and lessons are also about those two critical issues.

The changes in the CPC's historical position can be summarized as follows: Passing through revolution, construction and reform periods, Party has evolved from a party that led the people in fighting for state power to a party that has led the people in exercising the power and thereafter has long remained in power. It has developed from a party that led national reconstruction under external international blockade conditions and a planned economy to a party that is leading national development while the country is opened to the outside world and when a socialist market economy was established. These two historical changes can be summarized into one sentence: The Party has become a ruling party which has been remaining in power for a long period and leading national development under the brand new conditions of all-round reform and opening-up. Here, "remaining in power" and "reform and opening-up" are the two key phrases marking the new historical position of the CPC. Thus all the new problems concerning Party building could be studied along with the accurate grasp of current historical position of the Party.

The above two changes have brought several changes for the Party. Its environment and position, the surroundings, tasks and major contradictions confronting it, and its own conditions have all undergone in-depth changes. Marxist scholars and activists should reflect creatively and stand up to meet new challenges arising in the process of solving the two big historical topics: One is how to enhance the Party's art of leadership and governance; the other is how to increase its capability of fighting corruption and guarding against degeneration and risks.

In recent years, in several occasions the Party leaders have attached great importance to the studies on basic Marxist theories and the important doctrine "Three Represents". Outstanding Party leaders have delivered many speeches and acknowledged the important position and role of philosophy and social sciences, comparing them to "two wheels of a bike and two wings of a bird." In particular, the nationwide education to maintain the progressiveness of Party members has greatly invigorated the theoretical studies on Party building, and fruitful achievements in theory and practice were gained. I certainly believe that the theoretical studies on Party building will enjoy a rising position among philosophy and social sciences.

Compared with other disciplines, Party building has five features: First is its distinctive class character, or Party spirit, as Marxists believe, which distinguishes it from general studies on political parties. Second is its profound theoretical character, as it is guided by Marxist Party Theory. Third is its requirement of high-levelness, as its objects for study are all critical problems having a bearing on the overall situation. Fourth is its strong practical character. It is not purely academic; it is a theory arising from and developing in practice and a practice guided by theory. All the problems it studies come from practice, while practice is the only criterion for testing its results. Fifth is its extensiveness in its scope, as it is a comprehensive subject covering many fields. As a grand systematic project, Party building is more than the Party itself; it takes into consideration the objective environment for the Party and the undertakings that the Party leads, which means that this discipline involves politics, economy, culture, society and other aspects.

In light of the above features of Party building, I suggest the following research methods:

Firstly, the studies should be guided by scientific theories. Marxist Theory of Party Building in China has experienced three stages in its development: Karl Marx and Friedrick Engels had laid the foundation for the theory; Lenin has enriched and developed the theory in practice; Chinese Communists have assimilated the riches of the first two stages and later formed three successive native Party building theories in the third stage: Party Building in Mao Zedong Thought, Party Building in Deng Xiaoping Theory and Party Building in the important thought of Three Represents. Some viewpoints and principles are almost the same in the three stages, such as the nature, goal, organizational principle and maximum program of proletarian parties. Meanwhile, due to different historical conditions, major social contradictions, realities and tasks of the proletarian parties in the three stages made Marxist Theory of Party Building keep developing in some aspects, such as social foundation—classes, stratums, standards for Party members, minimum program and the Party's working style. Marxist Theory of Party Building should be evaluated from the perspective of development, and each component has piled up rich assets. All above theories should be employed to understand and analyze problems concerning Party building studies in China.

Secondly, combine theory and studies with practice. According to theoretical circles in China, further research should be focused on three spheres: the laws governing the rule of the CPC, the laws governing modernization, and the laws governing the development of human society. The research on these three spheres is to study key social topics. In the practice of building the Party, theoretical and practical problems should be solved while always bearing people in mind and serving the society. In today's China, several hot and difficult issues regarding Party building attract enthusiasm and are keenly studied by theoreticians and activists. How to maintain and improve the Party's advanced vanguard nature, governance capacity, and arts of leadership and governance are targets of exploration and practical efforts. Generally accepted description of the specific topics or problems could be formulated as follows:

How to continue strengthening the Party's vanguard nature ideologically and theoretically, and maintain and improve the vanguard nature reflected in its theoretical basis which is wrapped in the guiding ideology of the Party.

How to continue strengthening the Party's vanguard nature in ruling and leading the country, so as to maintain and improve the Party's vanguard nature in the practice of promoting scientific development and building a harmonious socialist society.

How to continue strengthening the Party's vanguard nature in respect of its ultimate program, so as to maintain and improve the Party's vanguard nature in establishing lofty ideals and firm beliefs.

How to continue strengthening the Party's vanguard nature organizationally and among its members, so as to maintain and improve the Party's vanguard nature in solidifying its organizational basis and in improving training mainstay leaders.

How to continue strengthening the Party's vanguard nature regarding the Party's working style and clean government conduct, so as to maintain and improve the Party's vanguard nature in its working style and image.

How to continue strengthening the Party's vanguard nature regarding inner-Party institutions, so as to maintain and improve the Party's vanguard nature in leadership mechanisms and working mechanisms.

Thirdly, studies should consider global world trends. The world today is volatile, and political parties in all countries are facing severe challenges and seeking solutions through reforms. Political parties in different countries demonstrate a variety of characteristics and systems and they also have some common aspects. Studies and comparisons could reveal both their merits and shortcomings, but some political parties, due to their nature, can be compared and some cannot. Anyway, through comparative studies some aspects could be borrowed from other parties' practices in Party building and their operational mechanisms. We suggest studies should attach importance to the research on the world political and economic situation and development trends of political parties, so as to absorb and utilize all the fruits of human civilization.

Fourthly, Party Building discipline demands comprehensive and complex studies but research methods used by other social sciences such as politics, administration and law could be adopted.

In summary, in studying the Party building theories, Marxists should emancipate their minds, advance with the times, inherit historical practices and learn from global other countries.

I hope this book will contribute to more comprehensive studies on Marxist Theory of Party Building and strengthen the process of its establishment as an academic discipline. Hence Marxists and class conscious workers will grasp the Party issue deeper, have a firmer belief in the socialist cause and a stronger sense of historical mission and social responsibility, and voluntarily devote to great undertakings.

Wu Meihua,
Beijing, 2007

Contents

Chapter 1

Marxist Theory of Party Building: Classics and Innovations in China

Marxist Theory of Party Building is a developing discipline and advances with the times. Karl Marx and Friedrick Engels have co-founded the theory and laid its theoretical basis. Vladimir Ilyich Lenin developed the theory in practice by leading the socialist revolution and construction in Russia and thus brought into being a complete theory of party building. Chinese Marxists, combining the theory with the concrete practice in China, have assimilated and inherited the main essence of those theories and later formed three successive native Party building theories in China: Party Building in Mao Zedong Thought, Party Building in Deng Xiaoping Theory and Party Building in the important thought of Three Represents. These innovations in China have contributed significant progress and improvement to the Theory.

1.1 Marx and Engels' Theory of Party Building

Marx and Engels' Theory of Party Building appeared in Europe in the 1840s when England, France, Germany and other typical capitalist countries were in the stage of "free competition" (laissez-faire) capitalist development. Social, economic and political development and vigorously growing labor movements provided historical conditions for the theory to come into being.

England was the first country to realize Industrial Revolution at the end of the 1830s and became the "Workshop of the World." The second was France, from the late 1840s to 1860s. Germany was a bit later, achieving Industrial Revolution by the 1870s. The success of capitalist industrialization enabled capitalist countries to make astounding advances and had led to sharper contradictions between the proletariat and the bourgeoisie. The bourgeoisie used every means to exploit workers' absolute surplus value and relative surplus value; workers including women and children had to start working in their very early years of life—10 to 15 years old—with high labor intensity and longer work-days up to 15 or 16 hours per day, facing high labor casualties and diseases and having extremely low standard of life. In particular since the first economic crisis erupted in England in 1825, capitalist economic crises broke out more frequently, almost once every few years, resulting in sharp decrease in workers' income and massive unemployment waves. Consequently, the working class became poorer. Harsh and cruel oppression on the working class had naturally led to fertile and strong rebellion. Against such a historical background, labor movements in Western Europe had boomed since the 1830s. The three labor movements in Europe (revolts of the Lyon's silk weavers—the Canuts, the Chartist movement in England, the revolt of the Silesian textile weavers in Germany) marked that the European proletariat had staged onto the historical arena as an independent political force. The flourishing labor movements, workers' associations and trade unions called for and bred proletarian parties.

In June 1847, Marx and Engels restructured the League of the Justice (Bund der Gerechten) in Hamburg and founded the Communist League, the first international proletarian party under the guidance of the theory of scientific socialism. In November and December 1847, the Communist League held its second congress, at which the "Rules of the Communist League" was discussed and adopted, and Marx and Engels were mandated to draw up a new program for this organization (See Appendix 1: Draft Rules of the Communist League-1847). In February 1848, "The Manifesto of the Communist Party," drafted by Marx and Engels, was published, marking that Marx and Engels' Theory of Party Building was established and that Marxism was formally brought into being. Later, under the guidance of Marx and Engels, the Communist League took part in the European Revolution in 1848; after the revolution, it re-assembled in late 1849 and continued its activities in Germany. In November 1852, the organization was formally ended due to cruel oppression and abuses of the reactionary authorities. From the 1860s to the 1890s, Marx and Engels personally initiated the founding of the International Working Men's Association (also called the First International) and contributed to the establishment of independent national proletarian parties in European countries and in the United States. After Marx passed away, Engels was one of the outstanding leaders in early-stage activities of the Second International. In the long practice of founding proletarian parties, Marx and Engels had written a series of programmatic and essential works covering various key aspects of the newborn socialist-communist movement, including the "Inaugural Address of the International Working Men's Association" (1864), "General Rules of the International Working Men's Association" (1864), "The Civil War in France" (1871), "On Authority" (1872), "Critique on the Gotha Program of German Social Democrat Party" (1875) and "Socialism: Utopian and Scientific" (1880). These creative works had laid a comprehensive ideological basis for the new established proletarian parties.

The major contents of Marx and Engels' Theory of Party Building could be summed up as follows:

The necessity of establishing proletarian parties: Marx and Engels summarized the lessons and experience learned from European labor movements and proposed that the primary premise for the proletariats to fulfill their self historical mission was to establish proletarian parties. As promulgated in the "Resolution Relating to the General Rules of the International Working Men's Association" adopted at the Hague Congress in September 1872, "In its struggle against the collective power of the propertied classes, the working class cannot act as a class except by constituting itself into a political party, distinct from, and opposed to all old parties formed by the propertied classes. This constitution of the working class into a political party is indispensable in order to ensure the triumph of the social revolution, and of its ultimate end, the abolition of classes."[1]

Exposition of the nature and features of the Communist party: As Marx and Engels pointed out, the Communist party is the most advanced class organization, integrating class character and progressiveness. This nature is displayed mainly in three aspects: In terms of class foundation, a proletarian party publicly declares that it represents the interests of the proletariat as a whole, and "they (the Communists) have no interests separate and apart from those of the proletariat as a whole."[2] Theoretically, a proletarian party takes a scientific worldview as its guiding ideology and theoretical basis, and thus "they have over the great mass of the proletariat the advantage of clearly understanding the line of march, the conditions, and the ultimate general aims and results of the proletarian movement."[3] They can master the law governing social development and assume the role as the leader of revolutions. Practically, a proletarian party has a political foresight and a spirit of self-sacrifice, and the Communists "are the most advanced and resolute section of the working-class parties of every country, the section which pushes forward all others."[4]

Basic principles for organizational and political activities of proletarian parties: According to Marx and Engels, a proletarian party should be an organized force, and political activities and the party's style of activities

[1] *Marx & Engels Selected Works* (2nd edition), Volume 2, p.611. Beijing: People's Press, 1995.
[2] *Marx & Engels Selected Works* (2nd edition), Volume 1, p.285. Beijing: People's Press, 1995.
[3] *Ibid.*
[4] *Ibid.*

should conform to the political goal of the party. Although they did not expose a clear definition on "democratic centralism" principles and did not use that term, Marx and Engels had formulated concrete regulations on the organizational system, organizational structure and style of activities of proletarian parties in the "Rules of the Communist League" and the "General Rules of the International Working Men's Association," which indeed fully demonstrated the principle of democracy. In the meantime, they had emphasized that the party should strictly observe discipline and correctly deal with inner-party debates and struggles, so as to safeguard the unity, purity, and solidarity of the party and exclude any opportunist or religious schism and split.

Program and strategies of proletarian parties: According to Marx and Engels, a proletarian party should formulate a common program guided by scientific socialism and take it as a public banner to coordinate ideologies and actions of individual party members and call upon the masses to expand its ranks. As the first classical program of the proletarian parties, the Manifesto of the Communist Party had made that point quite clear: The ultimate goal of the Communists is to abolish private property, exploitation and class distinctions and establish a Communist society, while the immediate aim of the proletariat is to overthrow the bourgeois supremacy and conquer political power. Marx and Engels had also believed that to realize its program, a proletarian party should adhere to correct principles and strategies: combining immediate, partial interests with long-term, overall interests; combining strictness and consistency of principles with flexibility of strategies; integrating economic struggles with political struggles, and legal struggle with outlawed struggle; and persisting in the united front and the principle of internationalism, uniting with all the forces that can be allied and directing the strike at the main enemy.

In the practice of establishing proletarian parties, Marx and Engels had made a scientific exposition of a series of basic problems concerning Party building, set up its theoretical framework and laid a solid foundation for the formation and development of the Marxist Theory of Party Building. Thus they had pointed out a clear direction for the founding and building of the early proletarian parties in the world.

1.2 Lenin's Theory of Party Building

Lenin's Theory of Party Building had emerged and developed in Russia in the late 19th century and early 20th century. During this era, several tremendous changes had occurred in social and historical conditions: capitalism had progressed from the stage of laissez-faire capitalism onto the stage of imperialism; the inherent contradictions of capitalism had become more acute; and the class antagonism between the proletariat and the bourgeoisie was unprecedentedly intense. Since developed capitalist countries were transforming from exporters of commodities into exporters of capital, the bourgeoisie, in order to consolidate its rule in respective countries, domestically initiated some reformist measures and ideas to compromise with the rising labor movements, thus providing conditions for a reformist political movement. After Engels passed away, opportunists, represented by Eduard Bernstein and Karl Kautsky, had assumed the control in the Second International; they adopted and advocated reformist policies, totally losing the Marxist stand and thus becoming unqualified to lead labor movements. Lenin, in such a crucial historical juncture in the practice of founding a new-type proletarian party, combined Marx and Engels' Theory of Party Building with the realities and demands of the Russian revolution, and hence brought into being Lenin's Theory of Party Building.

Indeed, Lenin had creatively inherited and further enriched and developed the Marxist Theory of Party Building. Since 1893, Lenin had studied labor movements and criticized Russian populist-Narodnism movement; on this basis, he actively contributed in the founding and programmatic debates of the Russian Social Democratic Labor Party (RSDLP). The party was formally established in 1898. However, since revolutionary leaders including Lenin were arrested and sent into exile and the opportunism dominant in the Second International had exerted an important negative influence, the RSDLP fell into ideological chaos and organizational laxity. To tackle these problems, Lenin started to criticize the "economists," the most influential group in the RSDLP. He created *Iskra*, an all-Russia political newspaper, and he himself undertook the post of editor-in-chief and leadership of the revolutionary wing of the Party. Based on this newspaper, Lenin worked hard to spread Marxism and criticize opportunism and organize the local disconnected Marxist circles. Gradually the core of revolutionary Marxists—the Iskra faction—came into being. In 1903, the Second Congress of the RSDLP was held. An intense struggle unfolded in the party, between Marxists, represented by Lenin, and opportunists, represented by Julius Martov, and later divided into Lenin's Bolsheviks and opportunist Mensheviks. From then on, Bolshevism has been a political thought as well as a political party. For this reason, the academic circles generally suggest that the new-type proletarian party of Russia had started by 1903.

In the practice of founding a new-type proletarian party of Russia, Lenin had penned a series of his famous works about party building, including "Our Program" (1899), "The Urgent Tasks of Our Movement" (1900), "Two Tactics of Social-Democracy in the Democratic Revolution" (1905), "The Historical Destiny of the Doctrine of Karl Marx" (1913), "The Three Sources and Three Component Parts of Marxism" (1913), "Karl Marx: A Brief Biographical Sketch with an Exposition of Marxism" (1914), "On the Slogan for a United States of Europe" (1915), "The Military Program of the Proletarian Revolution" (1916), and "The State and Revolution" (1917). The two most representative works were *What Is to Be Done?* (1902) and *One Step Forward, Two Steps Back* (1904). Published in March 1902, the pamphlet *What Is to Be Done?* had exposed the ideological root of opportunism in the Second International, elaborated the great significance of revolutionary theories for the proletarian party in Russia, and had established the guiding ideology for a new-type proletarian party, and at the same time, the ideological foundation for the new-type proletarian party organization was elucidated. His famous comments such as "without revolutionary theory there can be no revolutionary movement" and "the role of vanguard fighter can be fulfilled only by a party that is guided by the most advanced theory" had exerted a far-reaching influence on the Russian Bolsheviks and even proletarian parties of other countries. Published in May 1904, the pamphlet *One Step Forward, Two Steps Back* was written from the organizational aspect and had exposed those Menshevik opportunist views such as "member's autonomy and laxity, opposing and ignoring centralization" thus systematically explained the organizational principles of the proletarian party. To sum up, *What Is to Be Done?* and *One Step Forward, Two Steps Back* had marked the formation of Lenin's Theory of Party Building.

The major contents of Lenin's Theory of Party Building could be summarized as follows:

Regarding the party nature, Lenin put the main emphasis on the party's advanced, vanguard nature while paying due stress to its class character. The proletarian party should be the leading force of the proletariat; only after the Communist party is elevated to the vanguard of the working class, could it become the core motivator leading the working class to fulfill its historical mission.

Regarding the party's guiding ideology, Lenin attached special importance to theoretical building of the party, and emphasized the role of revolutionary theories as the guide. He demanded the proletarian party should apply Marxism independently and creatively based on national realities while carefully avoiding opportunist exaggeration on national particularity, and at the same time oppose revisionism that misinterprets or falsifies basic tenets of Marxism and reject dogmatism that copies Marxism mechanically and applies it indiscriminately.

Regarding the party's organizational principles, Lenin had raised the theory of relative system of democratic-centralism principle. He stressed that the proletarian party should strictly carry out democratic-centralism, promote inner-party democracy, achieve high centralization, adhere to the rule of majority while protecting rights of the minority, and prohibit any factions within the party. He stressed the principle of collective leadership, asserting that any individual should not be allowed to decide on any major political or organizational problem by himself. He also stressed that the proletarian party should formulate and carry out strict discipline, oppose both left-wing and right-wing tendencies in her ranks, and safeguard the unity and solidarity in the party.

Regarding the party's program and strategies, Lenin had stressed that a proletarian party should make a correct program based on the current historical conditions of the country. He had for the first time raised the idea and terming of maximum and minimum programs as the two dialectical components of the party program. He carefully attached more importance to the latter and the dialectical relationship between the two. According to Lenin, correct strategies are critical to the proletarian party; the party should combine the consistency and strictness of principles with flexibility of strategies, fully utilizing all forms of struggles that can be realized, including necessary compromising tactics, and the party should energetically and rapidly be able to shift from one form of struggle to another responding to changing circumstances.

Lenin had made great contributions to Marxist Theory of Party Building, and had enriched the basic tenets of Marxist Theory of Party Building with his vigorous ideas, and moreover, in his later works and practices had put forth series of important ideas about the building of the proletarian party which has assumed and exercises power. Hence, Lenin had developed Marxist Theory of Party Building into a rather complete, scientific system. After the success of the October Revolution in 1917, Lenin had focused on transforming the revolutionary opposing party into a ruling party. Before he passed away, he indeed penned outstanding works about the party in power in his seven-year practice as the core leader of the Party and the Soviet state. "The Immediate Tasks of the Soviet Government" (1918), "A Great Beginning" (1919), "The Workers' State and Party Week" (1919), "Purging the Party" (1921), and "Left-Wing Communism: An Infantile Disorder" (1920) were his main important works on this subject. According to Lenin, the Communist party should be the leading force in a socialist country and should exercise political leadership over national organs of political power, and thus maintain its leading role and functions in the state and in social and political life. The central task of the ruling party was to lead the socialist economic construction, and the development of social productive forces should be the fundamental task of the party and state, and all party members should study and grasp the art of administrating the state and economic affairs of the country. The ruling party should set strict requirements for its member candidates, constantly improve the quality of its party members, purify them, and strengthen education and management of them; and should maintain close contact with the masses of people and prevent the tendencies of bureaucracy and isolation from them. Lenin's ideas had directly guided the ruling party building in Russia, the first socialist country in the world, starting the ruling party building era both theoretically and practically.

In the practice of leading the Russian proletariat to seize state power and build socialism, Lenin had solved a series of important problems on building a new-type proletarian party in a backward capitalist country and later problems of consolidating it under socialist construction stage, thus greatly contributing to the world socialist movement.

1.3　Communist Party of China and Its Party Building Theory

The CPC was founded in China, an Eastern country with extremely lagging economy and culture. The social and historical conditions of its founding, path of development and mode of self-building were all different from those of Western proletarian parties. Consequently, its theory of Party building was quite unique. Since the CPC was founded, the Chinese Communists have striven to combine the Marxist Theory of Party Building with the concrete practice of revolution, later construction and reform in China and with the practice of building the CPC, and thereafter have brought into being consecutive theories of Party building with distinctive Chinese characteristics: Party Building in Mao Zedong Thought, Party Building in Deng Xiaoping Theory and Party Building in the important thought of Three

Represents.

Party Building Theory of the Mao Zedong Thought

Party Building Theory is an indispensable component of the scientific system of Mao Zedong Thought, and a theoretical summary of the Chinese Communists' collective practice of building the CPC as well. Like other components of the Mao Zedong Thought, it was the crystallized, collective wisdom of the CPC.

In May 1945, in his report to the Seventh CPC National Congress about the amendment to the Party Constitution, Liu Shaoqi had raised for the first time the concepts and Mao Zedong's Line of Party Building, and made preliminary elaboration on this theoretical system. In July 1977, in his speech at the Third Plenary Session of the Tenth CCCPC, Deng Xiaoping had made a speech affirming the significance of this theory and made a pithy exposition of the social background and historical process of the formation, development, major contents and great contributions of it. The Decision of Central Committee of the Communist Party of China on Several Historical Problems of the Party since the Founding of New China, adopted at the Sixth Plenary Session of the 11th CCCPC in 1981, and the *Program for Studying Deng Xiaoping Theory of Party Building*, compiled by the Policy Research Office and Organization Department of the Central Committee and Party School of the CPC in 1998, both had given an objective, comprehensive, accurate and scientific summary of Party Building Theory of the Mao Zedong Thought.

Party Building Theory of the Mao Zedong Thought was created in the semi-feudal and semi-colonial China with lagging economy and culture and in the face of imperialist invasion or yoke and world-wide ascending proletarian revolution tide. Compared with Communist parties in capitalist countries, the CPC building in the Mao Zedong era had following features:

The CPC was founded following the example of the Russian communist party under the guidance and with the help of the Comintern (Communist International, also known as the Third International), which had enabled the CPC to stay away from revisionism and reformism of the Second International. Since it was not part of China's social practice and could not accurately understand Chinese situation, the Comintern had given some wrong directions for the Chinese revolution; and her interactions with the Russian Communist Party had both positive and negative impacts on the CPC.

The CPC was founded in a country with a large number of peasants and petty bourgeoisie greatly surpassing the number of the industrial workers, and it had indeed expanded its organizational base uniting with the peasants and petty bourgeoisie. This unique particularity had brought several problems for the CPC in ideological and organizational spheres and exerted an arduous task as to maintain its nature: vanguard of the proletariat.

The CPC had developed in a unique practice: allying with while at the same time struggling against the bourgeoisie, which had posed severe challenges in maintaining correct political line and the leadership of the proletariat.

The CPC had been illegal for a long time, and expanded its political influence through long-term armed struggle, which had demanded higher requirements in combining Party building with armed struggle, especially in how to guarantee and establish the CPC's absolute leadership over armed forces.

The CPC had developed on rural revolutionary bases and was for a long time located in the rural China, and its many branches and organs had been disconnected and encircled by the enemy forces. This had also brought some problems to the CPC about how to maintain its unity and solidarity.

The above five features show that what the CPC had faced was quite different from European Communist parties. The old China was quite different from those Western capitalist countries in which Marx and Engels organized revolutionary activities, and the same was true when compared with the pre-October Revolution Russia in which Lenin led the revolutionary practice. The situation that the CPC had faced was much more complicated, and the task of Party building was much more difficult and arduous. The first generation of the collective leadership of the CPC, with Mao Zedong as its core leader, applied Marx and Engels' Theory of Party Building and Lenin's Theory of Party Building and combined them with native conditions in its long practice; thus Party Building Theory of the Mao Zedong Thought was established.

Five Stages of Theoretical Forming

Party Building Theory of the Mao Zedong Thought experienced a long historical process in its formation and evolution, which can be roughly divided into five stages:

The first stage (1920-1927) covers the period from initial preparation efforts extending through the founding of the CPC—the Party was officially founded in 1921—till the failure of the 1927 Great Revolution, which witnessed the sprouts of Party Building Theory of the Mao Zedong Thought. The main issue was about what kind of party shall be built in China. The three important correspondence between Mao Zedong and Cai Hesen, and Mao's "Analysis of the Classes in Chinese Society" (1926) and "Report on an Investigation of the Peasant Movement in Hunan" (1927) had raised some basic problems concerning Party building, such as the class foundation and nature of the CPC. These works marked the sprout of Party Building Theory of the Mao Zedong Thought.

The second stage (1927-1935), from the failure of the 1927 Revolution to Zunyi Conference, witnessed the Party Building Theory of the Mao Zedong Thought taking shape. The focus was on the ideological leadership and ideological building of the CPC. Mao's "The Struggle in the Jinggang Mountains" (1928), "Resolution of Gutian Conference" (1929) and "Oppose Book Worship" (1930), and the "Letter from the Central Committee to the Front Party Committee of the Red Army's Fourth Army" (1929) dictated by Zhou Enlai and drafted by Chen Yi together had advocated correcting and overcoming non-proletarian ideologies in the party, which in fact was expounding the principle of building the Party ideologically. These works had revealed that Party Building Theory of the Mao Zedong Thought had taken shape. To be accurate, the major unique exposition was released in the "Resolution of Gutian Conference."

The third stage (1935-1945), extending from Zunyi Conference to the Seventh CPC National Congress, witnessed that Party Building Theory of the Mao Zedong Thought was maturing. As the CPC grew from a child up to an adult, Party Building Theory of the Mao Zedong Thought had been put into practice in many aspects in Yan'an main base area and had gradually formed a system. In this stage, Mao Zedong had penned "On Practice" (1937), "On Contradiction" (1937), "Combat Liberalism" (1937), "The Role of the Chinese Communist Party in the National War"(1938), "Introducing the Communist" (1939), "Reform Our Study" (1941), "Rectify the Party's Style of Work" (1942), "Oppose Stereo-Typed Party Writing" (1942), "Some Questions Concerning Methods of Leadership"(1943), "Our Study Works and the Current Situation" (1944) and "On Coalition Government" (1945). Liu Shaoqi had penned "How to Be a Good Communist" (1939), "On Inner-Party Struggle" (1941) and "On the Party" (1945). Major contents of these works had directed theoretical attention to the following formulations: the three "magic weapons" of the Chinese revolution (united front, armed struggle and Party building), taking Party building as a "great undertaking," dialectically combining Party building with political line, prioritizing and putting stress on the Party's ideological building, a systematic theory on how Party members should cultivate and temper themselves, the thoughts on correct attitudes during inner-Party struggles, and lastly scientific concepts on Party style and style of work which had essentially covered three notions: integrating theory with practice, forging close links with the masses and practicing self-criticism. These works showed that Party Building Theory of the Mao Zedong Thought had become a rather complete theoretical system. The academic circles generally suggest that Liu Shaoqi's work "On the Party" marked that Party Building Theory of the Mao Zedong Thought had grown into maturity and all-round systematic development.

The fourth stage (1945-1949), from the Seventh CPC National Congress to the Second Plenary Session of the Seventh CCCPC, witnessed Party

Building Theory of the Mao Zedong Thought progressing. In his works "On Setting Up a System of Reports" (1948), "On Some Important Problems of the Party's Present Policy" (1948), "A Circular on the Situation" (1948), "On Strengthening the Party Committee System" (1948) and "Methods of Work Committees" (1949), Mao Zedong had put forward the thoughts on Party policies and strategies and on science of leadership, which had greatly improved Party Building Theory of the Mao Zedong Thought.

The fifth stage (1949-1976), from the Second Plenary Session of the Seventh CCCPC to the end of the Cultural Revolution, was an important stage in which Party Building Theory of the Mao Zedong Thought had finally shaped but had also witnessed serious complications. As early as in the 1930s since the CPC took power in China's Soviet Area, Mao Zedong and Liu Shaoqi had started to think about possible problems that might arise after the Party took power. They warned Party cadres and members against conceit, corruption and degeneration, which can be regarded as the sprout of Party Building Theory of the Mao Zedong Thought. Before the victory of Chinese revolution, in 1949 Mao Zedong had presided over the Second Plenary Session of the Seventh CCCPC and made a report, in which he brought forward the issue of shifting the focus of Party work from revolution to re-construction and warned the Party against possible problems that might arise after the Party has assumed the ruling status. This report signified that Party Building Theory of the Mao Zedong Thought had already taken shape. After the New China was founded in 1949, the old generation of leading veteran Marxists had made active explorations in theory and practice on various new aspects of the ruling party building, and had penned a lot of works about how to shift the focus of Party work under new conditions, how to improve members of the ruling party, how to guard the Party against corruption and degeneration, how to maintain close ties with the masses, and how to strengthen democratic-centralism and promote the unity and solidarity of the Party. Major works written in this period were: Mao Zedong's "Combat Bureaucracy, Commandism and Violations of the Law and Discipline" (1953), Liu Shaoqi's "Eight Qualifications for Communist Party Members" (1951) and "Strive for Higher Qualifications for Party Members" (1951), and Deng Xiaoping's "Report on the Revision of the Constitution of the Communist Party of China" (1956). In particular, the report to the Eighth CPC National Congress in 1956 made comprehensive summary of building the Party ideologically, organizationally and in style of work spheres and put forth new and higher requirements, marking the formation of Party Building Theory of the Mao Zedong Thought. After the Eighth CPC National Congress, as Mao Zedong had strayed away from his previous correct road, the Party collective had suffered "left" mistakes in its guiding ideology and therefore witnessed setbacks in Party building. However, Mao Zedong had still brought forward several correct and fore-sighted thoughts on preventing against "peaceful evolution from socialism to capitalism" policies of imperialist forces and brilliant ideas on cultivating and training millions of successors to the proletarian revolutionary cause.

Party Building Theory of the Mao Zedong Thought: Six Major Points

The major contents of Party Building Theory of the Mao Zedong Thought could be summarized as follows:

Firstly, priority should be given to and emphasis should be put on ideological building of the Party. The unique national conditions of China determined that there were a small number of industrial workers, and Chinese Communists must adopt armed struggle and take the strategic path of encircling cities from the countryside to develop the Chinese revolution. For a rather long time, Chinese Communists had concentrated their revolutionary efforts on the countryside and recruited revolutionary farmers and petty bourgeoisie for their armed forces. Consequently, there were a large number of Party members who belonged to farmer and petty bourgeoisie class origins, and the Party was always surrounded by farmer and petty bourgeoisie ideologies. Naturally, Mao Zedong had believed that priority should be given to ideological building of the Party, so as to maintain the nature of the Party as vanguard of the working class. In November 1928, he had penned "The Struggle in the Jinggang Mountains" in which he had raised the question of proletarian ideological leadership, where he had for the first time explicitly mentioned giving priority and stressing ideological building of the Party. In December 1929, he drew up a resolution for the Ninth CPC National Congress of the Fourth Army of the Red Army, entitled "On Correcting Mistaken Ideas in the Party" (this text is also called "Resolution of Gutian Conference"). The resolution marked that both the principle of giving priority to and stressing ideological building of the Party and Party Building Theory of the Mao Zedong Thought had started its forming. As generally agreed, this principle is the most important part of Party Building Theory of the Mao Zedong Thought, and has proved as the most successful practice of the CPC in Party building.

Secondly, the building of the Party should be closely inter-related with its political line. Mao Zedong had believed that the formulation and implementation of a correct political line would affect and determine the fate of the Party, and consequently Party would wax successfully or wane by failure. In December 1936, in "Problems of Strategy in China's Revolutionary War" Mao Zedong pointed out, "We need a correct Marxist military line as well as a correct Marxist political line."[1] In October 1939, in "Introducing the Communist" he summarized the historical record as to how the CPC had developed and won the battles, and elaborated the idea that the building of the Party should be closely linked with its political line. He said, "For eighteen years, the building and bolshevization of the Party had been closely linked with its political line, i.e., the correct or incorrect handling of the political questions of the united front and armed struggle."[2] Later in his other works, Mao also emphasized that the Party must take it as a central task to formulate and implement a correct political line, and strengthen education on Party members' acute consciousness of the political line, so as to maintain political consensus among the whole party ranks.

Thirdly, the organizational building of the Party should be strengthened in accordance with the principle of democratic-centralism. The CPC lacked a

---

[1] *Selected Works of Mao Zedong* (2nd edition), Volume 1, p.186. Beijing: People's Press, 1991.
[2] *Selected Works of Mao Zedong* (2nd edition), Volume 2, p.605. Beijing: People's Press, 1991.

sound tradition of democracy within itself, while feudal patriarchal thoughts and the petty bourgeoisie individualistic aversion to discipline had negative impacts on the Party conduct. Moreover, Party organizations were segmented by the enemy, and some were even far away from the Central Committee and difficult to contact and control or manage. Such circumstances could easily breed de-centralism, "mountain stronghold" mentality (or factionalism) and other negative mentalities and attitudes. To tackle such problems, the old generation of revolutionaries, including Mao Zedong, more than often expounded and reviewed the dialectical relation between democracy and centralism in the practice of Party building; summarized and concretized several fundamental rules of democratic-centralism; stressed that the purpose of democratic-centralism was to give play to the initiative of the whole Party members and safeguard the unity and solidarity in the Party; and brought forward correct approaches on democratic-centralism principle such as expanding inner-Party democracy; members observe others and in turn accept others' critics in strict accordance with the disciplinary rules of the Party. All these efforts had indeed enriched and developed the Marxist principle of democratic-centralism.

Fourthly, cultivating a fine working style for the Party should be an important part of Party building. This was a major creative innovation of the CPC in respect of Party building, and a unique and important part of Party Building Theory of the Mao Zedong Thought. In February 1942, in "Rectify the Party's Style of Work", Mao Zedong used the term—"the Party's style of work"—for the first time. In April 1945, in "On Coalition Government" he summarized the CPC's fine traditions that were formed in long revolutionary struggles and formulated as "three major features of the Party's style of work": integrating theory with practice, forging close links with the masses and practicing self-criticism. Mao Zedong had further pinpointed that "closely integrating theory with practice is the hallmark distinguishing our Party from all other political parties."

With Mao Zedong's efforts, the CPC formulated a complete system of effective principles and measures for building a fine work style for the

Party. These principles and measures explicitly reflect the class origins and ideological origins of a fine style of work and a bad style conversely, and include the notion that the Party's style of work could only be improved on the basis of worldview and party spirit. Moreover, the wisdom was to include relevant standards and conducts of style into the Party Constitution and important Party resolutions, thus making it clear in the form of inner-Party rules explicitly pointing to what should be spread and what should be abandoned in order to guide or restrain Party members. Another concrete formulation was to issue the principle of depending on the whole Party to improve its style of work, lay stress both on ideological education and necessary organizational and disciplinary means to rectify bad styles with collective efforts and regular sequences. And lastly, a key measure was formulated as putting the Party work under critical supervision of entire Party members and non-Party people, making it clear that any leading cadre should set an example by his own individual acts, and advising them to practice the conduct of self-improvement, which is also a rational wisdom of traditional Chinese culture, thus guide surrounding Party members in tempering themselves, while at the same time breeding fine styles and overcoming bad ones.

Fifthly, a correct cadre guideline and cadre policies should be adopted. Mao Zedong had paid great attention to the decisive role of cadres in realizing the Party's guidelines and policies, and strongly believed that cadres would play a decisive role after the Party has formulated its political line. He put forth several criteria for assessing cadres' "integrity and competence" and set a guideline for the "appointment of cadres by their merits." And together with other leaders, he formulated a series of correct cadre policies: upholding unity and opposing "mountain stronghold" mentality (factionalism) and rejecting sectarianism; evaluating each cadre with consideration of his or her complete record and whole work instead of a short period or a single practice; uniting with and loving cadres and helping them in self-improvement; correctly approaching to those who made mistakes; strengthening education and cultivation of cadres; working to improve cadres' ideological, political and professional competence; and tempering and testing them in practice.

Sixthly, inner-Party conflicts should be handled in a correct manner. Mao Zedong had analyzed the root causes of inner-Party conflicts and proposed to carry out constructive ideological struggles. He had raised a correct guideline formulation: "learn from past mistakes to avoid the future ones, and criticize a person in order to help him" which contrasted the "left" conduct in previous inner-Party struggles that had advocated and applied "ruthless struggle and merciless blows." Thus, he had highlighted the aim of the inner-Party struggle: settle ideological problems while uniting with all comrades, and create a new model form for rectifying the Party's style of work by employing criticism and self-criticism and base yourselves on Marxist and Leninist ideological education. Liu Shaoqi had also penned a lot of works about treating inner-Party conflicts, including "Eliminate Closed-Doorism and Adventurism" (1936), "Against All Kinds of Unhealthy Tendencies within the Party" (1941), "Eliminate Menshevist Ideology within the Party" (1943), and "Several Questions Concerning Party Building" (1944). His famous work "On Inner-Party Struggle" was a speech delivered at the Central Party School in July 1941, which was then telegraphed to Yan'an Party Headquarter and published in the Yan'an-based *Liberation Daily* in October, 1942. In this speech, Liu Shaoqi had given a comprehensive and systematic exposition on the objectivity, necessity, roots, nature and forms of inner-Party struggle, and reviewed previous negative conducts and lessons of the Party in this regard, and proposed several principles, policies and methods for constructive inner-Party struggle. This speech was delivered at a certain historical time when the CPC was suffering from "left" and right type of mistakes that had emerged in several inner-Party struggles. The speech had preceded the well-known rectification campaign aiming improvements in Party's style of work, and this three-year long campaign was initiated in 1942. At that time, the ideological guidelines of the CPC was not yet clearly defined, and the whole Party didn't have time to summarize experiences and lessons of previous struggles, which made the lecture more significant. The speech had marked a major progress for Marxist-Leninist conduct in treating inner-Party conflicts. After the speech was published in *Liberation Daily*, Mao Zedong wrote a comment, praising that every member should read and study that work which clarified the major problems of inner-Party struggle in theory and in practice.

Apart from the above contents, Party Building Theory of the Mao Zedong Thought has many other important components, such as building Party branches at the company level in armed forces, building basic primary Party organizations as strong fighting forts, adhering to the principle that Party commands the army, and ensuring the absolute leadership of the Party over the army. All these principles were sound practices that CPC had summarized during the process of building the Party, and had produced major progress when exercised in the practice. Under the guidance of Party Building Theory of the Mao Zedong Thought, the CPC had successfully built itself into a united, disciplined and strong Marxist political party, and was closely connected with the masses.

The Ruling Party Notion

In its many aspects, Party Building Theory of the Mao Zedong Thought was a theory inherited and developed from Lenin's Theory of Building the Ruling Party in many aspects.

The ruling party should have a stronger sense of governance and solidify its ruling position. Mao Zedong had asserted that the core task of a proletarian party's leadership is to hold and control the state power. He had pointed out, "The Communist Party of China is the core of leadership for the whole people in the country. Without such a core, the socialist cause will never succeed."[1] In his famous work "On the Correct Handling of Contradictions among the People" (1957), Mao Zedong had suggested a criterion to be applied in political activity: to judge whether a person's words and deeds were right or not should be evaluated by whether they helped to strengthen the leadership of the Communist Party of China and this should be the most important criterion. Later on many occasions he had criticized those

---

[1] *Collected Works of Mao Zedong*, Volume 7, p.303. Beijing: People's Press, 1999.

improper speeches undermining the leadership of the CPC, to heighten the sense of governance among Party members.

The ruling party must prioritize economic construction as its central task: Mao Zedong had believed that the leadership of a ruling party must be demonstrated in its guiding work to emancipate and develop the social productive forces. He pointed out in "On Coalition Government" (1945): "To judge the impact, good or bad, great or small, of the policy and the practice of any Chinese political party among the people should depend on whether and how much it helps to develop their productive forces, and on whether it fetters or liberates these forces."[1] At the Second Plenary Session of the Seventh Central Committee of the CPC held in March 1949, Mao Zedong had proposed a timely focus shift in the Party work, concentrating on country (national) construction. After the People's Republic of China was founded, he had presided at the important meetings over the formulation of the general guidelines of the Party for the transitional period. And later he had published his work "On the Ten Major Relationships" in 1956 on the basis of in-depth investigation and research, in which he had for the first time proposed the idea of realizing socialist modernization in line with the national conditions. In 1956 at the Eighth National Congress of the CPC, a correct line was promulgated as follows: the chief task confronting the Party and the people is to concentrate all efforts on developing social productive forces, industrializing the country and gradually meeting the people's growing material and cultural needs. Based on this guiding line, Mao Zedong had stressed many times that the Party should not only do well in leading politics, military affairs, culture and foreign affairs, but also in leading economic construction; and that Party should strive hard to improve its knowledge basis, and act as a "central committee of science"[2] and reform the former conduct; Party cadres should follow the leadership of common people. In his works, including "National Industrialization and Growing Living Standard of the People" (1950) and "Future Tasks of the Communist Party of China"

---

[1] *Selected Works of Mao Zedong* (2nd edition), Volume 3, p.1079. Beijing: People's Press, 1991.

[2] *Collected Works of Mao Zedong*, Volume 7, p.102. Beijing: People's Press, 1999.

(1951), Liu Shaoqi had also highlighted that economic construction was the central task of the Party. He had also explained the notion behind developing productive forces and concentrating on economic construction. We should note that, though, generally the older generation of veteran revolutionists had understood the necessity of economic construction in China's reality and had proposed some correct policies. They had failed to concentrate their endeavor due to some reverse historical factors.

The ruling party should firmly prevent and combat against corruption: As early as in the late period of the War of Resistance against Japan (1937-1945), Mao Zedong had started to consider on how to prevent the Party from decaying and degenerating after it assumes power. In 1944, Guo Moruo had published an article titled "Commemorating the 300th Anniversary of the Jia-shen Year"[1] in the Chongqing-based *Xinhua Daily*, and Mao Zedong immediately included that article into the reading bibliography for high-level Party cadres in the campaign of rectifying the Party's style of work, and warned the Party to "learn from the lesson of Li Zicheng, and never repeat his mistake—becoming so proud after successes."[2] In 1949 at the Second Plenary Session of the Seventh Central Committee of the CPC, Mao Zedong had proposed the famous "two musts": "The Chinese revolution is great, but the road after the revolution will be longer, our work greater and more arduous. This should be made clear now in the Party. The comrades must be educated to remain modest, prudent and free from arrogance and rashness in their style of work. The comrades must be educated to preserve the style of plain living and hard struggle."[3] After the founding of New China, Mao Zedong put into practice the policy of resisting corruption and decadence and personally led the Party in the Three-Anti Campaign (anti-corruption, anti-waste and anti-bureaucracy) and Party Rectification Movement. Mao urged the Party to conduct more ideological and educational campaigns aiming at the members and cadres, so as to improve their awareness of resisting against

---

[1] The Jia-shen year refers to 1644 when the Ming Dynasty perished after a peasant uprising led by Li Zicheng (1606-1645).

[2] *Selected Works of Mao Zedong* (2nd edition), Volume 3, p.948. Beijing: People's Press, 1991.

[3] *Ibid.*, pp.1438-1439.

corruption and decadence. Each member should be able to understand the social and historical roots and ideological and moral causes of corruption and its harm to the Party's undertaking, and embrace the organizational principle of serving the people wholeheartedly and sharing weal and woe with the people. He advocated that the Party should follow a strict policy in combating corruption among Party members, that is, to resolutely rectify any inner-Party corruption and root out decadent elements. He had considered rectification campaigns—generally regarded as a component of Party's style of work—an important tool against corruption in the Party, and had extended this practice into the state organs aiming to achieve a clean government. Thus, the theory of rectifying the Party's style of work became fundamental in theory and practice for preventing and combating corruption after the Party had assumed the ruling position. Mao Zedong generally emphasized that anti-corruption struggles should start from high-level cadres. He was personally involved in handling the first case of corruption against Liu Qingshan and Zhang Zishan after the founding of New China. Moreover, Mao advocated that the CPC should accept and enable supervision from inside the Party, the common people, the other eight democratic parties and news media. Liu Shaoqi had also raised unique ideas: to restrict powers of leaders, make no exception for leading cadres, and borrow some relevant systems from capitalist countries. Zhu De, another prestigious top-level leader, made some speeches on how to strengthen the Party's discipline inspection systematically and rectify the Party discipline when he was the Secretary of Central Commission for Discipline Inspection of the CPC. Zhou Enlai had often warned cadres on delicate issues: ideology, politics, social relations, relatives and personal life. The anti-corruption theories and practices of the first generation of the central collective leadership group of the Party had effectively curbed corruption sprouts after the Party had assumed power, and played a significant role in maintaining the clean working style of the Party and clean government in the early days of the New China.

The ruling party should strive for higher membership qualifications: In 1951, to face several new facts, a high increase in new Party members and impurity phenomenon in ideology, organization and style of work spheres, the Central Committee of the CPC held a conference on organizational issues. In the conference, Liu Shaoqi proposed the "Eight Qualifications for Communist Party Members" and penned a summarizing report for the conference titled "Strive for Higher Qualifications for Party Members." He personally presided the meeting to formulate the Party decree titled "Decision on Rectifying Primary Base Party Organizations" and "Decision on Admitting New Party Members". His expositions on the issue and suggestions for strict regulations on Party members' qualifications had played an important role.

The ruling party must adhere to and improve democratic-centralism and safeguard the unity of the party: In February 1957, Mao Zedong had given an in-depth exposition on the dialectical relation between democracy and centralism in his work titled "On the Correct Handling of Contradictions among the People." He had written: "Within the ranks of the people, democracy is correlated with centralism and freedom with discipline. They are the two opposites of a single entity and contradictory as well as combined, thus we should not one-sidedly emphasize one of them to the exclusion of the other. Within the ranks of the people, we cannot do without freedom, nor can we do without discipline; we cannot do without democracy, nor can we do without centralism. This unity of democracy and centralism, of freedom with discipline, constitutes our democratic centralism."[1] In July of the same year, he stated in another article "The Situation in the Summer of 1957": "Our aim is to create a favorable political situation in which we have both centralism and democracy, both discipline and freedom, both unity of will and individual ease of mind and liveliness." Those views had contributed a significant enrichment to the democratic-centralism, and had set higher requirements for the ruling Party. In practice, Mao Zedong had often warned against two opposing erroneous tendencies: decentralism and individual arbitrariness, and suggested conducting educational campaigns on democratic-centralism among all Party members and enhancing their

---

[1] *Collected Works of Mao Zedong*, Volume 7, p.209. Beijing: People's Press, 1999.

conscientiousness in implementing the principle.

The ruling party must train new successors for the cause of proletarian revolution: In the 1950s, evaluating the requirements of large-scale economic construction, Mao Zedong proposed new requirements for Party cadres: study hard and be both red and professionally high caliber. In several key working conferences in the early 1960s, Mao Zedong had advocated a two faceted combined struggle: oppose to the revisionist trend together with opposition to "peaceful evolution" policy of imperialism. Due to tense atmosphere in that era he had proposed several strategic measures: conducting Marxist educational campaigns, criticizing revisionist trend, and training tens of thousands of new successors for the cause of proletarian revolution. Mao Zedong had regarded the cultivation of successors a significant issue for the Party and the state and calculated that this measure would highly guarantee the leadership of the proletariat as a class. Thus he suggested higher and stricter requirements for Party members and cadres, and stressed that cadres should be inspected, selected and evaluated according to their long-term practice in mass struggles. He proposed the policy of combining two tasks: the building among the ranks of Party members and cadres with the cultivation of new successors for the future, and formulated the five famous criteria for successors. Today, scholars researching Party theories and Party history generally suggest that "the five criteria" containing some notions undermining professional qualities and highly emphasizing political awareness were historically blended with the "left" trend of that period characterized by the tense political and ideological atmosphere, though the main essence in them was basically correct. They generally agree that "the five criteria" could also be applied today with some revision.

The first generation of the central collective leadership group of the CPC, with Mao Zedong in the core position, integrated Marxist and Leninist theories of party building with the realities of China, creatively solved special contradictions and complicated problems cropping up in the building of the CPC, and brought into being Party Building Theory of the Mao Zedong Thought. As specified above, Mao Zedong had personally penned and contributed quite much to the Party's ideology, politics, organization and style of work spheres, thus enriching and developing Marxist and Leninist theories of party building. As Deng Xiaoping had once pointed out, "It was Mao Zedong who had developed Lenin's theory of Party building comprehensively."[1] Here, the term "comprehensively" refers to that it has covered and studied many aspects of the issue, and not one single or a few aspects. Generally scholars also suggest that Mao Zedong had developed Lenin's Theory of Party Building and brought into being an ideological system unique to China: a quite advanced Marxist theory of Party building. However, relatively speaking, the CPC had not been enjoying power for a long period and still lacked a comprehensive understanding, especially on the issue of governance. Consequently, we may suggest that Party Building Theory of the Mao Zedong Thought was historically not complete or imperfect. Chinese academy suggests that Mao Zedong Thought should not include his erroneous ideas in his late years and Party Building Theory of the Mao Zedong Thought should not include those of his late years, either. I agree that the mistakes should not be credited to the Party Building Theory of the Mao Zedong Thought but it does not mean they could be ignored.

1.3.1 Party Building in the Deng Xiaoping Theory

As early as in the democratic revolution period and later in the early period after the founding of the New China, Deng Xiaoping had also made in-depth research on many issues concerning the building of the CPC, and had accumulated a series of insightful ideas. In 1941, in his work "The Party and the Anti-Japanese Democratic Government," he expounded the relationship between the Party and the government, and had raised the idea that the Party should exercise political leadership over the government and people's mass organizations. In 1950, he had emphasized the necessity of enhancing the Party spirit in his report titled "Overcome the Current Unhealthy Tendencies in the Party Organizations of Southwest China." In 1954, at the Fourth Plenary Session of the Seventh Central Committee of

---

[1] *Selected Works of Deng Xiaoping* (2nd edition), Volume 2, p.44. Beijing: People's Press, 1994.

the CPC, Deng had delivered a speech entitled "Conceit and Complacency Are the Arch-Enemies of Party Unity", pointing at the significance of maintaining the Party unity and solidarity. Later, he put forward many other ideas about the building of the ruling party in the "Report on the Revision of the Constitution of the Communist Party of China" which was delivered in 1956 at the Eighth National Congress, "The Communist Party Must Accept Supervision" (1957), "Questions Concerning Cadres of the Party in Power" (1962) and "Build a Mature and Combat-Effective Party" (1965). All these works indeed reveal Deng Xiaoping's contribution to the Party Building Theory of the Mao Zedong Thought, and also demonstrate how he himself developed a unique theory of Party building.

In the period after the Third Plenary Session of the 11th Central Committee of the CPC held in 1978, the objective environment and historical conditions for the Party had encountered several significant changes when compared with the previous periods. In this new era, Party's own situation, tasks, problems concerning Party building had also altered. In the late 1980s and early 1990s the general international social and political environment had changed a new situation in which peace and development had become two outstanding trends that had emerged. The world seemed to enter into a new period, generally termed as the post-Cold War era. But on the other hand the Cold War mentality still exerted its power, and hegemony and power politics were still major factors threatening world peace and stability. After the dramatic changes in Soviet Union and Eastern European socialist countries, worldwide socialist movements had suffered severe setbacks, but later socialist forces in many countries had began to recover and shown significant signs of progress. As for China's domestic environment, CPC had re-evaluated the country's general realistic historical position in regard to an advanced socialist society, as envisaged by Marx and Engels, and concluded that the country was still in the primary stage of socialism, and shifted its focus from class struggle to economic construction and transformed the society from a relatively isolated pattern of planned economy to a market economy. A long-term new economic development mode was decided:

reform and opening-up. Specifically, as for the Party itself, it was confronted by a prominent problem that the Party's ideology, organization and style of work needed a significant improvement after the negative effects of the Cultural Revolution. In this new period, Deng Xiaoping had led the Party to analyze the characteristics of the new phenomena and summarized the experiences and lessons from the building of the Party, and put forward a series of new ideas, concepts and conclusions about what kind of Party shall be built and how to build it during the reform, opening-up and modernization drive period. Thus in this new era the Party Building of the Deng Xiaoping Theory was established.

The major contents of the Party Building of the Deng Xiaoping Theory contain the following features:

Regarding the Party's program and historical mission, the Deng Xiaoping Theory has put forth the new theory on primary stage of socialism. According to this theory, the ultimate goal of the Party is to realize communism, and socialism is the primary stage of communism while China will be for longer time in a stage—termed as the primary stage of socialism. And the other important aspect of this theory envisages that the Party's current task is to build socialism with Chinese characteristics.

Regarding the Party's nature and the goal of Party building, the CPC is the vanguard of the Chinese working class. The Party should build itself into a Marxist political party with militant combat effectiveness, and should be a strong core, leading the people in realizing material, cultural and ethical progress.

Regarding the Party's leadership, the most important component and core of the Four Cardinal Principles (adherence to the socialist road, the people's democratic dictatorship, the leadership of the Party and adhering to Marxism-Leninism and Mao Zedong Thought) is adherence to the leadership of the Party. To achieve this, efforts should be made to improve the leadership of the Party. Deng Xiaoping had made in-depth exposition on the relationship between adherence to the Party's leadership and improvement of that quality. He had stressed the need to improve the Party's style of leadership, ways of organization, style of work and forms of activities to adapt to the new situation, and hence developed an advanced theory of the Party leadership.

Regarding the Party's political development, Deng formulated the basic line of "one central task and two basic points" and stressed that the basic line should not change for 100 years and the Party should center its work on this basic line and never interrupt or endanger the central task as economic development. Deng decisively reviewed and corrected the classic official mantra in the Party, known as "struggles between two lines and the two classes" and instead proposed to realistically carry out struggle in the two battlefronts while guarding against and opposing both "left" and "right" trends, especially the "left" trends which had deeper historical roots in the Party.

Regarding the Party's guiding ideology, Deng re-established and developed the Party's ideological line, not only adhering to Mao Zedong's basic principle: proceeding from reality and seeking truth from facts, but also combining emancipation of minds with seeking truth from facts and making it a basic point of the Party to adhere to and develop truth in practice. He stressed that Mao Zedong Thought must be completely and accurately grasped concentrating on its real essence, and Marxism-Leninism and Mao Zedong Thought must be learned, carried forward and developed in practice. Moreover, on the basis of the criterion of practice, he put forward the idea of "three favorables" (every act should be judged whether it is favorable for the growth of the productive forces in a socialist society, for the increase of the overall strength of the socialist state and for the improvement of the people's living standards) as criteria for measuring the results of socialist reforms, thus further expounding the Party's ideological line comprehensively.

Regarding the Party's organizational development, Deng Xiaoping had stated that a correct political line needs to be guaranteed by a correct organizational line, and special attention should be paid to the building of the ranks of cadres and primary basic Party organizations. He proposed that cadres in the new era should be politically highly revolutionary, younger on the average, better educated and professionally more competent, and being politically highly revolutionary should be the prerequisite. He advocated respect for intellectual knowledge and for trained personnel, breaking with the classic notions and practices as overstressing seniority in the cadre selection and appointment, and he opposed promoting and employing outstanding personnel. He stressed that the core of building the ranks of cadres should be focused on the leadership building and special attention should be paid to selecting qualified leaders and forming rationally structured collective leadership with leaders complementing each other. He also put forth new contents, policies and principles for the reform of cadre policy and personnel system of the Party and the government. The idea was to break with the old tradition as lifelong tenure for leading cadres in the Party and proposed a new system in which a generation of collective leaders should give way—collectively—to the next generation including the Party's central leadership. He proposed to solve the problem of promoting and demoting cadres by improving the cadre system and then to gradually bring into being a rational mechanism of recruiting and employing personnel. He had demanded to strengthen the building of primary Party organizations and the ranks of Party members, pay special attention to the problem of unqualified Party members and ideological purity criteria, to inspect the work of primary Party organizations on a regular basis and improve them, and to give full play to the role of primary organizations as political cores and fighting forts.

Regarding the Party's style of work, Deng stressed that the style of work of the ruling Party was a matter of vital importance. Fine traditions in the style of work should be carried forward; bureaucracy, formalism and subjectivism should be opposed; and corruption should be resolutely fought against throughout the whole process of reform and opening-up and integrity should be the most important quality being upheld. He had advocated that anti-corruption qualities and upholding integrity were two major factors contributing to close relationship between the Party and the masses, and thus demanded leading cadres at all levels set examples for others and fight against unhealthy tendencies to stand up to the two hard tests of being in power and leading the reform and opening-up tasks. He held the opinion that the Party should rely on self-education and at the same time obey the legal system—of both the Party and the state—to improve its style of work and uphold integrity.

Regarding the Party's ultimate goal and line of work, Deng stressed the Party's task was to serve the people wholeheartedly, and thus the Party should maintain close ties with the masses and uphold the mass line through all kind of work. He stressed that whether the masses would support, agree to, be pleased with or approve the policy should be the starting point and goal of the Party in formulating any policies, as well as a criterion determining the success or failure of all the work. He pointed out that maintaining close ties with the masses was fundamental to uphold and improve the Party's leadership.

Regarding the Party's institutional improvement, Deng stressed that the system of leadership and the system of organization should be regarded as fundamental and those systems should be stable, long-lasting and advocated that systems have a major bearing on the overall situation. He stressed that democratic-centralism was a basic system for the Party and the state and a most rational and convenient system, and never be discarded. He asked to set up and improve systems based on democratic- centralism, improve the Party's rules and regulations, make inner-Party activities more democratic and institutional-based, connect the improvement of the Party's institutions with that of socialist democracy and the country's legal system, and open up a new method of relying rather on institutional improvement instead of political campaigns in Party building.

Regarding the Party's self-discipline and being strict with its members, Deng stressed that the Party should be strict first with its members and second with its cadres, especially top-level cadres. Both inner-Party and non-Party supervision should be strengthened over the Party and its members. He demanded to strictly implement the Party discipline and to uphold the principle of equality preceding the principle of discipline, so as to safeguard the authority of the Party discipline and state laws.

Regarding the CPC's relations with foreign political parties and countries, Deng proposed the four principles—independence and autonomy, complete equality, mutual respect, and non-interference—to deal with and promote relations between the Party and foreign parties. He stressed that the parties and people of each country should select a development road by themselves, and explore their own ways to settle internal affairs. Every Party should be respected that they are best to judge the quality of their policies. And China should not decide on bilateral relations with a country by ideological criteria, but focus on strategic interests of the country.

Party Building of the Deng Xiaoping Theory had inherited, enriched and developed Marxist Theory of Party Building and Party Building Theory of the Mao Zedong Thought, and was a new breakthrough; the CPC had achieved during the process of exploring the laws of building the Party which is in the ruling position. It was a development of Party Building Theory of the Mao Zedong Thought in many respects, especially some components of it had played a major bearing on the overall situation. It naturally reflects the qualities accumulated in the Party and the new features of the era. Scholars generally agree that Deng Xiaoping had supplemented Party Building Theory of the Mao Zedong Thought with new contents conforming to reform, opening-up and modernization strategy, added more ideas to Mao Zedong's Party theories and elevated Mao's Party theory from its relatively narrower content to more macroscopic, open, systematic and comprehensive system. The two outstanding examples would be to fight against inner-Party corruption rather by legal means and to advocate advancing in Party building through a style of reform and development. Thus, Party building has been integrated with the great systematic program of reform, opening-up and socialist modernization, and thus attained a new vitality.

1.3.2 Jiang Zemin and Party Building Theory in the Important Thought of Three Represents

At the Fourth Plenary Session of the Thirteenth CPC Central Committee in June 1989, Jiang Zemin was elected General Secretary of the Central Committee of the CPC and hence the third generation of the new central collective leadership group, with him as its core leader, was formed. Confronted with the highly volatile world situation and arduous domestic tasks, the third generation of the central collective leadership, with Jiang Zemin as its core, had agreed on the perspective as: "the key concern should be the Party," and concentrated its efforts on the Party building. In this new period, under the new circumstances the Party leadership had agreed to insist on the reform strategy and avoid any hesitate on that policy, and that was a courageous stand in that point of time. With this general background, a series of important statements about the Party building responding to the new circumstances and the important thought of Three Represents was developed and established. Based on Deng Xiaoping theory, this thought has produced a more complete content to the question: what is socialism and how to build it. Its Party theory has also given a more complex answer to the question: what kind of Party shall be built and how to build it. The important thought of Three Represents is a theoretical system that embodies closely related new thoughts and new ideas concerning reform strategy, development style, stability factor, style in handling internal affairs, foreign affairs, national defense, Party building, state affairs, management and administration of military affairs. The part of the important thought of Three Represents concerning the building of the ruling party is hereby called the important thought of Three Represents on Party Building, which is embodied in Jiang Zemin's works titled "On Three Represents," "On the Party Building," "Special Excerpts on Strengthening and Improving the Building of the Ruling Party," and his works published in the three-volume *Selected Works of Jiang Zemin*.

The major contents of Party Building in the important thought of Three Represents are as follows:

About the Party's nature: The CPC is the vanguard both of the Chinese working class and of the Chinese people and the Chinese nation. Hereby the nation as a subject is included in the new concept. And the Party is the core of leadership for the cause of socialism and represents the development trend of China's advanced productive forces, represents the orientation of

China's advanced culture and also represents the fundamental interests of the overwhelming majority of the Chinese people. At the same time the Party should maintain its pivot nature as the vanguard of the Chinese working class, and its proletariat style as serving the people wholeheartedly, maintain its vanguard nature, strengthen its working class foundations, expand its general mass base, and enhance its social influence.

The Party's ideological line is to proceed from reality in handling all matters, to integrate theory with practice, to seek truth from facts, and to verify and develop the truth through practice. The Party should emancipate the minds, seek truth from facts, advance with the times, and make theoretical, institutional, scientific, technological and other innovations to meet practical demands. Among all the innovations, striving for theoretical innovation is the prerequisite and key, guiding and driving all the other innovations. The Party should view Marxism with a scientific attitude, and work to enrich and develop it in practice. The Party should make the truth-seeking and pragmatic spirit the core of its ideological line, and widely promote this new style.

About the Party's basic line: The Party must build itself in line with its political line, its central task and at the same keenly consider its future ultimate goal. The thought propounds the Party's basic program for the primary stage of socialism, and expounds the Party's basic theories, basic line and basic program and their relations. All the Party members should unwaveringly adhere to the Party's basic program for the primary stage of socialism; integrate the central task of economic development and the two basic points—the Four Cardinal Principles and Reform and Opening-up—into the great practice of building socialism with Chinese characteristics; concentrate on the priority of governing and rejuvenating the country; carry out the scientific outlook concept on development issues in all respects. The Party should have a good understanding on and appropriately handle the relations between reform, development and stability; develop the advanced productive forces and promote the advanced culture and respond to the fundamental interests of the overwhelming majority of the Chinese people in order to demonstrate the Party's vanguard nature and the superiority of the socialist system; and promote social progress in all respects and all-round development of citizens.

About the Party's ideological building: The Party should highlight its ideological building; make the Three Represents a guiding ideology for the Party work and state affairs; work hard to build itself into a learning party; and constantly improve all the Party members' theoretical attainment in Marxism. The Party should strengthen Marxist research and development; make the Party's ideological and theoretical work more creative, persuasive and appealing; carry out the project of Marxist research and development; and boost philosophical and social science studies. The Party should work hard to promote the Marxist style of learning that integrates theory with practice; combine the transformation of the objective world with that of the subjective world; and enhance Party members' ability in utilizing basic Party theories to solve practical problems.

About the Party's fundamental organizational system and leadership system: Inner-Party democracy is the life of the Party, and is an example and propeller for people's democracy in the country. The Party's leadership system and working mechanism should be improved to institutionally guarantee better implementation of democratic-centralism. In order to strengthen democratic centralism, Party committees should follow the principles of "collective leadership, democratic-centralism, individual consultations among committee members and decisions should be produced in the meetings." Party organizations at all levels and all the Party members, particularly leading cadres, should strictly observe the Party discipline, safeguard the authority of the Central Committee of the Party, and enhance the Party's vitality, unity and solidarity.

About the building of a contingent of high-caliber Party cadres and strong leadership: It is a matter of vital importance for maintaining prolonged stability of the Party and state to build a contingent of high-caliber leading cadres capable of assuming heavy responsibilities and withstanding the test of trials and tribulations, and in particular, and train a large number of outstanding leading cadres for the tasks of running the Party, state and army. The Party should build a contingent of competent personnel for the Party and government, for corporate management and with sound expertise. Leading cadres at various levels must stress study, political awareness and integrity, and develop a correct view on evaluating their performances and all these acts should conform to the scientific outlook on development. The Party should adhere to the principle that the Party is in charge of cadre management and personnel management; deepen the reform of the cadre and personnel system; carry out the principle of making the ranks of the cadres more revolutionary, younger in average age, better educated and more professionally competent; promote cadres to leading posts who have political integrity, professional competence and outstanding performance and enjoy popular support. Work hard to form a vigorous personnel mechanism under which the Party can gather large numbers of talented people, put them for the best use and get them prepared for both promotion and demotion; and strengthen leaderships at all levels in accordance with the requirements of being politically reliable, truth-seeking and pragmatic, pioneering and innovative, hard-working and clean, and having teamwork spirit.

About the building of the Party's primary organizations: The Party should, by focusing on the central task and serving the overall interests, broaden the fields of its endeavor, intensify its functions and expand the coverage of the Party's work so as to increase the rallying power and combat effectiveness of primary organizations. Primary Party organizations should organize, motivate and practice the implementation of the Three Represents. The Party should work harder to build the Party at the primary level in rural areas, state-owned enterprises, communities, and Party and government organs. The Party should set up Party organizations and strengthen Party building in enterprises belonging to non-public sectors, and intensify efforts to establish Party organizations in mass organizations and intermediary organizations.

About the building of Party membership: The Party should build a membership that is highly qualified, rationally structured, in moderate numbers and performs well. In accordance with the principle of "maintaining strict standards, guaranteeing the quality, improving the structure and progressing prudently," the Party should make a point of recruiting Party members, study the features and rules of recruitment under the new circumstances of reform, opening-up and market economy, and develop a mechanism for regular work in this sphere. The Party should recruit Party members mainly from among workers, farmers, intellectuals, servicemen and cadres, thus expanding the basic components and backbone of the Party. In addition, the Party should admit members from advanced elements of other social strata, those who accept the Party's program and Constitution, work for the realization of the Party's line and program consciously and meet the qualifications of Party membership after a reasonable long period of test.

About the improvement of the Party's style of work: The key to improving the Party's style of work lies in keeping the flesh-and-blood ties between the Party and the people. The Party should make effective efforts to resolve major problems in respect of its way of thinking, study and work, its style of leadership and its cadres' way of life by acting on the principle of the "eight do's" and "eight don'ts" proposed by the Central Committee. The "eight do's" and "eight don'ts" are: (1) Emancipate the mind and seek truth from facts; do not stick to old ways and do not stand still without making any progress. (2) Combine theory with practice; do not copy mechanically or apply book worshipping. (3) Keep close ties with the people; do not practice formalism and bureaucracy. (4) Adhere to the principle of democratic-centralism; do not act arbitrarily or stay feeble and lax. (5) Abide by Party discipline; do not pursue liberalism. (6) Be honest and upright; do not abuse power for personal gains. (7) Work hard; do not indulge in hedonism. (8) Appoint people on their merits; do not resort to malpractice in personnel placement.

About the Party's discipline promotion and anti-corruption: To run the state well, the first thing is to run the Party well. To do this, strict discipline should be observed for Party members. To be strict with Party members, Party discipline should be enforced. The essential way to enforce the Party discipline is to make Party members abide by Party rules and regulations, and study hard, conscientiously observe, carry out and safeguard the Constitution of the Party. To meet the requirement of strictness with Party members, the Party should build itself ideologically, politically, organizationally, institutionally, and in the style of work and discipline, and educate, manage and oversee its organizations at various levels, its members and cadres. To combat and prevent corruption resolutely is a political battle of vital importance to the Party and state, and thus the Party should take a clear stand and a resolute attitude to persistently combat and prevent corruption. The Party should follow the general idea of fighting corruption in a comprehensive way, addressing both its symptoms and root cause and combining punishment with prevention, putting the emphasis on prevention, and work hard to set up and improve a system for punishing and preventing corruption that emphasizes education, institutions and oversight and conforms to the socialist market economy.

About the ultimate goal of the Party work: The Party should display its ultimate goal of serving the people wholeheartedly in its practice of remaining a ruling Marxist party that is solely built for public interests and exercises governance for the people. It must adhere to the consistency and coherence between the law governing social development and the principal position of people making the history, between struggling for the lofty ideals and for the interests of the people, and between carrying out Party work and serving the people's interests. All the Party members should bear in mind that the aim and outcome of making and implementing all the policies is to represent the fundamental interests of the overwhelming majority of the people. The Party should establish and improve a working mechanism for properly handling contradictions among the people, care for the life and production conditions of the masses, take effective measures to deal with practical problems that involve the immediate interests of the people, and put into practice the principle of exercising power solely for the people, showing concern for them and working for their interests.

About strengthening the Party's governance capability: Strengthening the Party's governance capability is one of the fundamental undertakings of the Party after it has assumed power. Its significance is reiterated from the perspective of solidifying the Party's ruling position by summarizing experiences and lessons of Chinese and foreign ruling parties. Guiding ideology, general goal and major tasks for strengthening the Party's governance capability are identified in the important thought of Three Represents of Party Building, which demands to improve the theoretical system of the Party's governance and its styles of leadership and governance from the aspects of concept, foundation, strategies, institutions, style, resources and environment of governance, and to constantly strengthen the Party's governance capability while exploring the laws governing social development, socialist construction and the governance of Communist parties.

The important thought of Three Represents of Party Building is an important component of the important thought of Three Represents, a continuation and development of Marxist Theory of Party Building. In November 2002, the 16th National Congress of the CPC was held successfully in Beijing, the first of its kind held by the Party in the new century. The Congress witnessed a smooth succession of the Party's old central collective leadership group by the new. Since the Congress, the new generation of central collective leadership, with Hu Jintao as General Secretary, has held high the great banner of Deng Xiaoping Theory and the important thought of Three Represents.

The important thought of Three Represents has developed theories of building the ruling party mainly in following aspects: put forward the scientific outlook on development style as a major guiding ideology that must be adhered to for pushing forward economic and social development; ask the Party to launch a new campaign among all the Party members, requiring them to learn and implement the important thought of Three Represents, thus solidify the guiding position of this Thought; make Party members carry forward the truth-seeking and pragmatic spirit; ask Party members to bear in mind the "two musts" and carry forward the Party's fine traditions in her style of work; require the Party to put into practice the principle of exercising power solely for the people, showing concern for them and working for their interests, and always make sure that the aim and outcome of all the work of the Party is to realize, safeguard and expand the fundamental interests of the overwhelming majority of the people. Substantial breakthroughs were achieved in improving the Party's capacity for democratic, scientific and law-based governance and combining this conduct with the need to uphold the Party's leadership and the principle that the people are the masters of the country which also requires to rule the country by law; demand to set up and improve a system for punishing and preventing corruption that stresses education, institutions and oversight and conforms to the socialist market economy; make the point that strengthening the Party's governance capability is one of the fundamental undertakings of the Party after it has assumed power and that the Party's art of leadership and governance capability should be improved constantly; and make endeavors to strengthen the Party's vanguard nature and improve the permanent mechanism whereby the Party always retains its vanguard nature.

Chapter 2

Basic Marxist Ideas on Proletarian Parties and the CPC

According to Marxism, a proletarian party represents the fundamental interests of the proletariat as a whole and the working people is an advanced and organized force of the proletariat, and shoulders the historical mission entrusted by the proletariat and the working people, and is the highest form of union of the proletariat and a tool of the proletariat to accomplish specific historical mission in a specific period. The goal of a Communist party is to wholeheartedly serve the working class and the laboring people for their interests.

2.1 The Nature of Proletarian Parties

Nature means the essential qualities or characteristics of something, namely, the unique inborn stipulations distinguishing it from the others. The nature of a political party refers to the party's inherent stipulations, that is, the basic qualities distinguishing it from other parties. Marxism maintains that every political party in the world is based on a certain class foundation, acts on behalf of a certain class, strata or social groups, and is composed of people from this certain class who are the firmest, the most faithful and enthusiastic in safeguarding the class interests. Any political group that bases itself on the bourgeoisie, takes a firm bourgeois standpoint, acts on behalf of that class, and conscientiously serves them is a bourgeois party. Any political group that bases itself on the proletariat, takes a firm proletarian stand, acts on behalf of and conscientiously serves the proletariat is a proletarian party. There is no political party in the world that stands "above classes" or represents the interests of the whole nation or all the citizens.

2.1.1 Marxist Classics on the Nature of Proletarian Parties

The earliest statements of Marx and Engels on the nature of proletarian parties can date back to around 1845. In the first co-authored book *The Holy Family* (1844), they had pointed to the nature of political parties: "Any political party is a political representative of a certain class," and thus laid the foundation of Marxist theory of political parties. In the "Manifesto of the Communist Party" (1848), they had re-stated the point. During the First International period, Engels stressed, "Contrary to the previous sectarian organizations, with their vagaries and rivalries, the International is a genuine and militant organization of the proletarian class of all countries, united in their common struggle against the capitalists and the landowners, against their class power organized as the state."[1] Even during the Second International period, Engels had persisted in the proletarian nature of the party. In the letter to Gerson Trier on December 18, 1889, he wrote, "For the proletariat to be strong enough to win on the decisive days, it should—and this Marx and I have been arguing ever since 1847—form a separate party distinct from all others and a conscientious political party of the proletariat."[2]

---

[1] *Marx & Engels Selected Works* (1ˢᵗ Chinese edition), Volume 18, p.36. Beijing: People's Press, 1964.

[2] *Marx & Engels Selected Works* (2ⁿᵈ Chinese edition), Volume 4, p.685. Beijing: People's Press, 1995.

During his struggle against opportunists in the Second International and founding of the Russian proletarian party, Lenin had carried on and developed Marx and Engels' ideas about the nature of proletarian parties. His major points were: Firstly, class character is an essential quality of any party, and any "non-class political party" or a party standing "above classes" is ridiculous in theory and harmful in practice. "In one form or another, the idea of a 'non-class party' is still advocated, but the 'force of historical conditions' has invariably refuted this idea and has shattered this illusion. The attempts or efforts to include different classes in 'one party' have always been characteristic of bourgeois democracy at the time when it had chosen its main enemy in the past, and not in the future, i.e., when it fought against the feudal lords, and not the proletariat."[1] "All attempts to establish a party standing 'above classes,' to unite the peasants and the workers in one party, to represent a non-existent 'working intelligentsia' as a class by itself, are extremely harmful and ruinous to the cause of Russian political freedom, since such attempts can bring nothing but disillusionment, a waste of strength, and confusion in people's minds."[2]

Secondly, a Communist party is a political party of the proletariat, but a party and a class are different. "The (Russian) Economists erred by confusing party with class. Reviving those old mistakes, the Iskrist group of today confuses the total sum of democratic parties or organizations with the organization of the people. That is empty, false, and harmful phrase-mongering. It is indeed empty because it offers no specific meaning whatever, and lacks any reference to definite democratic parties or trends. It is false because in a capitalist society even the proletariat, the most advanced class, is not in a position to create a party embracing the entire class, and as for the whole people creating such a party, that is entirely out of the question."[3]

Thirdly, a Communist party is the vanguard of the proletariat, which

---

[1] *Collected Works of Vladimir Lenin* (2nd Chinese edition), Volume 21, p.249. Beijing: People's Press, 1990.

[2] *Ibid.*, p.278.

[3] *Collected Works of Vladimir Lenin* (2nd Chinese edition), Volume 11, pp.362-363. Beijing: People's Press, 1987.

can never be a vanguard only because of its class character. "The Party is the politically conscious, advanced section of the class; it is its vanguard. The strength of that vanguard is ten times, a hundred times, more than a hundred times, greater than its numbers."[1] And "the Party should be only the vanguard, the leader of the vast masses of the working class, the whole (or nearly the whole) of which works 'under the control and direction' of the Party organizations, but the whole of which does not and should not belong to a 'party'."[2]

After the success of the Great October Socialist Revolution of Russia, Stalin enriched Lenin's views about the nature of proletarian parties in socialist revolution and construction period. He pointed out that the dictatorship of the proletariat was composed of "transmission gears" and "directing force" with trade unions, Soviets and youth leagues being the "transmission gears" while the party being the "directing force." "The Party is a higher form of a class organization of the proletariat as compared with the other forms of proletarian organization (labor unions, cooperatives, state organization) and, moreover, its function was to generalize and direct the work of these organizations." "The dictatorship of the proletariat may be realized only through the Party as its directing force." "The dictatorship of the proletariat can be complete only if it is led by a single Party, the Communist Party, which does not and should not share its leadership with any other parties."[3] However, the Party's leadership should not be replaced with the proletarian class it represents because "the Party carries out the dictatorship of the proletariat" and thus "whoever identifies the leading role of the Party with the dictatorship of the proletariat substitutes the directives given by the Party for the will and actions of the class."[4]

---

[1] *Collected Works of Vladimir Lenin* (2nd Chinese edition), Volume 24, p.38. Beijing: People's Press, 1990.

[2] *Collected Works of Vladimir Lenin* (2nd Chinese edition), Volume 7, pp.270-271. Beijing: People's Press, 1986.

[3] *Collected Works of J. V. Stalin* (1st Chinese edition), Volume 10, pp.90-91. Beijing: People's Press, 1954.

[4] *Collected Works of J. V. Stalin* (1st Chinese edition), Volume 8, pp.37-38. Beijing: People's Press, 1954.

In summary, in their statements about the nature of proletarian parties, Marx, Engels, Lenin and Stalin had always stressed the class character and opposed any denial of this basic quality by any reason or excuse. In the meantime, they had insisted that proletarian parties were only a part of the proletarian class, a force composed of advanced elements of this vanguard class, and that the vanguard nature of the proletariat should never be substituted for that of proletarian parties.

2.1.2 Chinese Communists on the Nature of the Proletarian Party

In the long practice of revolution, construction and reform periods, the Chinese Communists have inherited previous classical ideas about the nature of proletarian parties, and integrated them with Chinese conditions and developed their own thoughts in practice of building the CPC. To be specific:

Firstly, they have also stressed the class character and political nature of proletarian parties. According to Mao Zedong, a political party is a kind of society, a political society. The No. 1 category in a political society is political parties. A party is an organization of a certain class. Jiang Zemin had also underlined that quality: "A political party is a political group organized under a political program and a political line and for the fulfillment of its political goals. A party will never be a real party when departing from politics, its political program, line and goals. Our party is a Marxist political party, and thus should stress politics of Marxism, politics related to the building of socialism with Chinese characteristics, and politics that realizes, safeguards and develops the interests of the people."[1] The Chinese Communists believe that it is nonsense to discuss the issue of proletarian parties disregarding society, class, politics or the vanguard nature.

Secondly, a party's nature should not be judged based on the social origin of its members. China was a big agricultural country, with numerous farmers and small industrialists. In the New Democratic Revolution, the CPC had a large proportion of members from the class of farmers or petty

---

[1] *Selected Works of Jiang Zemin*, Volume 3, pp.360-361. Beijing: People's Press, 2006.

bourgeoisie. In the process of building itself, the CPC has always attached special importance to educating Party members with proletarian ideas, so as to build the Party ideologically and uplift members from the class of farmers or petty bourgeoisie into true, advanced fighters of the proletariat. "It is not just the social origin of Party members…that decide things." "Marxist-Leninist education will enable Party members of petty-bourgeois origin to undergo a thoroughgoing ideological remolding to change their former petty-bourgeois character and gain the qualities of advanced fighters of the proletariat. A party founded, steeled and educated in such a manner is certainly not inferior—to say the very least—to any proletarian party of the capitalist countries."[1] In the new era of reform and opening-up when the society became more diversified and plural, Jiang Zemin stressed, "To judge whether a political party is advanced or whether it is the vanguard of the working class, we should mainly consider whether its theories and programs are Marxist, whether it represents the correct direction of social development, and whether it represents the fundamental interests of the overwhelming majority of the Chinese people,"[2] instead of referring to the social origin of its members. "We should admit members into the Party from the advanced elements of other social strata who indeed accept the Party's program and Constitution, work for the realization of the Party's line and program consciously and meet the qualifications of Party membership following a long period of test."[3]

Thirdly, the Party is a tool of the proletariat and the people. Political parties are all political tools used in class struggle. A bourgeois party is a tool that the bourgeoisie uses to realize their interests, while a proletarian party is a tool that the proletariat and the laboring people utilize to realize their interests and self-emancipation. In the period when class struggle was quite intense, Mao Zedong had pointed out, "We are Marxists and we believe in instrumentalism." "The Party is a tool for class struggle; the

[1] *Selected Works of Liu Shaoqi*, Volume I, p.325. Beijing: People's Press, 1981.
[2] *Selected Works of Jiang Zemin*, Volume 3, p.285. Beijing: People's Press, 2006.
[3] *Ibid.*, p.286.

government is a tool; and the Central Committee and administrative organs of the Party are both tools of the Party and are for the class struggle. Our Party is the leader of the working class, and the Central Committee is the leader of the whole Party. We regard both of them as tools." "To achieve success, our class should select a vanguard. It is in practice that the people select their tool of leadership and leaders. Those selected would be wrong if they became arrogant and regard themselves as big potatoes, instead of conscientiously acting as a tool. To make the people succeed, our Party should act as a tool, consciously. All the members of the Central Committee and administrative organs should understand this."[1] In the peaceful period of economic construction after the Party became the core of leadership and assumed power, Deng Xiaoping still highlighted the character of the Party as a tool: "A political party of the working class, unlike the political parties of the bourgeoisie, never regards the masses as its tool, but consciously regards itself as their tool for carrying out their given historical mission in a given historical period." "The Communist Party is the collective body of the advanced elements among the working class and the laboring people, and there can be no doubt as to its great role in leading the masses. But the Party is able to play its part as vanguard and lead the masses forward precisely and solely because it wholeheartedly serves the masses, represents their will and interests, and works hard to help them organize themselves to fight for their own interests and for the fulfillment of their own will."[2]

Fourthly, the Party is also a kind of historical phenomenon. Marxist theoreticians maintain that after seizing of power from exploiting classes, the proletariat will abolish the exploiting ownership of the production means, implement the socialist public ownership, and vigorously develop and emancipate the productive forces. Based on this, the proletariat will gradually eliminate disparities between urban and rural areas, between brain-workers and manual workers, and between workers and farmers, and

---

[1] *Selected Works of Mao Zedong*, Volume 3, pp.373-374. Beijing: People's Press, 1996.

[2] *Selected Works of Deng Xiaoping* (2nd edition), Volume 1, pp.217-218. Beijing: People's Press, 1994.

surrender traditional and conservative forces that are closely connected with small-scale production. Classes and class disparities which emerge when productive forces develop into a certain level and remain throughout a period when productive forces are still underdeveloped will ultimately disappear in the future when the conditions are ripe. What's the destiny of political parties, as representatives of class interests, particularly proletarian parties? Mao Zedong had given such an explanation on this issue: "The Communist Party and the democratic parties are all products of history. What emerges in history disappears in history. Therefore, one day the Communist Party will disappear, and so will the democratic parties.... Our task is to hasten their extinction."[1]

Therefore, on the basis of stressing its class character, the CPC always integrates its vanguard nature with the mass line, and its leading role with the function as a tool, and maintains that the CPC's vanguard nature and leading role are demonstrated through its mass line and the function as a tool. Moreover, from the standpoint of historical materialism, the CPC acknowledges the historical limitation of the existence of political parties and advocates transforming Party members with non-proletarian origin into true, advanced fighters of the proletariat by means of ideological education. We think such ideas have enriched Marxist theories about the nature of proletarian parties.

2.2 The New Vanguard Formulation of the CPC

The nature of the CPC refers to the innate qualities distinguishing it from all the other parties and social organizations in China. Among the qualities, the basic ones are its class character and vanguard nature. An accurate description of the CPC's nature was stated in the Program of the CPC promulgated in 2002: "The Communist Party of China is the vanguard both of the Chinese working class and of the Chinese people and the Chinese nation." This statement is a new development in the previous classical

---

[1] *Selected Works of Mao Zedong*, Volume 7, p.35.

formulation: "The party is an advanced force of the working class," a Marxism-Leninist idea on the nature of proletarian parties. Although the CPC has used different expressions about its nature in different periods to respond to the time features, the scholars on Party building have suggested that the essence had always remained unchanged.

2.2.1 The Party as an Advanced and Organized Force of the Working Class

As soon as it was founded, the CPC gave clear expressions about its nature. The Resolutions on "Trade Union Movements and the Communist Party" adopted at the Second National Congress of the CPC in 1922 had stressed, on the one hand, the vanguard nature of the Chinese proletariat among all the exploited classes and strata: "The struggle of the proletariat and laboring people to liberate themselves from the exploitation of the bourgeoisie should be accompanied by the struggle of the proletariat—the most advanced and militant section of the working class—for their interests." On the other hand, the Resolutions underlined the vanguard trait of the CPC among the Chinese proletariat: "The Communist Party is an organization of the proletarian people with class consciousness, the vanguard of the proletariat"; and "if the Communist Party is the brain of a person, then all the workers constitute the body. Therefore the Communist Party should be the 'vanguard' and 'brain' in any labor movement."[1] The contents in the above formulations can be summarized into one sentence: Since the Chinese proletariat is the "most advanced and militant section" of "the proletariat and laboring people" in China and while the CPC is the vanguard organization and the core of leadership of the working class, the CPC is naturally the vanguard organization and the core of leadership of "the proletariat and laboring people."

After the practice of the Great Revolution period (1924-1927), also called the First Revolutionary Civil War, and the Agrarian Revolutionary

---

[1] *Selected Documents of the Central Committee of the Communist Party of China*, Volume 1, p.48, pp.51-52. Beijing: The Party School of the Central Committee of the CPC Press, 1982.

War period (1927-1937), also called the Second Revolutionary Civil War, and the War of Resistance against Japan (1937-1945), the CPC got a deeper understanding of the class structure and stratum structure of the Chinese society, and made a more explicit statement on its nature. The Constitution of the Communist Party of China adopted at the Seventh National Congress of the CPC in 1945 had pointed out, "The Communist Party of China is an advanced and organized force of the Chinese working class, the highest form of its class organization. It represents the interests of the Chinese nation and people." Liu Shaoqi had explained the formulation from two aspects. "The interests of the Chinese proletariat are at all times identical with those of the Chinese people…. The Communist Party of China can succeed only when it stands for the interests of the whole people, instead of merely for the partial and immediate interests of one class. The proletariat cannot win its own emancipation if it fails to emancipate the people as a whole. On the other hand, the Chinese working class and the working people as a whole constitute the main body of the Chinese nation. It is their interests that form the foundation of the interests of the Chinese nation and people. In fighting for an independent, free, democratic, united, prosperous and powerful new China, the Communist Party of China is representing the interests of the entire Chinese nation and people as well as those of the Chinese working class. The same will be true in the future when it fights for socialism and communism, because the realization or a socialist and Communist society will mean final emancipation of all mankind."[1] These were actually scientific expositions of the classical statement of the Communists—"Only by emancipating all mankind can the proletariat achieve its own final emancipation."—when integrated with the historical mission of the CPC.

The Constitution of the Communist Party of China adopted at the Eighth National Congress of the CPC in 1956 had pointed out, "The Communist Party of China is the vanguard of the Chinese working class and the highest form of its class organization." Such a statement was made at a time when profound changes took place in the class relations of the Chinese society after

[1] *Selected Works of Liu Shaoqi*, Volume I, pp.331-332. Beijing: People's Press, 1981.

the socialist transformation was mainly realized: the working class became the ruling class of the state; most farmers had been organized in cooperatives; and the bourgeoisie, as a class, was dying out. What's more important was that the CPC had taken power and played a leading role in all the state affairs. The emphasis on the nature of the CPC as the vanguard of the working class was to make the CPC maintain its vanguard nature while adhering to the mass line in face of new tests after it had assumed power. In this sense, this statement also embodied the connotation that "the CPC represents the interests of the Chinese nation and people." As Deng Xiaoping pointed out in the Report on the Revision of the Constitution of the Communist Party of China, discussed and approved at the above Party Congress: "The Communist Party is the collective body of the advanced elements among the working class and the laboring people."[1]

During the Cultural Revolution (1966-1976), serious errors had occurred in the Party line. The Constitution adopted at the Ninth National Congress of the CPC in 1969 stated, "The Communist Party of China is composed of the advanced elements of the proletariat; it is a vigorous vanguard organization leading the proletariat and the revolutionary masses in the fight against the class enemy." The Constitution adopted at the Tenth National Congress of the CPC in 1974 stated, "The Communist Party of China is a party of the proletariat, the vanguard of the proletariat." Although there were no errors of principle, the two formulations had replaced "the working class" with "the proletariat" and used such languages as "the fight against the class enemy," revealing a strong "left" hue—"stressing the class struggle as the central task."

In the new era, the Constitution adopted at the 12th National Congress of the CPC in 1982 agreed on another formulation: "The Communist Party of China is the vanguard of the Chinese working class, the faithful representative of the interests of the people of all nationalities in China, and the force at the core, leading China's cause of socialism." It restored the more accurate expressions used by the Party before, particularly that about

---

[1] *Selected Works of Deng Xiaoping* (2nd edition), Volume 1, p.218. Beijing: People's Press, 1994.

the class character, vanguard nature, national character and mass character, as formulated in the Constitution adopted at the Seventh National Congress of the CPC in 1956. Moreover, the 1982 formulation had highlighted the significance of upholding the Party's leadership and ruling position under new historical circumstances. The Constitutions adopted at the 14th and 15th national congresses of the CPC both continued using this formulation.

2.2.2 The Idea of Two Vanguards

As the reform and opening-up strategy had deepened, particularly after the reform of establishing and improving the market economic system was fully unfolded, the class structure and stratum structure of the Chinese society have changed a lot, compared with the past. The ranks of the working class had kept expanding in numbers, with growing ideological, ethical, science & tech and cultural attainments, while the inherent connotations and forms of the vanguard nature of the working class had also changed; in sum the class foundation of the CPC had been much stronger. In a socialist society generally regarded as part of the working class, intellectuals have added much to the science & tech and cultural levels of the working class. In the meantime, during the course of reforms, some workers have practiced a change in their posts and laboring modes which, however, had not changed their status as the working class. Naturally, in the long run, these changes will improve the overall qualities of the working class and give play to their class advantages. Reforms have produced other social groups and strata, and there have emerged businessmen and women, technical professionals group working in private sci-tech enterprises, managerial and technical professionals group employed by foreign-funded enterprises, self-employed people, personnel of intermediary agencies, and people working on a freelance basis. Moreover, a quite big number of individuals frequently float and move among different ownership systems, professions and places, and their occupations and identities see frequent changes. It seems such phenomena will be a developing trend. Under the guidance of the CPC lines and policies, these people belonging to those new social strata, and increasing to a large number have made their contributions to the development of productive forces and other undertakings of the socialist China by means of honest work and lawful economic operations. They unite with workers, farmers, intellectuals, cadres and soldiers of the People's Liberation Army, and can also be regarded as subjects of the socialist cause.

Against such a new background, the Program adopted at the 16th National Congress of the CPC in 2002 has agreed on a new formulation on the issue of Party's nature: "The Communist Party of China is the vanguard both of the Chinese working class and of the Chinese people and the Chinese nation. It is the core of leadership for the cause of socialism with Chinese characteristics and represents the development trend of China's advanced productive forces, the orientation of China's advanced culture and the fundamental interests of the overwhelming majority of the Chinese people."

Many scholars suggest that, it has been a realistic and a significant change to develop the exposition of the CPC's nature from "one vanguard" to "two vanguards." Firstly, this new statement unambiguously confirms the identity of the class character and vanguard nature of the CPC. After the Second World War, a few European working-class parties gradually gave up the ideas about class character in their party constitutions or programs in order to win more votes in the general elections, and consequently evolved into "all people's parties." Before and after the Cold War ended, working-class parties in the Soviet Union and Eastern Europe have lost their leading or ruling positions, and some had even vanished. In the newly established nation-states in the developing countries, only few parties—including left-wing ones—prefer to highlight their class character, explicitly. As the world progresses in the 21st century, the CPC firmly believes that the Chinese working class is always a basic force pushing forward China's advanced productive forces, and thus the Party should always maintain its vanguard nature—that of the working class—and wholeheartedly rely on the working class. Secondly, the new formulation stresses that the CPC is both the vanguard of the Chinese people and the Chinese nation, integrating the idea of vanguard nature of the working class with the idea of the mass line; thus it can be regarded as a new conclusion drawn on the basis of reviewing CPC's historical position under the new conditions. It is generally suggested that the new formulation offered a new view on the closed-door practices in the history of the CPC building and reached a conclusion on them. It seems the Party had gone too far in criticizing or when describing dividing lines with the "all people's parties."

The new formulation integrates the **Two Vanguards** idea together with **Three Represents** thought as important aspects of the CPC nature, enriching the connotation of the CPC's nature. Three Represents thought expands the previous formulation as: the CPC is "the faithful representative of the interests of the people of all nationalities in China", which was stipulated in the CPC Program since the 12th National Congress in 1982. It conforms to the realities of a Party practicing ruling position and also meets the overall requirements of the recent times for the connotation of Party building. Another concern is that it fulfils the wish of Party members and cadres; and is favorable for giving full scope to the initiative and creativity of Party members on a most extensive scale, and uniting and leading the people in the building of socialism. Three Represents thought has thus offered not only a new guiding principle but also a fundamental approach for the CPC to maintain its vanguard nature.

The new formulation has changed the phrase "the force at the core leading China's cause of socialism" with "the core of leadership for the cause of socialism with Chinese characteristics," and thus has further clarified the position of the CPC in accordance with the actual conditions of the CPC and the country. This change suggests that the Party has reached a new view in its new practice of nearly 20 years on the question of "what is socialism and how to build it" explored since the Third Plenary Session of the 11th Central Committee of the CPC in 1978. It also embodies the new conclusions that the CPC has reached in questing for the laws of building socialism, views on the world historical development following an unbalanced and non-linear course, a deeper view on unique national conditions of each country, and probability for diverse paths of socialist revolution and construction. It seems the Party has assumed a more solid belief: Only when working-class parties integrate Marxist tenets with national conditions, can they open up a path of socialist construction in line with national conditions and pleased to publicize it.

The Program adopted at the 16th National Congress of the CPC integrates Two Vanguards, Three Represents and "core of leadership" connotations in one complete formulation in defining the nature of the CPC, which is an inheritance as well as an elaboration and development of the classical statement—"the Party is an advanced force of the working class," and conforms with general expressions about the nature of Marxist polities while on the other side reflecting the Party's unique practice and her evaluation on time spirit.

2.3 The Values of a Marxist Party

The purpose of a political party refers to the aim and value that it exists and works for. It is determined by the nature of the party, and is the starting point and goal of all the policies of the party. Bourgeois parties represent the interests of the bourgeoisie of the capitalist societies, and all their policies serve the few capitalists who only account for a small proportion in the total population; whereas Marxist political parties stick to the goal of fighting for the interests of the overwhelming majority.

When founding the International Communist League, Marx and Engels had explicitly summarized the essential difference between the proletarian movement led by Communist parties and the previous political movements launched by exploiting classes offering several complementary aspects in their different statements: "All previous historical movements were movements of minorities, or for the interest of minorities. The proletarian movement is the self-conscious, independent movement of the immense majority, for the interest of the immense majority." The proletarians "have nothing of their own to secure and to fortify; their mission is to destroy all previous securities for, and insurances of, individual property."[1] Meanwhile,

---

[1] *Marx & Engels Selected Works* (2nd edition), Volume 1, p.283.

as the leader of the proletarian movement, the Communists "have no interests separate and apart from those of the proletariat as a whole," and "they do not set up any sectarian principles of their own, by which to shape and mold the proletarian movement." And compared with other proletarian parties, "the Communists do not form a separate party opposed to the other working-class parties." "The Communists are distinguished from the other working-class parties by this only: (1) In the national struggles of the proletarians of the different countries, they point out and bring to the front the common interests of the entire proletariat, independent of all nationalities. (2) In the various stages of development which the struggle of the working class against the bourgeoisie has to pass through, they always represent the interests of the movement as a whole."[1] In summary, the proletariat is the most revolutionary class, while their leading force—the Communists—form the most selfless political party in the world, whose purpose is to wholeheartedly fight for the complete liberation of the proletariat until realizing communism. Marx and Engels' statements served as a guide to later Communist parties in deciding upon their purposes and values.

At the Second Congress of the Communist International, Lenin delivered a "Speech on Affiliation to the British Labor Party," saying that "whether or not a party is really a political party of the workers does not depend solely upon a membership of workers but also upon the men that lead it, and the content of its actions and its political tactics. Only this latter determines whether we really have before us a political party of the proletariat."[2] As he believed, a true proletarian party should meet three qualifications: whether its leadership has firm political beliefs, strong revolutionary will, ambitious political aspirations, and a lofty political purpose to build the party for the public; whether it always fights for the immediate interests of the proletariat and people; and whether its political policies can truly reflect the demands and will of the proletariat and people and realize their interests.

---

[1] *Marx & Engels Selected Works* (2nd edition), Volume 1, p.285.

[2] *Collected Works of Vladimir Lenin* (2nd Chinese edition), Volume 39, p.246. Beijing: People's Press, 1986.

Based on historical materialism and its mass line idea, the CPC has also carried on and developed Marxist theories about the purpose of Communist parties. Mao Zedong had stated in his work "On Coalition Government": "Our point of departure is to serve the people wholeheartedly and never for a moment divorce ourselves from the masses, to proceed in all cases from the interests of the people and not from the interests of individuals or groups, and to understand the identity of our responsibility to the people and our responsibility to the leading organs of the Party."[1] Liu Shaoqi had also pointed out, "The interests of the people are precisely the interests of the Party. The Party has no special interests of its own beyond the people's interests. The maximum good for the greatest number of people is the highest criterion of truth, and consequently, the highest criterion of all the activities of our Party members."[2]

How to build a Party that will always serve the people wholeheartedly? According to Marxism, party cadres, particularly leading cadres, should completely understand and put into practice the historical materialism, bear in mind the masses and adhere to the mass line. To achieve the above, cadres should believe that the masses are true heroes and should be open-minded in learning from the masses; they should believe that the masses can emancipate themselves, and that any idea of bestowal or giving up mass struggle is wrong; they should give priority to the interests of the people and always take a responsible attitude to the people when organizing any activity or formulating policies; and they should collect the masses' opinions, then explain the opinions to the masses and make them stick to and act upon these opinions, and thus prove the opinions in mass activities.

According to Marxism, a party member should always stick to the proletarian world outlook, class outlook on life and values, and transform himself into a noble-minded and pure man, a man of moral integrity and above vulgar interests, a man who is of value for the people. As Liu Shaoqi had stated, "Every Party member should completely identify his personal

[1] *Selected Works of Mao Zedong* (2nd edition), Volume 3, pp. 1094-1095.
[2] *Selected Works of Liu Shaoqi*, Volume I, p.350. Beijing: People's Press, 1981.

interests with those of the Party both in his thinking and in his actions.... Unhesitating readiness to sacrifice personal interests and even one's life, for the Party and for the proletariat and for the emancipation of the nation and of all mankind—this is one form of expression of what we usually describe as 'Party spirit,' 'Party sense' or 'sense of organization.' It is the highest expression of Communist morality...."[1]

The reason why the CPC had managed to grow stronger and finally assumed power in those epochs of revolutionary wars is that its line, policies and practice had always represented and reflected the fundamental interests of the overwhelming majority of the people in China, and that countless Communist warriors had sacrificed themselves for the purpose of serving the people wholeheartedly. Throughout those periods of revolutionary wars, so to speak, the CPC had realized its purpose of serving the people wholeheartedly.

2.4 A Marxist Party Is Built for Public Interests and Exercises State Power for the People

After a Marxist party assumes power, it is of great significance to carry on the principle of serving the people wholeheartedly. The Party had also explored on this problem before the People's Republic of China was founded. Mao Zedong had suggested raising the qualities for the whole party: "The comrades should be taught to remain modest, prudent and free from arrogance and rashness in their style of work. The comrades should be taught to preserve the style of plain living and hard struggle." After the New China was founded, the CPC Central Committee demanded that the whole party, particularly cadres, always bear in mind the key question that "who has given us the power," consciously fight with bureaucracy which divorces Party members from the masses, and maintain the purity of the Party.

After the Third Plenary Session of its 14th Central Committee in 1992, the CPC, on the basis of summarizing its goal, has put forth the new idea: "The Party is built for public interests and exercises state power for the

[1] *Selected Works of Liu Shaoqi*, Volume I, pp.130-131.

people." This idea was first declared in the celebration meeting of the 80th anniversary of the founding of the CPC. Jiang Zemin had pointed out, "The radical difference of our party from all parties of exploiting classes is that our party serves the people wholeheartedly, is built for public interests, and exercises state power for the people."[1] In the report to the 16th National Congress of the CPC, it was stated that: "The implementation of the important thought of Three Represents is, in essence, to keep pace with the times, maintain the Party's progressiveness and exercise the state power in the interest of the people. All Party members should be keenly aware of this basic requirement and become more conscious and determined in implementing this important thought."[2]

Professor Yang Deshan has given a detailed explanation and several aspects of this idea as follows: To achieve the goal, "the Party is built for public interests and exercises state power for the people." the CPC should, at any time, respect both the laws of social progress and the mainstay status of the people—making history integrate the struggle for the lofty ideals with the efforts to gratify the interests of the people, and proceed the Party work in line with realizing the interests of the people. Yang Deshan has also suggested the following new notions in that direction:

Firstly, the Party and government policies should be designed and implemented in line with this goal. At present, profound changes have taken place in the Chinese society, presenting a trend of plurality in economic subjects, ways of employment, other forms of distribution and thus changes in people's values. Meanwhile, among the people various interest groups have emerged, presenting a situation of increasing interest differences. Under such circumstances, it is more critical to evaluate and take the fundamental interests of the people as the starting point and goal in designing and implementing the policies of the Party and the government.

Secondly, leading cadres at all levels should be oriented to this goal in ideology and practice. While holding positions of power, leading cadres

[1] *Selected Works of Jiang Zemin*, Volume 3, p.279.
[2] *Ibid.*, p.537.

should work to put into practice the principle of exercising power for the people, showing concern for them and working for their interests and doing positive and practical things for them with heart and soul. They should oppose formalism and bureaucracy in any form. Leading cadres should go to people, obtain first-hand information and learn about the people's life and working conditions. They should make investigations and research in a factual and realistic style, and try to enhance their abilities of discovering and solving problems.

Thirdly, exercise that goal in the work concerning people's life, so that people can gain economic, political and cultural benefits. Economic interest is the basis of the people's subsistence and development, and it is mainly demonstrated in the improvement of working conditions, food, clothes, housing and transportation including health and clean environment. Political interest is demonstrated in that the people enjoy the rights of information, election, supervision and direct participation and involvement in administrating state affairs. Cultural interest combines the above two, that is, the people have the rights to accept education and enjoy various cultural achievements. Leading cadres at all levels should watch these interests of the people.

Fourthly, give full play to the people's enthusiasm, initiative and creativity. Today, the Party faces a more complicated situation and more arduous tasks. Experiences have proven that the fundamental guarantee for the Party to overcome difficulties and achieve success was to rely on the people and promote their enthusiasm, initiative and creativity. Without the people's enthusiasm, initiative and creativity, the Party would never have succeeded in revolutionary wars, and would never have made eye-catching achievements since the reform and opening-up.

Professor Wang Haijun has stressed on the study and cultivation aspect of this goal and has made the following suggestions: For Party cadres, the key for achieving this goal and grasping its significance lies in whether they can establish a correct idea on power and appropriately handle the relationship between interest and position. The primary point in establishing a correct idea of power is to maintain close ties with the people. To sustain and solidify the Party's ruling position in the long run, Party members and cadres, as they did in revolutions and when the Party first came into power, should maintain their vigor and vitality, dashing spirit and integrity, giving priority to the interests of the people. They should overcome those negative conducts as bureaucracy and enjoying the post without facing any troubles and should also overcome negative practices such as confusing the subject and object of power, power abuse, and infringement of the people's interests. In this way the Party can win the endorsement and support of the overwhelming majority of the people.

To form a correct idea of power, the Party members and cadres should strengthen theoretical study and enhance their ideological and moral attainments. Only by diligently studying Marxist universal theories and those developed in China can they become more conscious and determined in implementing the important thought of Three Represents. They should also study the basic Marxist theories, to grasp historical materialism, have a firm faith in communism and socialism, have a keen understanding of the relationship between individual interests and the people's interests, and correctly understand and exercise power in their works. Through careful study, they can cultivate their temperament, improve moral integrity, and understand those quite common phenomena like individual fame, position and interest and correctly deal with them. Thus they will be able to conscientiously devote themselves to working for the collective interests, and will not care about individual gain or losses, and not use power to gain profit from the people or seek individual interests.

To establish a correct idea of power, they should put in the first place the interests of the country, the whole nation, the people and the collective, and strive to form themselves as individuals with lofty pursuit and good cadres esteemed by the people. Leading cadres at all levels should strengthen their sense of public servants ideologically, practically and in the style of work, and deal well with their relationship with the people. They should adhere to the mass line idea, go to the masses, particularly to problem stricken areas, make thorough investigations and researches, modestly listen to opinions from the masses, and then use those knowledge to improve Party and government work, so as to truly work for the interests of the people, and strengthen their ties with them in practice.

To establish a correct idea of power, they should break down the conventional official hierarchy, and transcend the remnants of feudal thoughts and practices. Leading cadres at all levels should bear in mind that a communist should work for a lofty ideal instead of striving for position, and wealth should never be a target. If a position is gained by "asking" or "buying" instead of serving the people, those will naturally violate the political morality for the communists, and will soon or later conflict the discipline rules. They should devote themselves to gratifying the interests of the people, be prepared to accept any choice or selection of the Party and the people, and keep calm with promotion or demotion. As long as they are in the position of power, they should try their best to work for the people, living up to the Party and the people's expectations.

To establish a correct idea of power, the Party spirit should be cultivated. With the Party spirit, leading cadres will be able to view and use power correctly. Party members and cadres should have a strong sense of the Party, always follow the Party's line, and safeguard the Party's image and prestige in every word and deed. They should have a faith in the Party's cause and be prepared for any difficulty or risk on the road ahead. They should actively work with vigor and practical style, and rally the masses closely around the Party with their acts.

The Party members—in the whole—should establish the idea that "the Party is built for public interests and the Party members are the vanguard of the people." Party members practicing their vanguard and exemplary roles constitute an important conduct of a Marxist party. In the history of the Party, such vanguard and exemplary conduct has reflected to different requirements. For example, in the years of revolutionary wars, the Party had demanded that Party members should be exemplary as brave and seasoned warriors, "be first in charging and last in retreating"; in the 1950s and 1960s, the Party had demanded that Party members be exemplary hard workers in economic construction, "be first in bearing hardships and be last in enjoying fruits". Naturally in the new era, in face of new tasks and environment, the Party has designed new requirements for the members:

Firstly, in the new historical era, the Party members should reflect an exemplary role in "emancipating the minds, being realistic and advancing with the times" and adhere to the Party's ideological line. It is a decisive factor for the Party to maintain its vanguard nature and develop its creativity. Party members should have a firm faith in the scientific character of Marxism while opposing any dogmatism in following Marxism, and keep pace with the times, so as to be more conscious in understanding and implementing the basic Party line, basic Party program and current policies of the Party, make brave explorations in practice, do well at work and play an exemplary role among the masses.

Secondly, they should reflect an exemplary role in "working hard, selfless dedication and serving the people heart and soul."

Thirdly, they should reflect an exemplary role in "observing the discipline and practicing democratic-centralism." Discipline is the premise and guarantee for the implementation of the Party's line and tasks. Today when the society turns more plural, it is of vital importance to observe the discipline. It is a responsibility that every Party member should accept to observe the Party discipline, and also the country laws and the rules in their work units. Only when Party members observe discipline or rules of the country and society, will the masses consciously follow suit. As the organizational principle of Marxist state politics, democratic-centralism is the core of socialist democracy. To realize that principle, Party members should always attend to and report the people's opinions, collect mass wisdom, open themselves to the people's supervision, and combine the people's opinions with Party policies in their work. Only in this way, can the people understand and make good use of democratic-centralism in political and social life.

Fourthly, they should reflect an exemplary role in "working hard in a down-to-earth manner and being devoted to duty." Party members should foster the lofty ideal of communism, have a firm faith in it, and push themselves with high ideological and moral standards. On the other hand they should be fully aware that it will be a long process to realize a communist society, which can only be realized on the basis of a fully developed socialist society, whereas China is still at the primary stage of socialism, the beginning phase of the long process of building socialism with Chinese characteristics. Thus every Party member should work hard in a down-to-earth manner for realizing the Party's basic program suited for the primary stage of socialism, do well in every work while keeping in mind the current stage, and set an example for the people with a hardworking spirit.

Fifthly, they should reflect an exemplary role in "opposing any forms of decadency and corruption and carrying forward the new ethos of socialism." Practices of decadency and corruption spoil the Party's style and image, and undermine social morality and the image of the Chinese nation. It is a long-term, arduous and complex political task of the Party, as well as an important content of the people's political life, to eliminate such practices. Thus it is a high mission for the Party members to resolutely combat all forms of decadency and corruption. In such combat, Party members should first understand the harm and keep themselves away from such practices, and at the same time dare to criticize, educate or expose anyone else with such practices.

In summary, the idea that "the Party is built for public interests and exercises state power for the people" highlights the basic goal of the Party and reflects the essence of the important thought of Three Represents, and is a political stance of the Party. When the Party is oriented to act and work for public interests, it could be built more stably, and exercise the state power for good. If a Marxist party cannot give expression to the will and desires of the people, seek interests for them and win their support, it will lose the aim and ground for its governance and the source of its strength.

Chapter 3

Democratic-Centralism Principle and the Organizational System of the Party

S ince modern times, every party in the world has its own organizational principle and system. Compared with bourgeois parties that target mainly at election and have slack organization and lax discipline, proletarian parties are quite different. Marxist proletarian parties are generally still positioned in the edge of political power and aim to overthrow the rule of the bourgeoisie, establish the dictatorship of the proletariat and ultimately realize the system of communism. They have developed their own organizational systems emphasizing the spirit of democracy to be carried inside the parties, attaching importance to building a rigorous organizational system and strict discipline, organically combining inner-Party democracy with centralism, and member's freedom with discipline. The scholars of party building generally define democratic-centralism as the fundamental organizational principle and the system of new-type Marxist parties. This principle integrates democracy and centralism, and is the Marxist epistemology and the mass line applied in the Marxist parties' political activities and organizational improvement.

3.1 Origin and Development of Democratic-Centralism

Marxist parties are organized based on democratic-centralism. This fundamental organizational system has also experienced a process of development.

3.1.1 Origin of Democratic-Centralism

The year 1847 witnessed the founding of the Communist League, the first international proletarian party under the guidance of the theory of scientific socialism in the world. Shortly after that, when Marx and Engels personally participated in discussing and drafting the "Rules of the Communist League," they pointed out that the proletariat should change the traditional way of secret discussions and set up like communities. They had suggested that proletariat should organize in circles, leading circles, the Central Authority and the Congress from bottom to top according to democratic-centralism. The League Congress should be the highest authority for the whole League and held annually; the Central Authority is the executive organ of the whole League and should regularly give a report to the Congress; all members are equal and as such owe each other maximum assistance and solidarity in every situation, and should strictly observe and follow to the aim of the League in their every activity, acknowledge the program of the League and subordinate to the decisions of the League. (See Appendix 1: Draft Rules of the Communist League-1847)

In 1864, when the International Working Men's Association was founded, the "General Rules of the International Working Men's Association" drafted by Marx stipulated: the General Working Men's Congress is the highest authority, and General Council is the executive organ. The core of the General Council is its Standing Committee, consisting of a chairman (but this position was abolished in 1867), a general-secretary, a treasurer, and corresponding secretaries for different countries. The association of each country should include a central committee, district federations, leading communities, communities and groups. As the Association gradually expanded, with regard to its organizational principle and system, it had correspondingly strengthened the organizational centralization on the basis of democracy: the functions and powers of the General Council had been enlarged, and the Congress was also authorized to accept and dismiss communities. Other new principles were that: no religious organization should be allowed in the Association; all attached country organizations were restricted to adopt a program against the Association's principles; all members of the Association should not join other organizations opposing the Association.

Thus, we can see that both the Communist League and the International Working Men's Association had always put into practice the spirit of democratic-centralism in their organizational principle and system. However, it was Lenin who explicitly established and termed "democratic-centralism" as the fundamental organizational principle and system of proletarian parties. At the Second Congress of the Russian Social Democratic Labor Party (RSDLP) held from July to August in 1903, Lenin had pointed out, "A prerequisite condition of a party organization is that it should be approved and endorsed by the Central Committee." "It should not be misinterpreted that Party organizations should consist solely of professional revolutionaries."[1] One year later, he had emphasized, "Without the subordination of the minority to majority there can be no working-class party at all worthy of the name."[2] In 1905, when the Russian Revolution broke out and great changes took place in the struggle conditions of the proletarian

---

[1] *Collected Works of Vladimir Lenin* (2nd Chinese edition), Volume 7, p.269.

[2] *Collected Works of Vladimir Lenin* (2nd Chinese edition), Volume 9, p.5. Beijing: People's Press, 1987.

party, Lenin promptly put forward the idea of giving full play to democracy inside the party. From February to March 1905, he pointed out, "The Party itself is *obliged* to see to it that its Rules are observed by its functionaries, that 'to see to' here does not only mean to criticize by words but to rectify by deed." And he had emphasized, "He, who is unable to demand *successfully* from his organs, and the discharge of their duties towards those who entrusted them is unworthy of the name of a politically free citizen."[1] In May, he had pointed out, "It is clear to anyone who has any idea of the general principles of Party organization that discipline in regard to a lower body is conditional upon discipline in regard to the higher body; the discipline which the Council may command is conditional upon the Council's subordination to its principals, that is, to the committees and their totality, the Party Congress."[2] In March 1906, he had clearly stated that democratic-centralism was now a publicly acknowledged principle. From then on, "centralism" and "democracy" started to appear as a combined principle in Lenin's articles. In April 1906, the RSDLP approved its party Constitution at the Fourth Congress, stating that "all the Party organizations to be set up according to the principle of democratic-centralism." From July to August in 1917, the new party Constitution approved at the Sixth Congress of the RSDLP had stated that all the Party organizations should be based on *democratic-centralism* and explained this system: all the leading organs of the party are elected from bottom to top; Party organs at all levels shall regularly report work to their respective Party organizations; all Party members shall strictly observe discipline, and the minority shall be subordinate to the majority; organs at lower levels and all members should without question obey and carry out decisions of higher bodies.[3]

The October Revolution in 1917 had proved the success of a proletarian party in building itself in accordance with democratic-centralism. Thus,

[1] *Collected Works of Vladimir Lenin* (2nd Chinese edition), Volume 9, p.292.

[2] *Collected Works of Vladimir Lenin* (2nd Chinese edition), Volume 10, p.208. Beijing: People's Press, 1987.

[3] *Concise History of the Communist Party of the Soviet Union (Bolshevik)*, p.245. Moscow: Foreign Languages Publishing House, 1946.

after the Communist International (the Third International) was founded in 1919, Lenin emphasized, "Parties belonging to the Communist International should be organized on the principle of democratic-centralism. In this era of acute civil war, the Communist parties can perform their duty only if they are organized in a most centralized manner, marked by an iron discipline bordering on military discipline, and have strong and authoritative party centers armed with wide powers and enjoying the unanimous confidence of their membership."[1] Lenin's requirements were based on the domestic political environment—intense civil war in Russia and the general conditions of post-war Europe, and were a summary of experience and lessons that Russian communist organizations accumulated over the process of establishment and development, that is, especially when hardly or unable to protect themselves in public, the communist parties should strictly follow democratic-centralism while central organs, especially the executive organs, should have wide powers.

3.1.2 The CPC's Theories and Practice of Democratic-Centralism

The CPC was founded with the help of the Communist International. At the Second Congress, the CPC made the decision to join the Communist International; and as a branch attached to it, CPC should abide by "democratic-centralism." However, although the CPC Constitutions adopted or revised before the Fifth National Congress embodied the spirit of "democratic-centralism" in their articles related to "Party meetings" or "Party discipline," they didn't contain a clear statement or stipulation about "democratic-centralism" principle. It was not until June 1927 that the Political Bureau of the CPC Central Committee approved at a meeting the Third Amendment to the Constitution of the Communist Party of China, and democratic-centralism was set as the guiding principle. The Constitution adopted at the Sixth National Congress of the CPC in 1928 had made an

---

[1] *Collected Works of Vladimir Lenin* (3rd Chinese edition), Volume 4, p.254. Beijing: People's Press, 1995.

explicit statement: "Organizational Principle: The Communist Party of China, like other branches of the Communist International, abides by the organizational principle of democratic-centralism." That statement had also explained the three points of the principle.

After the Sixth National Congress, Mao Zedong, who was in Jinggang Mountains at that time, started to explore the ways to realize democratic-centralism in the practice of Party building, army building and governance. In the next year (1929), he pointed out in the Decision of the Ninth Party Congress of the Fourth Red Army, "In the sphere of organization, we should ensure democracy under centralized guidance."[1] The Decision had also stipulated the ways for the implementation.

The peaceful solution of Xi'an Incident in 1936 had lessened the conflict between the CPC and the Kuomintang and brought relative political stability to the Soviet Areas controlled by the Party. Under the new conditions of the total resistance struggles against the Japanese invaders, the CPC had adjusted its program and policies while raising a requirement to make the Party's political activities "more democratic." In May 1937, the Outline of the Report on Organizational Problems of Party Congresses in the Soviet Area pointed out, "To fulfill new and great tasks facing the Party, all Party organizations and members in the Soviet Area shall work enthusiastically and actively; to achieve this goal, we should promote democracy within the Party. The objective conditions of the Soviet Area now allow us to greatly promote inner-Party democracy. Thus Party organizations in the Soviet Area should expand democracy in their political activities on the basis of democratic-centralism. Democratic-centralism means: (1) the Party's leading bodies at all levels are elected; (2) the Party's leading bodies should report on their work to Party members; (3) the lower level is subordinate to the higher level; and (4) the minority is subordinate to the majority."[2] The Outline had also put

---

[1] *Selected Works of Mao Zedong* (2nd edition), Volume 1, p.89.

[2] Archives Bureau of the CPC Central Committee, *Selected Documents of the CPC Central Committee*, Volume 10, pp.211-212. Beijing: Party School of the CPC Central Committee Press, 1985.

forward seven ways for implementation.

As the Anti-Japanese War had entered into the stage of stalemate after October 1938, major changes had occurred in the domestic class relations. In response to Zhang Guotao's betrayal and Wang Ming's undisciplined behaviors, Mao Zedong had presented a report entitled "The Role of the Communist Party of China in the National War" at the Sixth Plenary Session of the Sixth Central Committee of the Party in October 1938. In the report, when expounding on "Party discipline" Mao had pointed out, "In view of Zhang Guotao's serious violations of discipline, we should affirm anew the discipline of the Party, namely: (1) the individual is subordinate to the organization; (2) the minority is subordinate to the majority; (3) the lower level is subordinate to the higher level; and (4) the entire membership is subordinate to the Central Committee. Whoever violates these articles of discipline disrupts Party unity."[1] From then on, the principle of the Four Subordinates has been formally applied in the Party's political activities.

On the eve of overall success of the Anti-Japanese War, the CPC had approved a new Party Constitution at its Seventh National Congress, which stated, "The Party's organizations are built in accordance with democratic-centralism. Democratic-centralism is a combination of centralism on the basis of democracy and democracy under centralized guidance. Its basic conditions are as follows: (1) The Party's leading bodies at all levels are elected. (2) The Party's leading bodies at all levels report their work regularly to Party organizations that elect them. (3) Individual Party members are subordinate to the Party organization, the minority is subordinate to the majority, the lower Party organizations are subordinate to the higher Party organizations, and all the constituent organizations are subordinate to the Central Committee of the Party. (4) All Party members shall strictly observe Party discipline and carry out Party decisions unconditionally."

Soon after the Party had assumed power, Gao Gang and Rao Shushi's attempt to split the Party was exposed and later Nikita Khrushchev's secret

---

[1] *Selected Works of Mao Zedong* (2nd edition), Volume 2, p.528.

report at the 20th Congress of the Communist Party of Soviet Union had produced a chaos in the international communist camp, reflecting on these events; the Party had developed a new understanding on the application of "democratic-centralism." In 1956, the CPC adopted its first Constitution as a ruling Party at the Eighth National Congress, which made in-depth exposition on democratic-centralism and attached special importance to the role of democratic-centralism in safeguarding the Party's unity and solidarity. Article 19 stipulated, "The Party is organized on the basis of democratic-centralism. Democratic-centralism is a combination of centralism on the basis of democracy and democracy under centralized guidance." The Constitution also raised six basic conditions for the practice of democratic-centralism, among which the most important one was, "Party organizations at all levels should function on the principle of combining collective leadership with individual responsibility. All major issues shall be decided collectively, while individuals should be able to play their proper role."

However, in that period as the CPC and Mao Zedong had made a wrong judgment of domestic and international situations, particularly in those days when the Party had advocated the slogan of "taking the class struggle as the central task," the above stipulations about "democratic-centralism" were seriously damaged. "Centralism" was such applied that the power of decision-making highly depended—more and more—on individuals, which had finally enabled the top leader of the Party to "personally" launch the decade-long Cultural Revolution in 1966. Although democratic-centralism had remained as the organizational principle or organizational system of the Party, in the Constitutions at the Ninth and Tenth National congresses of the Party during the Cultural Revolution and in the Constitution adopted at the 11th National Congress held shortly after the Cultural Revolution, its real contents were quite different. For instance, leading bodies at all levels "are elected and through democratic discussion"; members of leading bodies at all levels should meet the "five qualifications" and the organ building structure should follow the principle of "including senior, middle-aged and young cadres". Also the fourth point of the Four Subordinates was misinterpreted to replace the following rule: "all the constituent organizations of the Party are subordinate to the National Congress and the Central Committee of the Party" with "the entire membership is subordinate to the Central Committee." The collective leadership of the Party was actually destroyed, the power of the CPC chairman was highly exaggerated, and extreme individualism and disorganization was encouraged within the Party; these conducts when practiced, had indeed produced two negative phenomena—"a high degree of centralization" and "ultra-democracy"—which seemed contradictory but were identical in nature.

After the Third Plenary Session of the 11th Central Committee, restoring and improving the Party's combat effectiveness and making it the hard core of leadership for the cause of socialist modernization was formulated as a central task in party building. The Party undertook a hard job to overcome the high degree of centralization, patriarchal style, anarchism, and weak or lax organization modes that had prevailed during the Cultural Revolution and to restore the principle and system of democratic-centralism. At the Fifth Plenary Session of the 11th Central Committee, the CPC adopted Several Norms for Political Activities within the Party, to rectify the high degree of centralization conduct within the Party. The resolution explained: "Collective leadership is one of the highest principles of the Party's leadership. Based on this principle, Party committees at all levels, from the central to grassroots, will function on the system that combines collective leadership with individual responsibility based on division of work." And, it resolutely opposed arbitrary decision-making by any individual, commenting: "Secretary or First Secretary will gather others' opinions, and will not practice 'what I say counts' or patriarchal style." As the baneful influence of disorganization within the Party had not yet been eliminated, the resolution had emphasized: "Democratic-centralism is the Party's fundamental organizational principle." "We should reaffirm the principle that 'the individual is subordinate to the organization, the minority is subordinate to the majority, the lower level is subordinate to the higher level, and the entire membership is subordinate to the Central Committee.' For every Party member, safeguarding the Party's unity and solidarity and strictly observing the Party discipline should be the standards for words and behaviors."[1]

The new Party Constitution adopted at the 12th National Congress in 1982 made a new summary of the Party's organizational system; emphasized that the Party is a united whole organized on the basis of its program, Constitution and democratic-centralism; stated that the organizational system is a high degree of centralization on the basis of a high level of democracy; and raised six principles for practicing democratic-centralism, one of which was: "The Party forbids all forms of personality cult." Over the 20 more years from the 12th to the 16th National congresses, the structure and the basic articles on democratic-centralism in the Constitution of the Party— except for some statements—has remained unchanged. For example, the Constitution adopted at the 14th CPC National Congress revised the phrase: "a high degree of centralization on the basis of a high level of democracy" as "a combination of centralism on the basis of democracy and democracy under centralized guidance." The Constitution adopted at the 16th CPC National Congress made an additional phrase as: "Party organizations at all levels should keep Party members better informed of these affairs and to provide them with more opportunities to participate in them"; it had also clarified the system that combines collective leadership with individual responsibility based on division of work: "All major issues shall be decided upon by the Party committees after discussion in accordance with the principle of collective leadership, democratic-centralism, individual consultations among them and decisions should be made in the meetings. The members of the Party committees should earnestly exercise their functions and powers in accordance with the collective decisions taken and according to the division of work." These stipulations marked the CPC's progress in the theory and practice of democratic-centralism, playing an active role in strengthening Party building under new circumstances.

---

[1] *Selected Important Documents since the Third Plenary Session of the 11th Central Committee of the Communist Party of China*, Volume 1, pp.417-419.

3.2 Connotations and Essential Requirements of Democratic-Centralism

Democratic-centralism is the fundamental organizational principle and fundamental organizational system as well as the fundamental system of leadership of the Marxist parties and the CPC. Marxist parties should creatively employ democratic-centralism and also formulate basic norms and specific systems that should guide political activities and inner-party relations, which is a distinctive feature of the organizational development. Democratic-centralism has rich scientific connotations and many specific requirements. The purpose of practicing this principle is to create within the Party and among the people a political situation in which there are both centralism and democracy, both discipline and freedom, both unity of will and personal ease of mind and liveliness, and thus improve Party building and promote the cause of socialism under the leadership of the Party.

3.2.1 "Democracy" in Democratic-Centralism

"Democracy" in democratic-centralism is that Party members and organizations can fully express their wishes and opinions and give full scope to their enthusiasm and creativity. "Centralization" in democratic-centralism means that the whole Party's will and wisdom is coherent and the actions are uniform. These are two aspects of the same thing, and thus are interrelated, interdependent and interactive, and supplement each other, are of equal importance and can not be disjoined. The "centralization" without "democracy" will produce a trend that some individuals could make decisions arbitrarily and wrong decisions cannot be corrected promptly, which in turn would breed negative relations and dissension and discord among Party members, and weaken the Party's combat effectiveness, dismantle the Party's cohesion, stifle creativity and thereafter cause setbacks for the Party's cause. The "democracy" without "centralization" will produce disorganization and indiscipline within the Party. Consequently, the Party's line, principles and policies cannot be implemented, and the Party will not be able to advance or make achievements in its cause. Therefore, to apply the principle of democratic-centralism, a Marxist party should give full play to democracy while practicing centralization correctly, and should not slide from one extreme to the other.

From the perspective of institutional designing, democratic-centralism offers a scientific, sound and efficient system. It is optimal for reflecting the people's fundamental interests and desires, and for the correct formulation and implementation of the Party's line, principles and policies and timely and effective rectification of errors. Since institutional party building is fundamental, stable, long-lasting and concerns the overall situation, Marxist parties should improve all the systems of democratic-centralism, ensuring that they will not alter when new top leaders rise to authority or when leaders' ideas change or attention shifts. In particular, Marxists should enhance the conscientiousness of the whole Party, especially leading cadres, in applying democratic-centralism, oppose all the negative trends violating and negating this principle, and try to prevent arbitrary decision-making by any individual and/or leading to ultra-democracy.

Inner-party democracy is the life of a Marxist Party. It is a concentrated expression of the "democracy" value of democratic-centralism to promote inner-party democracy and give full play to the whole Party's enthusiasm. Without democracy, there would be no socialism and no socialist modernization—it is a scientific conclusion of the socialist-communist movement in the long struggles. The essence of socialist democracy is that the people are the masters of the country, and this broadest possible people's democracy is essentially different from bourgeois democracy, and is totally opposite to anarchism that gives no consideration to discipline and order. The promotion of inner-party democracy can certainly play an important exemplary and leading role in establishing and developing people's democracy in the country and I think this could be major starting point in building socialist democracy and politics in a socialist society, under certain conditions. Inner-party democracy should be promoted from all levels, all aspects and by all means. Inner-party democracy should be promoted with the aim to realize the Party's program and regarded as the starting point of guiding, protecting and giving play to Party members' enthusiasm, and should also be applied in the sphere of the Party organizations' functions and powers and Party members' rights and duties. Party members should be encouraged to emancipate their minds, seek truth from facts, boldly probe into everything and stick to the truth. Democracy should be fully promoted in all Party organizations from the Central Committee to every branch of the Party, and in all Party activities from decision-making at leading bodies to Party meetings and policy discussion on the Party's newspapers and periodicals, from inner-Party elections to the evaluation and oversight of leading cadres.

Democratic decision-making is an important component of inner-Party democracy, as well as the prerequisite to scientific decision-making. It is a basic requirement for the Party in enabling its style of leadership and a more democratic governance, law-based and scientific, and also in establishing and improving the decision-making mechanisms and incorporating leaders, experts and the masses. Leading bodies and cadres of a Marxist party should promote a democratic style of work, adhere to the mass line that from the masses and to the masses, fully respect the masses' pioneering spirit, and summarize those rich practices of the grassroots and in a timely manner. Marxists should listen to views from all sectors of society, including objections. When a Party organization at the higher level makes any important decision concerning its subordinate Party organizations, it should listen to views of subordinate Party organizations.

Effective measures on inner-Party democracy should be employed to protect the democratic rights of Party organizations at all levels and the Party members. It is highly necessary to open up and expand concrete channels for inner-party democracy, keeping Party members better informed of the Party affairs and providing them with more opportunities to participate in them. The Party's principles, policies, orders and decisions should be transmitted to Party organizations at lower levels and Party members in a timely manner. Something important should be first discussed within the Party and the Party members should be informed of it as soon as possible. No organization or individual is allowed to encroach upon any right of Party members stipulated in the Constitution of a Marxist Party. The Party should observe the rules for protecting Party members' rights, and take clear and concrete measures to guarantee that Party members can exercise their rights.

3.2.2 "Centralism" in Democratic-Centralism

Effective centralization on the basis of democracy is a fundamental guarantee for effective enforcement of the Party's line, principles and policies. Democracy and centralization are supplementary to each other and uniform in nature. Without democracy, there would be no correct centralization; without centralization, there would not be correct line, principles and policies, let alone unity of will within the Party. Centralization means collecting the correct opinions and remolding them to form consensus ideas in the Party, then formulating correct decisions and resolutely carrying them out.

To safeguard the authority of the Central Committee of the Party is the most fundamental prerequisite to centralization. To safeguard this authority is to ensure that decisions of the Central Committee are carried out without failure, and seriously incorporated to the decisions at all levels. Regarding the Party's basic line, general principle, general policy, general objective and on the major issues having a bearing on the overall situation, the whole Party should keep in step with the Central Committee. When it is a ruling Party, the organizations at all levels and all the Party members should play an exemplary role in abiding by the Constitution and other laws. Local governments should take the overall situation into consideration, resolutely carry out resolutions and decisions of the Central Committee, work creatively in the light of realities, and ask for instructions from and report to superior authorities on major issues.

In China, after the period of Reform there has been a change in the content of centralization at the local and grassroots Party organizations level, and it does not include a high-degree concentration of power as practiced in the era of planned economy; instead, it aims to give full play to initiatives of local organizations under the leadership of the Central Committee—it is an important new content that the Party consistently advocates. To give play to initiatives of local organizations, it is suggested that they should combine the guideline of the Central Committee with local realities, and be accountable to both local people and the people in the whole country. To guarantee the authority of the Central Committee does not mean to withdraw the powers that should be conferred upon local authorities; instead it means to give full play to initiatives of central departments and local organizations on the basis of reasonable division of the functions and powers.

For central departments, centralization means to correctly exercise functions and powers endowed by the Central Committee, realistically transform their functions in light of the Reform strategy, handle well the relationship between sectored/partial interests and general interests, strengthen and improve macro-economic regulation and macro-management, and better serve local and grassroots organizations.

For Party committees and leading cadres of central and local state organs and mass organizations, centralization means to conscientiously accept the leadership of the central and local Party committees. Major issues should be submitted to the Party committee at the corresponding level for discussion, discussed among state organs and mass organizations, and dealt with according to law and regulations. The Party should strictly conduct its activities within the framework of the Constitution and laws of the country, be good at organizing and coordinating all forces, bring into play functions of all the organizations, and exercise correct leadership.

Regarding the system of leadership within the Party, centralization means that the Party should adhere to and improve the system that combines the conducts of collective leadership with individual responsibility based on division of work. Any issue concerning principles, policies, and the overall situation, or the recommendation, appointment, dismissal, rewards or punishment of important cadres should be decided by the Central Committee or local leading Party committees. When deciding on major issues, Party committees at all levels should first go through full deliberation and discussion, and afterwards try a vote-based decision on the principle of subordination of the minority to the majority. No individual should have the right to change any collective decision; if any individual or a few people disagree with any decision, they should be allowed to make reservations, but they should accept it unconditionally and carry it out resolutely when it is decided to be put in force. Collective leadership and individual responsibility based on division of work are regarded as equally important notions. A Marxist party should generally advocate the spirit of accountability among leading cadres, and oppose to the behavior of passing the buck and nobody taking charge or responsibility. Thus all the individual members of Party committees should, in accordance with the collective decisions and division of work principle, earnestly exercise their functions and powers, concern themselves with the overall situation, and take an active part in collective leadership. In any Party committee, the secretary and committee members should be equal and the Party secretary primarily should be responsible to maintain and develop the collective leadership, and should be the model in practicing democratic-centralism. Party committee members should trust, support, understand and help each other, including helping each other to overcome shortcomings and mistakes, thus strengthen the unity of leading bodies.

3.3 Six Basic Principles of Democratic-Centralism in the CPC

Specifically, to uphold democratic-centralism is to uphold its basic principles as stipulated in the Constitution of the Party. These basic principles have been improved since the Party put forward more explicit formulations in the Constitution at the Sixth National Congress in 1928. The current 2002 Constitution promulgated at the 16th Congress has formulated six basic principles of democratic-centralism.

The First Principle: Individual Party members are subordinate to the

Party organization, the minority is subordinate to the majority, the lower Party organizations are subordinate to the higher Party organizations, and all the constituent organizations and members of the Party are subordinate to the National Congress and the Central Committee of the Party.

These principles are generally called the Four Subordinates. They were raised at the Sixth Plenary Session of the Sixth Central Committee of the Party, and were formally included in the Party Constitution at the Seventh National Congress in 1945. Although they have changed a bit in expression and content, they have always included a certain part of previous Party constitutions. The Four Subordinates has led political activities and order within the Party, and has offered basic standards for handling all the relations within the Party.

That "individual Party members are subordinate to the Party organization" is the principle for handling the relationship between Party members and Party organizations, an important principle guaranteeing that the Party is an integral body. As prescribed in the Party Constitution, Party members should accept and carry out any resolution or decision adopted by Party organizations; in case of disagreement with a Party resolution or policy, Party members can make reservations and present their views to Party organizations at higher levels even up to the Central Committee, provided that they resolutely carry out the resolution or policy while it is in force. Party members should accept any job and actively fulfill any task assigned them by the Party. Every Party member, irrespective of position, should be organized into a branch, cell or other specific unit of the Party to participate in the regular activities of the Party organization and accept oversight by the masses inside and outside the Party. Leading Party cadres should attend democratic meetings held by the Party committee or leading Party members' groups. There should be no privileged Party members who do not participate in the regular activities of the Party organization and do not accept oversight by the masses inside and outside the Party. When an individual Party member is to express views on major issues beyond the scope of the existing decisions of the Party organization, **on behalf of the Party organization,** the content should be referred to the Party organization for prior discussion and decision, or referred to the next higher Party organization for instructions. No Party member, whatever his or her position, is allowed to make decisions on major issues on his or her own. In an emergency, when a decision by an individual is unavoidable, the matter should be reported to the Party organization immediately afterwards. No leader is allowed to take decisions arbitrarily or to place himself or herself above the Party organization.

That "the minority is subordinate to the majority" is the principle for deciding upon any matter within the Party, as well as a major sign of the Party as a modern political organization. There is often disagreement on some problems inside the Party, and thus it is necessary to uphold this principle to achieve unity in Party members' actions. Party members and members of Party committees are all equal within the Party and nobody has the power to decide anything alone, which determines that Party organizations should follow the principle of subordination of the minority to the majority when discussing any matter and take a vote when deciding upon any major issue. Serious consideration should be given to the differing views of a minority. In case of controversy over major issues in which supporters of the two opposing views are close in number, the decision should be delayed to allow for further investigation, study and exchange of opinions and decided by another vote, except in emergencies where action should be taken in accordance with the majority view. Under special circumstances, the controversy may be reported to the next higher Party organization. In Marxist parties this method is highly suggested for making correct decisions, avoiding mistakes and promoting solidarity of the Party.

That "the lower Party organizations are subordinate to the higher Party organizations" is the principle for handling the relationship between the lower Party organizations and the higher Party organizations. According to this principle, lower Party organizations should firmly implement the decisions of higher Party organizations. If lower organizations consider that any decisions of higher organizations do not suit the specific conditions in their localities or departments, they may demand modification. If the higher organizations insist on their original decisions, the lower organizations should carry out such decisions and refrain from publicly voicing their differences, but retain the right to report to the next higher Party organization. Of course, lower Party organizations resolutely accepting the decisions of higher Party organizations does not mean that individual members of lower Party organizations should obey the members of higher Party organizations. Generally under normal circumstances, when making decisions on important questions of the lower organizations, the leading bodies of the Party at all levels should solicit opinions of the lower organizations. Measures should be taken to ensure that the lower organizations can exercise their functions and powers normally. Except in special circumstances, higher leading bodies should not interfere in those matters that ought to be handled by lower organizations.

That "all the constituent organizations and members of the Party are subordinate to the National Congress and the Central Committee of the Party" is the principle for handling the relationship between all the constituent organizations and the Central Committee. The National Congress is the supreme organ of power and the producer of all the line, principles and policies of the Party. When the National Congress is not in session, the Central Committee carries out its resolutions, directs the entire work of the Party and represents the Party in its external relations.

Party building scholars generally suggest that the rule that "subordination to the National Congress and the Central Committee of the Party" primarily reflects the idea to accept the major decisions adopted at the National Congress, as it is the primary tool to keep in step with the Central Committee ideologically, organizationally and in action. But in reality, all the constituent organizations and members of the Party are subordinate to the National Congress and the Central Committee of the Party.

The Four Subordinates are correlated. Among them, "subordination of the minority to the majority" is the basis from which derive the other three. The rule that "all the constituent organizations and members of the Party are subordinate to the National Congress and the Central Committee of the Party" is the core of the Four Subordinates, the objective of the other three, and the basic guarantee for the Party's unity and solidarity.

The Second Principle: The Party's leading bodies at all levels are elected except for the representative organs dispatched by them and except the leading Party members' groups in non-Party organizations.

The electoral system is one of the major features of modern political and social organizations. Marxist parties have always regarded the electoral system as a major sign of and basic requirement for the realization of inner-party democracy, and the manifestation of subordination of the minority to the majority. The essence of practicing the electoral system within a party is to respect the will of rank-and-file party members, and to give party members the right to directly or indirectly manage party affairs. Since the First National Congress, the CPC has stipulated that Party's leading bodies at all levels should be elected. The Constitution adopted at the Seventh National Congress in 1945 made clear for the first time the methods of elections—secret ballot or voting. The Report to the 13th National Congress of the Party had for first time pointed out that the electoral system within the Party should be reformed and improved; the procedure for the nomination of candidates and methods of competitive election method should be clearer. The report had demanded, "The Party should expand the scope of competitive election method in the election of Party congresses at all levels, members and secretaries of grassroots Party organizations, members of local Party congresses and their standing committees, and members of the Central Committee of the Party."

The current Constitution of the Party stipulates, "The election of delegates to Party congresses and of members of Party committees at all levels should reflect the will of the voters. Elections shall be held by secret ballot. The lists of candidates shall be submitted to the Party organizations and voters for full deliberation and discussion. The election procedure in which the number of candidates nominated is greater than the number of individuals to be elected may be used directly in a formal election or this procedure may be used first in a preliminary election in order to draw up a list of candidates for the formal election. The voters have the right to inquire about the candidates, demand a change or reject a candidate in favor of another. No organization or individual shall in any way compel voters to elect or not to elect any candidate." Before the election of Party congresses or general membership meetings, the list of candidates drawn up on the basis of careful consideration and full deliberation generally enable the election to truly reflect the principle of democratic-centralism, reflect the will of the voters, and conform to Party work. Otherwise, it could be hard to ensure the solemnity of the election and to centralize the will of the voters. In Marxist parties to form an appropriate list of candidates is a very important link in the whole process of election. And competitive election method could enable the voters to elect the one that they consider the best, and better reflect the will of the voters, and is positive for promoting inner-party democracy.

In addition, the 2002 Party Constitution has also offered explicit stipulations on possible violations and defined corrective measures: "If any violation of the Party Constitution occurs in the election of delegates to local Party congresses at all levels or to Party congresses at the primary level, the Party committee at the next higher level, after investigation and verification, should decide to declare the election invalid and take appropriate measures. The decision should be reported to the Party committee at the next higher level for checking and approval before it is formally announced and implemented." The Party Constitution also makes strict stipulations on non-election cases: "The formation of a new Party organization or the dissolution of an existing one shall be decided upon by the higher Party organization. When the congress of a local Party organization at any level or the congress of a Party organization at the primary level is not in session, the next higher Party organization may, when it deems necessary, transfer or appoint responsible members of that organization. The Party's Central Committee and local Party committees at all levels may send out their representative organs."

The Third Principle: The highest leading body of the Party is the National Congress and the Central Committee elected by it. The leading bodies of local Party organizations are the Party congresses at their respective levels and the Party committees elected by them. Party committees are responsible, and report their work to the Party congresses at their respective levels.

It was since the Second National Congress that the Party had made clear statements on the highest leading bodies of the Party and defined their functions and powers. The Constitution adopted at the Fifth National Congress stipulated for the first time the four functions and powers of the Party's highest organ of power. The Constitution adopted at the Seventh National Congress had for the first time defined the content about the National Congress and its functions and powers. The Constitution adopted at the 12th National Congress classified the functions and powers of the National Congress of the Party into six points. And lastly, the Constitution adopted at the 16th National Congress has formulated the functions and powers of the National Congress of the Party as follows: to hear and examine the reports of the Central Committee; to hear and examine the reports of the Central Commission for Discipline Inspection; to discuss and decide on major questions concerning the Party; to revise the Constitution of the Party; to elect the Central Committee; and to elect the Central Commission for Discipline Inspection.

These provisions regarding the Party's system of leadership, particularly those regarding the status, functions and powers of the National Congress of the Party as the highest organ of power, are an important guarantee for the application of democratic-centralism; they fully reflect the democratic rights of all Party members, while organizationally guarantee the principle that "all the constituent organizations and members of the Party are subordinate to the National Congress and the Central Committee of the Party," which reflects centralization within the Party.

The Fourth Principle: Higher Party organizations should pay constant attention to the views of lower organizations and the rank-and-file Party members, and solve in good time the problems they raise. Lower Party organizations shall report on their work to, and request instructions from, higher Party organizations; at the same time, they shall handle, independently and in a responsible manner, the matters within their authority. Higher and lower Party organizations should exchange information and support and oversee each other. Party organizations at all levels should increase transparency in Party affairs in accordance with regulations to keep Party members better informed of these affairs and to provide them with more opportunities to participate in them.

This is a new and important supplementary support to the principle that "the lower Party organizations are subordinate to the higher Party organizations" and is the basic rule for handling the relationship between the lower Party organizations and the higher Party organizations. It points to the spirit of democracy for the higher Party organizations and their obligations to lower organizations, on the other hand to the spirit of centralization for the lower Party organizations in practical work and their responsibilities to the higher Party organizations. This principle coordinates the higher and lower organizations much better and increases their efficiency, and it suggests mutual trust, mutual help and mutual supervision relations between them. Moreover, it suggests that the higher Party organizations shall pay constant attention to the views of the rank-and-file Party members and orient the Party organizations to inform their members on the Party affairs—much better— and provide members with more opportunities to participate in them. This notion could positively improve the publicity and transparency in Party affairs, can make the Party's leadership more democratic, law-based and scientific, and help Party organizations to pool Party members' wisdom and power for better work.

The Fifth Principle: Party committees at all levels should function on the principle of combining collective leadership with individual responsibility based on division of work. As a system of leadership, the "party committee system" or the "system of combining collective leadership with individual responsibility based on division of work" was established in the era of Lenin as the principle for Marxist parties' system of leadership. During the new-democratic revolution, the CPC had absorbed and drew upon Lenin's statements about this issue, and made explicit stipulations on the operation of the "party committee system." Thus, all major issues should be decided upon by the Party committees after discussion in accordance with the principle of collective leadership, democratic-centralism, individual consultations among members and decisions should be produced in the meetings. The members of the Party committees should earnestly exercise their functions and powers in accordance with the collective decisions taken and division of work.

The Constitution adopted at the Eighth National Congress in 1956 had agreed as: "Party organizations at all levels function on the principle that combines collective leadership with individual responsibility. All major issues shall be decided collectively, while full play shall be given to the role of individuals." Constitutions after the 12th National Congress have further improved these notions. And, at the 16th National Congress, the CPC has agreed on a clearer formulation in the Constitution as "collective leadership, democratic-centralism, individual consultations among its members and decision produced in the meetings," thus developed this principle.

In the Marxist parties, "collective leadership" is the highest principle and the basic system of the Party's leadership. Only by relying on collective leadership, can the Marxist Party get a correct understanding of the situation, make correct decisions and avoid mistakes.

For the CPC that rules a big country and has to deal with various complicated problems under complicated conditions, individual wisdom and talent is far from enough; it has to pool the wisdom and efforts of all Party members and rely on collective leadership.

"Democratic-centralism" is the root approach to upholding collective leadership. Most correct decisions of the Party can be formed after collective discussion. Only by drawing on collective wisdom and absorbing all useful ideas on the basis of giving full play to democracy, can the Party be resourceful and decisive and make scientific decisions. Any member of a Party committee should have the power to decide on major issues alone and participate in decision forming.

"Individual consultation" among members is a necessary link and main method for scientific decision-making. Before holding meetings, members of the leading bodies should exchange opinions on the prerequisite of upholding principles and being pragmatic and try to reach a consensus, so as to resolve disagreements before meetings and find the best proposal for decision-making with brainstorming notion. This is good for promoting democracy, exchanging views, reaching a consensus and enhancing unity and solidarity within the Party.

"Decisions in the meetings" is the basic form and an important part of the procedure of realizing collective leadership. As stipulated by the Constitution and other regulations of the Party, from the aspect of procedure decisions by formal meetings can, reflect democracy and centralization and fairness and justice, and guarantee scientific and standard decision-making process. Here "meetings" point to mainly those held by Party committees and their standing committees. What kind of issues should be decided at which meetings by what means of voting? For this problem, a Marxist Party should formulate applicable rules of procedure and strictly follow it; it shall never replace formal Party meetings with brief, informal meetings, or decide upon major issues by oral statement.

The Sixth Principle: The Party forbids all forms of personality cult. It is necessary to ensure that the activities of the Party leaders are subject to oversight by the Party and the people, and at the same time the prestige of all the leaders who represent the interests of the Party and the people should be appreciated and honored.

In the Marxist party, personality cult arises when a leader is overly admired and his individual role is exaggerated, thus the trust and reliance on a leader is far more than those on a collective and people become blindly obedient to the leader; but it is an expression of the idealist conception of history. It undervalues and even denies the role of the rank-and-file Party members and the people, belittles collective leadership of the Marxist parties, and damages the principle of democratic-centralism; therefore, it results in such errors as arbitrary decision-making by individuals or patriarchal style and abnormal political activities. Lenin's Theory of Party Building had always attached importance to the clear distinction between several components of leadership: between protecting the authority of leaders and boosting personality cult, the collective power of Marxist parties, and the power of the masses, and Lenin had personally advocated a correct understanding of the relationship among leaders, parties, classes and the masses. However, both the history of international communist movement and that of the CPC had witnessed the personality cult, which brought a serious damage to the cause of communism and the image of Marxist parties. Before assuming power, the CPC had explicitly decided to oppose giving prominence to individuals or singing the praise of individuals within the Party. The Party had reaffirmed this principle at the Eighth National Congress in 1956, but had not included it into its Constitution. After the Third Plenary Session of the 11th Central Committee, the CPC drew lessons from history, and formally added this notion into the Constitution as: "the Party forbids all forms of personality cult" at the 12th National Congress, which was a first attempt in the history of international communist movement and in that of the CPC. This formulation supplements the principle of democratic-centralism, and is of great significance for correctly handling the relationship between the Party's leaders and leadership collectives and between the Party's leaders and the rank-and-file Party members, guaranteeing normal political activities within the Party, and improving the Marxist party at its top level leading organs.

The above six principles of democratic-centralism are correlated and supplement each other. The first principle highlights that the whole Party is an integral body on the basis of democracy; the second emphasizes that the electoral system is an important sign and basic requirement for inner-party democracy; the third underscores the system of Party congresses and the horizontal relationship among the Party's leading bodies at the same level; the fourth underlines the vertical relationship between the higher and lower Party organizations; the fifth attaches importance to the highest principle and the basic system of the Party's leadership; the sixth stresses the relationship between the Party's leaders and its collective leadership and between the Party's leaders and the rank-and-file Party members, a supplementary to the fifth principle. Hence, the six principles reflect democratic-centralism as an integral whole.

3.4 Improving Democratic-Centralism

As the fundamental organizational principle and system of the Party, democratic-centralism has gone through tests and developed in practice over a long period. Under new and ever changing circumstances, efforts to uphold and improve democratic-centralism involve both theory and practice and demand in-depth research by Party building scholars.

3.4.1 Several Misconceptions and Causes

During the history of Marxist parties serious deviations have propped in the practice of democratic-centralism. Those defects had particularly surfaced in the international communist movement when it suffered grave setbacks at the end of the 1980s, and China was no exception. Thus, some people doubted whether proletarian parties should continue to uphold democratic-centralism. Since China had established and started to improve the socialist market economic system, and economic and social life in China has become quite plural, some Party members were also confused whether Marxists should uphold the same principle. These factors and confusion on the issue constitute an important problem in the practice of democratic-centralism to varying degrees. I believe that the issue should be the concern of the academy and the Marxists. I would like to offer my suggestions on the problem as follows:

Is democratic-centralism outdated in China? Some people believe that it was a product of the revolutionary war time and the planned economy period when importance was attached to the collective and unified leadership of the Party and it was then necessary and practical in order to pool all forces for a great undertaking. But under the socialist market economy, this principle and system has lost its realistic value, is outdated and does not conform to the current economic and political system. Hence they conclude that the Party should gradually diminish and finally abandon it.

Is democratic-centralism antagonistic to the socialist market economy? Some people maintain that market economy stresses the initiative of people, self-management of localities and business enterprises, high efficiency, high yield and fast pace, while democracy demands higher costs and time; if the principle and procedures of democratic-centralism were to be continued, it will negatively affect the efficiency and yields, and even restrict economic development. Therefore, they conclude that democratic-centralism cannot be adapted or get along with the socialist market economy, and democratic-centralism cannot be practiced in the socialist market economy.

Are democracy and centralization contradictory? Some people hold that market economy underlines devolution of powers for the purpose of invigorating the market, and thus it should be necessary to pay more attention to democracy. On the other hand, some people think that market economy can hardly function well without macro-economic controls as some localities and business enterprises neutralize or by-pass the effects and the aims of government policies which lead to chaos in economic activities, thus it should be necessary to pay more attention to centralization or macro-economic control and regulation. The two views may be positive in the original intention, but they both put democracy against centralization, though they are two indispensable aspects of democratic-centralism.

Can the current chief executive responsibility system replace the system of democratic-centralism? Some people believe that the party committee system in democratic-centralism does not fit into the modern decision-making mechanism. They believe that the system of chief executive responsibility can better improve the authority of leaders and is convenient for decision-making and management, thus they suggest replacing the system of democratic-centralism with the system of chief executive responsibility.

In my opinion, the roots of the above misconceptions lie in the following aspects: Firstly, several past errors are attributed to democratic-centralism itself, and they don't indeed consider that the defects were due to distortion and malpractices of the Marxist democratic-centralism principles. Secondly, inner-party democracy is observed as contradictory with democratic-centralism. Therefore, it is a fundamental issue concerning the building of the Party and socialism to evaluate the practice of democratic-centralism in a historical aspect, and clarify how to uphold democratic-centralism under market economy conditions.

The history of the international communist movement and that of the CPC shows that the Communist Party of the Soviet Union in the Lenin period till 1920s and the CPC from Zunyi Meeting in 1935 to the mid-1950s both generally did a good job in applying democratic-centralism within the respective party, and thus their inner-party democratic activities were quite normal. However, when Stalin came to power, democratic-centralism was seriously damaged and political activities were abnormal within the Communist Party of the Soviet Union, and within the CPC from the late 1950s to the end of the 1970s. I suggest the following ideas as the roots: Firstly, in terms of historical environment, several socialist countries, including China, had experienced a rather long period of feudal despotism in the past; as historical inertia, the working-class parties in these countries surely could have been affected by social and historical environment and thus could not practice genuine democratic-centralism within the parties. Secondly, from the aspect of socialist practice, working-class parties that have assumed power were in reality transformed from revolutionary parties to ruling parties. In their revolutionary struggles, it was necessary to maintain a high degree of centralization within the party. But in the socialist construction period, some parties had still clung to their former understanding of democratic-centralism and continued to employ it within the party, thus democratic-centralism was not genuinely practiced. Thirdly, from the perspective of the theory of socialism building, the Soviet Union pattern as forerunner example had an impact on the most socialist countries, which considered highly-centralized political and economic systems as innate characteristics and laws of socialism building. Although such kind of systems and structures were relatively progressive and had played positive roles when socialist countries were just established, on the other hand, excess centralization had usually resulted in such malpractice as arbitrary decision-making by individuals, personality cult, bureaucracy, lack of distinction between the functions of the party and those of the state, and lack of oversight and supervision that would certainly destroy inner-party democratic-centralism and political life of the country. Fourthly, although all working-class parties had accepted democratic-centralism as the fundamental organizational principle and some had even fostered good style of work and traditions in their practice, they did not deeply institutionalize these traditions and style of work, resulting in randomness in the practice of democratic-centralism. For these reasons, democratic-centralism was distorted in practice, had departed from its essence and thus leading to misconceptions and confusions among sympathizers and even Marxists. Since the new period and in the new century, the CPC has become more powerful and has made remarkable achievements in socialist modernization, I think the main reason of which is that it seriously practices and keeps improving democratic-centralism.

3.4.2 Focal Point in Improving Democratic-Centralism

It is a very important question whether the Party should uphold and improve democratic-centralism in the process of establishing and improving the socialist market economic system. In fact, the CPC is always sober-minded in this question. In September 1994, at the Fourth Plenary Session of its 14th Central Committee the CPC had adopted the "Decision of the Central Committee of the Communist Party of China on Several Important Issues about Strengthening Party Building", which read as: "Combined with the basic system of socialism, the socialist market economic system is to make the market play a basic role in resource allocation under the national macro-control. To establish the socialist market economic system, we should mobilize all positive factors and give play to the initiative and creativity of the whole Party and the entire nation; make overall plans, coordinate and carry out them in orderly and step-by-step manner; get to know and use objective laws of economy in practice; and regulate and guarantee our efforts with an all-inclusive legal system. All these cannot do without the correct leadership of the Party and the Central Government based on democratic-centralism. It is not correct to evaluate that the socialist market economy does not need democratic-centralism in the leadership systems of the Party and the country, or that democratic democracy would take us back to planned economy."[1] In view of possible problems arising in practicing democratic-centralism, the Decision had pointed out, "We need to strengthen education on democratic-centralism around the Party, particularly among leading cadres, improve specific systems for implementing democratic-centralism, and improve the rules governing political activities within the Party."[2] During its 15th and 16th National congresses and the Fourth Plenary Session of the 16th Central Committee, the CPC made in-depth expositions on how to uphold and improve democratic-centralism, and had established quite important measures. I would like to offer the reader a summary on those new achievements since the Third Plenary Session of the 11th Central Committee, and also propose my own ideas on how to improve and develop democratic-centralism.

Firstly, inner-party democracy was promoted. The CPC had pointed at its 16th National Congress, "Inner-party democracy is the life of the Party and plays an important exemplary and leading role in the system of people's democracy." This formulation manifests that the Party had progressed in understanding the significance of inner-party democracy. In terms of institutional improvement, the CPC regards the protection of Party members' democratic rights as the foundation of promoting inner-party democracy and hence has released "the Regulations on Guaranteeing Rights of the Communist Party of China Members" (for Trial Implementation) in 1995, and this Regulation was officially endorsed and distributed in 2004. The regulation takes the improvement of Party congresses and Party committees system as the focus of institutional improvement for inner-party democracy, proposes

---

[1] The Party Literature Research Center of the CPC Central Committee, *Selected Important Documents since the 14th National Congress of the Communist Party of China*, Volume 2, p.960. Beijing: People's Press, 1997.

[2] *Ibid.*, pp.960-961.

the system of Party congresses with regular annual conferences—covering more cities and counties—in the new period, and offers several methods to give play to the role of delegates when Party congresses are not in session. In accordance with the principle of collective leadership, democratic-centralism, individual consultations among members and decision by meetings, it also focuses on improving the rules of procedure and decision-making mechanism within Party committees in order to increase the role of plenary sessions of Party committees to a higher level. To reform and improve the inner-party electoral system, the CPC has chosen a gradual development in enlarging direct election system for the posts in the primary Party organizations. Regarding the transparency of Party affairs, the Regulation promotes efforts to establish and improve inner-party information sharing and reporting systems and the system of soliciting opinions concerning major policy decisions, so as to increase transparency of Party organizations' work and keep Party members better informed of these affairs and to provide them with more opportunities to participate in them. I suggest that there is an inevitable link and relationship between inner-Party democracy and people's democracy and they should be designed so that the two appropriately complement each other, and if the relations could be well handled, a substantial progress could be achieved in promoting the inner-party democracy.

Secondly, the authority of the Central Committee of the CPC was improved. Concerning centralization aspect of democratic-centralism, since China started to establish and improve the socialist market economic system and the Reform policy, the CPC had continued to underline the key notion as: "The whole Party and the entire nation should maintain a high degree of unity with regard to the guiding ideology, line, principles and policies and major questions of principle." As China is a developing country with a vast territory and a large population, the Party faces arduous and complex tasks in reform and construction. So it is quite crucial that the authority of the Central Committee is maintained, the Party's rallying power and combat effectiveness can be enhanced, and our national unity, ethnic-national solidarity and social stability can be guaranteed, thus the reform, opening-up and modernization strategy could go on smoothly, and China can ultimately realize common prosperity covering all ethnic-national groups and develop economy, society, politics, culture and environment in a balanced way. Naturally, this notion is considered as the key for the optimal interests of the Party and the entire nation. It is desired that the Party members should consciously abide by the principle that individual Party members are subordinate to the organization, that the minority is subordinate to the majority, that lower Party organizations are subordinate to the higher ones and that all the constituent organizations and members of the Party are subordinate to its National Congress and Central Committee. It is desired that the authority of the Central Committee should be maintained and its decisions should be carried out without fail and Party organizations at all levels and the Party members, leading cadres in particular, should strictly abide by Party discipline and under no circumstances should they be allowed to go their own ways neglecting orders and prohibitions.

Thirdly, inner-party oversight and supervision was strengthened. The CPC regards the improvement of inner-party oversight and the promotion of Party discipline as an important content of promoting democratic-centralism. The content and aim of inner-party democracy concern that the Party serves the people's interests, and the Party exercises self-discipline and is strict with its members for improvement requirements. On December 31, 2003, the Central Committee had distributed the "Regulations on Inner-Party Oversight of the Communist Party of China" (for Trial Implementation), the first since the CPC was founded and assumed power and also the first about inner-party oversight in the world Marxist parties. The Regulations indeed includes detailed stipulations on inner-party oversight and supervision, and gives full play to the role of the Party's disciplinary organs at all levels and in the meantime combines inner-party oversight with the oversight from outside the Party, both from top to bottom and from bottom to top; thus sets up a powerful oversight framework. The Regulations has formulated ten systems of oversight and concretely defines responsibilities and rights for the six subjects of oversight. As prescribed in the Regulations, the major content of inner-Party oversight is to make sure whether Party organizations at all levels and Party members seriously and correctly carry out the Party's line, principles and policies, whether they abide by the Constitution of China and other laws, whether they properly exercise the power invested in them by the people according to laws, and whether they strictly abide by all the systems of democratic-centralism. It is quite natural that the main target of inner-party oversight focuses on leading Party organs and leading cadres at all levels, particularly chief leaders. It is generally suggested that under the new conditions of socialist market economy and Reform, the Party should pay special attention to preventing violations of Party discipline and laws among Party cadres especially against material corruption and misuse of power. The Regulations document stresses, "Whatever profession or position, Party members should strictly abide by Party discipline and conscientiously accept oversight from Party organizations and the masses, the equality of all Party members before the Party discipline should be guaranteed, and the Party should take stern actions to punish those who violate the discipline."

Chapter 4

Building a Contingent of High-Caliber Cadres for the Party

Building a contingent of high-caliber cadres is an important component of Marxist Party building, and an important organizational guarantee for the implementation of the Party's political line. It is a pressing and important task for Party building to build a contingent of high-caliber cadres capable of assuming heavy responsibilities and withstanding the test of trials and tribulations.

4.1 A Major Strategic Task for the Marxist Party

One of the distinguishing characteristics of modern political parties is a rather stable leadership group with its top leaders at the core of this group. Therefore, for any political party, it is very important to train high-caliber members as the backbone and give play to their role. It is especially true with proletarian parties.

4.1.1 A Central Issue for the Marxist Party

Proletarian parties always attach importance to the building of a contingent of cadres. Marx and Engels had also trained a large number of backbone people for labor movements and political activists during the Communist League and the First International. Lenin had proposed to cultivate a group of professional revolutionaries when founding a new proletarian party in Russia. After the victory of the October Revolution, he had stressed, "We need to study people and discover capable staff."[1] Stalin had also made many incisive statements on this issue. The most representative and famous statement was the phrase "cadres decide everything," which was included in his address to the graduates from the Red Army Academies in May 1935.

In May 1937, in his report to the Party Conference of White Areas held in Yan'an, Liu Shaoqi had pointed out, "All the work and changes rely on our cadres; therefore the problem of cadres is the central problem of our Party."[2] In October 1938, in his report to the Sixth Plenary Session of the Sixth Central Committee of the Party, Mao Zedong had pointed out, "Cadres are decisive factors, once the political line is determined."[3] After the Third Plenary Session of the 11th Central Committee of the Party was held, Deng Xiaoping had also commented on the organizational line and the building of a contingent of cadres on many occasions. He had pointed out, "Once a political line has been set, it has to be concretely implemented by people, and the results will vary depending on those who realize implementing, those who are in favor, those who are against, or the middle-of-the-roaders."[4] He stressed, "A correct organizational line should guarantee that a political line will be put into effect. The organizational line is now on our agenda. We'll be ashamed when we meet Marx 'there' if we fail to solve this problem well."[5]

---

[1] *Collected Works of Vladimir Lenin* (2nd Chinese edition), Volume 42, p.392. Beijing: People's Press, 1987.

[2] *Selected Works of Liu Shaoqi*, Volume 1, p.69.

[3] *Selected Works of Mao Zedong* (2nd Chinese edition), Volume 2, p.526.

[4] *Selected Works of Deng Xiaoping* (2nd Chinese edition), Volume 2, p.191.

[5] *Ibid.*, p.193.

In February 1992, Deng Xiaoping in his remarks during his inspection tour of South China had commented, "The implementation of the correct political line should be ensured by a correct organizational line. In a sense, whether we can manage our domestic affairs well, whether we can keep to the socialist road and adhere to reform and the opening-up policy, whether we can develop the economy more rapidly and whether we can maintain long-term peace and stability will all be determined by the people."[1] On the eve of new century, the core Party leaders of the CPC have also stressed the importance of this strategic task. It can be observed that the above comments evaluate the Marxist cadre principle from the aspect of relationship between the organizational line and political line of the Party.

4.1.2 Prolonged Stability of the Party and State

In a society where a Marxist is in the ruling position, naturally the quality of cadres has a direct bearing on the prolonged stability of the Party and state as well as the harmony and stability in the society. The reason is that those cadres possessing high qualities and a good style of work could better represent the fundamental interests of the broad masses, be more sensitive to public sentiments, interpret public opinion and pool the people's wisdom, thus maintain emotional ties with the people and win public support. Qualified cadres could better exercise the power for the people and seek concrete benefits for the people, be able to conduct their work effectively, and forge ahead with determination and in a pioneering spirit, practicing both realistic and pragmatic approaches. They could deal with more complicated problems and emergency cases with a higher dedication and strong sense of political consciousness, thus reflect higher leadership qualities and achieve better results in organization and coordination. In the report to the 16th National Congress of the Party in 2002, Jiang Zemin had commented, "It is a matter of vital importance for maintaining prolonged stability of the Party and state to train a large number of outstanding leading cadres for the mission

---

[1] *Selected Works of Deng Xiaoping* (1st Chinese edition), Volume 3, p.380.

of running the Party, state and army."[1] Article 33 in the Party Constitution formulates the nature of the Party cadres: "Party cadres are the backbone of the Party's cause and public servants of the people." Party cadres are the makers and implementers of the Party's line, its principles and policies, and they are the leaders and organizers of the people in revolution, construction and reform, and the link through which the Party maintains close ties with the masses. If a Marxist party has a good contingent of cadres, and the style of work is good, the relationship between the Party and the masses and between the cadres and the masses is harmonious, revolution develops, and the people live and work in peace and contentment. On the contrary, if some cadres are not open-minded and follow the beaten track, their work performance is mediocre; and if some are infirm in ideals and beliefs, seek ease and comfort and stay far above the masses and the reality, they may even become corrupt and degenerate, abuse power for personal gains, and violate the law and Party discipline, thus the revolution will not develop well and the masses will be dissatisfied.

Scholars generally agree that under the effect of radical changes, the CPC faces a challenging situation, bringing about serious challenges for the building of a contingent of cadres. Besides, recently the ranks of cadres are at a new round of succession of the old by the new: those who have started to work in the democratic revolution period and in the early days of New China have already retired from their posts; those who were promoted in the early period of reform in 1980s are retiring from their posts; and a large number of young and capable cadres are taking up those leading posts, but they still have to be tempered in practice. Statistical data available for the last years demonstrate that the cadres' education has been enhanced remarkably, and the knowledge structure has been improved. However, there are obvious facts and data suggesting that some cadres possess a weak consciousness on the Party's ultimate aim, have alienated from the masses, lack the spirit of plain living and hard struggle, are unwilling to go deep into the realities and go deep among the masses, cannot throw off their airs and work in a down-

[1] *Selected Works of Jiang Zemin*, Volume 3, p.571.

to-earth manner, and cannot do a good job in speaking to, acting for and dealing with the masses. This kind of evaluations in public is not rare and complements the researches made by Party building scholars. Thus it is quite understandable that the Party leadership has paid a keen attention to the issue during the last decade.

4.2 Basic Requirements for High-Caliber Cadres

Over the years, the Party has accumulated rich experience regarding the building of a contingent of cadres, and brought into being a set of correct line, principles and policies about cadre work. Meanwhile, it has put forth basic requirements for this work and improved them in new practice in the new period. The requirements are mainly embodied in the regulations on cadre work that the CPC Central Committee released in recent years. They are: "The Regulations on the Work of Selecting and Appointing Leading Party and Government Cadres" distributed in July 2002; "The Measures for the Supervision and Inspection of the Work of Selecting and Appointing Leading Party and Government Cadres (for Trial Implementation)" distributed in July 2003; "The Provisional Regulations on the Open Selection of Leading Cadres of the Party and Government", "Interim Provisions on the Work of Competition for Posts in the Party and Government", "Voting Methods for the Plenum of CPC Local Committees Concerning Candidates Nominated and Recommended as Head of a Party Committee or Government of an Immediate Lower Level", "Interim Provisions on the Resignation of Leading Party and Government Cadres", "Opinions on Leading Party and Government Cadres Being Engaged in Business Activities after Resignation", and "The Notice on the Clean-Up of Part-time Positions of Leading Party and Government Cadres in Enterprises" distributed in April 2004; "The Interim Provisions on the Tenure of Leading Party and Government Cadres", "Interim Provisions on the Avoidance of Leading Party and Government Cadres", and "Provisions on the Transfer of Leading Party and Government Cadres" distributed in June 2006. To build a contingent of high-caliber cadres, these documents form an important asset and meet basic requirements.

4.2.1 Four-Point Principle in Building a Contingent of Cadres

As early as in the new-democratic revolution period, Mao Zedong had raised a criterion for cadres—to have both ability and political integrity, and a merit-based line on cadres. In the early period of New China, he had put forth another principle—to be both socialist-minded and professionally qualified. In a rather long time, these had been the basic principles for the Party to select and appoint cadres. After the Third Plenary Session of the 11th Central Committee of the Party, Deng Xiaoping had proposed a **four-point principle** based on the reality of the ranks of cadres, so as to meet the need of the Party's central task (economic development) in the new period. He had made a comment on the issue in a central working conference: "While making sure that we select cadres who will keep to the socialist road, we should reduce their average age and raise the level of their education and professional competence. The cadre system should be gradually improved to ensure this. Of course, cadres should be revolutionary. This requirement takes precedence over considerations of age, education and professional competence. That is why we say adherence to the socialist road is the primary qualification for a cadre."[1] This was a complete statement of the four-point principle (making cadres more revolutionary, younger in average age, better educated and more professionally competent) for the cadre work in the new period. The Resolution on Several Historical Problems of the Party since the Founding of New China which was approved at the Sixth Plenary Session of the 11th CPC Central Committee in June 1981, Deng Xiaoping's opening speech and the political report approved at the 12th National Congress of the Party in September 1982 all included this four-point principle. The Party Constitution included this principle and made it the guideline for the building of the ranks of cadres in the new period.

The four-point principle is a summary of the international communist

---

[1] *Selected Works of Deng Xiaoping* (2nd Chinese edition), Volume 2, p.361.

movement and the Party's previous experience, and also includes Mao Zedong's standards as well as a creative development under the new historical conditions. I would like to give an explanation on them.

Being more revolutionary is a requirement for the political quality of cadres and a political standard for the building of the ranks of cadres, including the political stance, attitude, integrity, ideology and work style. The basic requirements for cadres to be more revolutionary at the current stage are: to have the firm ideal of communism, adhere to the Party's basic theories and basic line, bear in mind the Party's purpose of serving the people wholeheartedly, be honest and clean, fair and upright, and make selfless contributions. This point will enable Marxists to hold firmly the leadership of the Party and state at all levels.

Being younger in average age means that cadres, particularly leading bodies at different levels, should be younger, competent, energetic and able to assume heavy tasks. To make the ranks of cadres younger in average age, the Party should foster tens of thousands of successors to the revolutionary cause of the proletariat and realize the cooperation between elder cadres and younger ones and succession of the old by the new, with the goal to ensure that the Party has qualified successors. It should be noted that this point is not for individual cadres but for the ranks of cadres, requiring that the ranks of cadres, particularly leading bodies, be as younger as possible in average age. For individual cadres, aging is an irresistible natural law; they cannot choose to be young or not. This point does not mean that the younger the better, without considering other requirements; nor does it mean that there should be no flexibility regarding the problem of age.

Being better educated requires cadres to have certain educational attainment, which is a criterion of education for the building of the ranks of cadres. In recent years, the degree of education and knowledge of the ranks of cadres has grown a lot, with a big proportion of cadres having college degree and above. With the rapid development of science and technology, all the Party cadres should update their knowledge and try to learn, understand and apply basic knowledge of modern sciences including natural science, social science and management science, so as to make themselves cadres who are engaged in lifelong learning, are knowledgeable, understand science and are good at management.

Being professionally more competent requires cadres possess professional knowledge and competence that are needed within the extent of their leadership and become proficient in their work. Being better educated and being professionally more competent are correlated and have respective emphasis. The former mainly requires cadres have a broad range of knowledge, while the latter mainly requires cadres have intensive and comprehensive professional knowledge. The two points require selecting cadres who have comparatively higher educational attainment, more extensive scientific knowledge and stronger professional competence and enroll them into leading bodies, so as to make the leading bodies have a rational intellectual structure and exercise professional leadership in the socialist modernization drive. It is necessary to have a proper understanding on the two points, and not stress academic credentials too much while neglecting competence.

Among the four points, being more revolutionary is always at the first place; without it, the other three points will not have a correct orientation. But this does not mean that we can neglect the other three points; without them, being more revolutionary cannot be realized. If we can correctly understand the four-point principle, it could be possible to build up a contingent of high-caliber cadres.

4.2.2 Principles for the Selection and Appointment of Leading Cadres

According to "The Regulations on the Work of Selecting and Appointing Leading Party and Government Cadres", there are six principles in this work.

First, the principle that the Party is in charge of cadre management: This is the primary or elementary principle for cadre work, and also a general requirement for cadre work. It means that Party members are responsible for formulating and carrying out cadre line and policies, managing, supervising and examining the cadre and personnel work, and recommending leading cadres for important positions to state organs of state power. The essence of this principle is to ensure the Party's leadership over the cadre and personnel work and its right to manage cadres at important positions. Moreover, this principle should not be simplified; not all the cadres are directly appointed and removed by Party committees and the Party can manage more than cadres.

Second, the principle of merit, ability and political integrity: This principle is the criterion and the basic requirement of the cadre line for cadres. The requirements for ability and political integrity vary in different periods. We should understand them in accordance with Article 34 in the Party Constitution and refer to the essential qualifications for leading Party and government cadres stated in Article 6 in "The Regulations on the Work of Selecting and Appointing Leading Party and Government Cadres." To uphold this principle, the Party should be fair and honest in selecting and using cadres.

Third, the principle of wide acceptance and outstanding performance: This principle embodies the ideological line of seeking truth from facts and the Party's mass line. The first point means that we should fully respect the people's rights to be informed of, participate in, select and supervise the selection and appointment of cadres and expand the participation by the public—this is the most effective way to curb unhealthy practices in appointing cadres. The second point means that we should appraise, select and appoint cadres based on how they fulfill their job responsibilities and how their performance is, thus take into account the differences between cadres in the work basis and conditions, and carefully avoid appointing those who seek quick success and instant benefits and support vanity projects or image projects.

Fourth, the principle of openness, equality, competition and merit-based selection: This is an important measure in the reform of cadre work. Openness means to increase transparency in cadre work, publicizing the policies, principles, criteria and procedures of the selection and appointment of cadres and avoiding black-box operation. Equality is to offer equal opportunities for different people and put an end to any privilege for any people. Competition means that we should introduce the competition mechanism into cadre work, creating conditions for outstanding people. Merit-based selection means that the Party should select and appoint the superior or the best from among the good.

Fifth, the principle of democratic-centralism: This is the application of the Party's fundamental organizational principle in cadre work. It demands that Party committees at all levels should keep to the principle of group discussion and subordination of the minority to the majority in making decisions about the appointment and removal of any cadre; that is, they should take a voting before making the decision, allowing no individual or a few people to make the decision.

Sixth, the principle of acting in accordance with the law: This demonstrates the spirit of the rule of law, and conforms to a stipulation in the Party Constitution: "The Party should conduct its activities within the framework of the Constitution and laws of the country." Members of standing committee of people's congresses, members of people's governments, presidents of people's courts and chief procurators of people's procuratorates at all levels should be recommended by Party committees at their respective levels and elected and appointed according to legal procedures.

The above six principles are connected with each other and make up an organic whole, combining the principles that the Party has persisted in for cadre work with the new experience it has gained from making the cadre work more democratic, institutionalized, standard and law-based in the new period.

4.2.3 Procedures for the Selection and Appointment of Cadres

Strict procedures for the selection and appointment of cadres make up an important measure for ensuring fairness and justice in appointing cadres, curbing unhealthy tendencies and corruption from the root. As provided by relevant documents, the following procedures should be employed in the work of selecting and appointing leading party and government cadres.

Step one, democratic recommendation: Candidates should be nominated through democratic recommendation, including recommendation by meetings or through voting and recommendation by individuals. An individual who recommends a candidate for a leading post to the corresponding Party organization should write recommendation materials with a responsible attitude and sign his/her name. After the corresponding organization or personnel department examines and verifies the materials, democratic recommendation moves on according to established procedures.

Step two, observation by the corresponding Party organization: For a candidate determined through democratic recommendation, the organization or personnel department concerned makes strict observation on him/her within the scope of its authority and according to the requirements for selecting and appointing cadres and requirements of the leading post. The ways of observation are individual interview and asking for a comment in a certain range. The content of observation covers the candidate's political morality, professional competence, diligence, performance and honesty, with the emphasis on performance.

Step three, discussion and decision-making: To select and appoint a leading Party or government cadre, the Party committee or leading Party group concerned should hold meetings, discuss the matter and make the decision, or make a decision about recommendation or nomination. For such meetings, at least two third members of the Party committee or leading Party group should be present. After thorough discussion, a voting, either by voice, a show of hands or secret ballot, should be taken, and the decision is made when more than half of the present members vote for it. Then the result is reported to the next higher Party committee or leading Party group for approval or for the record.

Step four, public announcement before appointment: In December 2000, the Organization Department of the CPC Central Committee, based on the practical experience in local places, formulated a document: "The Opinions on Spreading the System of Public Announcement before

Appointment of Leading Party and Government Cadres", providing specific stipulations on the persons involved, range, content, methods, time and procedures of public announcement.

4.3 Focusing on the Leading Bodies

The building of leading bodies is the focus of the building of the ranks of cadres; to build a contingent of high-caliber cadres, the key is to do a good job in building leading bodies at all levels. At the Fourth Plenary Session of the 14th Central Committee, the CPC had approved the Decision of the Central Committee: "On Several Important Issues about Strengthening Party Building", raising an essential requirement for this work: "We should turn the leading bodies of the Party at all levels into staunch collectives that firmly implement the Party's basic line, serve the people wholeheartedly and are able to lead the modernization drive."[1] To adapt to the new situation and new tasks, the CPC has raised a higher requirement for the building of its leading bodies at the 16th National Congress: "We should turn the leading bodies of the Party at all levels into staunch collectives that firmly implement the important thought of Three Represents mainly by improving their qualities, optimizing their composition, refining their work style and enhancing solidarity."[2] In the Decision of the Central Committee of the Communist Party of China, "On the Enhancement of the Party's Governance Capability" adopted at the Fourth Plenary Session of the 16th Central Committee, the CPC had demanded: "We should turn the leading bodies of the Party at all levels into staunch collectives that are firm in politics, stay realistic and pragmatic, forge ahead in a pioneering spirit, are honest and diligent in governance affairs, and are united and coordinated."[3] In 2004, the CPC Central Committee had distributed "The Outline for the Building of

---

[1] The Party Literature Research Center of the CPC Central Committee, *Selected Important Documents since the 14th National Congress of the Communist Party of China*, Volume 2, p.970.

[2] *Selected Works of Jiang Zemin*, Volume 3, p.571.

[3] *Selected Important Documents since the 16th National Congress of the Communist Party of China*, Volume 2, p.292. Beijing: Central Party Literature Press, 2006.

Leading Bodies in Party Committees and Governments around the Country (2004-2008)", making overall arrangements for this work.

For the Party structure, the organizational system of the CPC is made of three levels: central organizations, local organizations and primary organizations. Correspondingly, the building of leading bodies also covers three levels: central leading bodies, local leading bodies and primary leading bodies. The central leading bodies of the Party refer to its Central Committee, Central Commission for Discipline Inspection, and Political Bureau of the Central Committee and its Standing Committee. The local leading bodies refer to Party committees and their standing committees from provinces, cities to counties, or from autonomous regions, prefecture to banners. The primary leading bodies refer to Party committees and their standing committees at primary organizations. Since the leading bodies at the three levels differ from each other in the rules of election, status, function and power, the respective requirements for them are different; but the general requirement is the same, that is, to build a strong core of leadership for the great cause of socialism.

For the state structure, the political system of China is made up of four main components: the people's congress system, multi-party cooperation and political consultation system under the leadership of the CPC, regional ethnic autonomy system, organizational system of the state administrative branch and other systems. Correspondingly, there are four sets of organized groups at different levels: people's congresses, the Chinese People's Political Consultative Conference (CPPCC), Party committees and people's government. The four are different in their nature, rules of election, status, function and power, and operational mechanism.

Here, I will mainly discuss about the building of the leading bodies in Party committees and governments.

4.3.1 Overall Capability of Leading Bodies

The cohesion and fighting capacity of leading bodies are mainly determined by their overall capability; therefore, to strengthen the building of leading bodies, the first thing to do is to enhance their overall capability. The report to the 16th National Congress of the CPC had commented on this issue: "Faced with profound changes in the conditions of governance and social environment, Party committees and leading cadres at all levels should, in response to the requirements of the new situation and new tasks, acquire new knowledge, accumulate new experience and develop new abilities in practice, thus living up to the mission assigned to them and the full trust placed on them. They should view the world with broad vision, acquire a correct understanding of the requirements of the times and be good at thinking on a theoretical plane and in a strategic perspective so as to improve their ability of sizing up the situation in a scientific way. They should act in compliance with objective and scientific laws, address promptly the new situation and problems in reform and development, know how to seize opportunities to accelerate development and enhance their abilities of keeping the market economy well in hand. They should correctly understand and handle various social contradictions, know how to balance the relations among different interests, overcome difficulties and go on improving their ability of coping with complicated situations. They should enhance their awareness of law and know how to integrate the adherence to Party leadership and the people being the masters of the country with ruling the country by law and improve their abilities of exercising state power according to law. They should base themselves on the overall interests of the work of the entire Party and the whole country, firmly implement the Party's line, principles and policies, work creatively in light of realities and keep enhancing their ability of commanding the whole situation."[1] The quality of leading cadres is reflected in their capabilities, while those of leading bodies at various levels are reflected in their capability to promote economic development and social progress. To build a good leading body, its members should follow the ideological guidance of the Party and should focus on the enhancement of governance capability, remain enthusiastic and diligent in their work, take the overall situation into consideration, work out practical measures and handle

---

[1] *Selected Works of Jiang Zemin*, Volume 3, pp.569-570.

concrete affairs in a down-to-earth manner, be willing to and capable of achieving development without making serious errors, and bring benefits to the people with concrete achievements.

4.3.2 Optimizing the Structure of Leading Bodies

Any leading body is an organism made up of various elements; that whether it can exert its function depends on not only the qualities of individual members but also the entire structure. To strengthen the building of leading bodies at all levels, primarily it is necessary to select the right people. We should select the cadres who have political integrity, professional competence and a good style of work and have made outstanding performance at work and put them in leading posts at different levels. The most important thing is to select qualified and competent chief leaders for Party committees and governments at different levels, because they can then help foster good leading bodies. Moreover, we should take into consideration the age composition, knowledge structure and composition of professions in leading bodies, apart from temperament and strong points of each member, and then rationalize these structures on the premise of guaranteed ideological and political qualities and according to the requirements for leading bodies at different levels. To rationalize the age composition, we should boldly select young, outstanding cadres into leading bodies, and promote them to be more energetic. To rationalize the knowledge structure, we should ensure that members of leading bodies have a certain level of educational attainment, comprehensive and reasonable knowledge composition, and in particular, modern high and new technologies; for the knowledge structure, members of leading bodies differ from each other but complement each other, enabling leading bodies to meet the needs of leading work at different layers and in different fields. To rationalize the composition of professions, we should ensure that each member of any leading body has his/her own professional background and expertise in some field, or even is expert in some field; thus members can complement each other in profession. To rationalize the temperament composition, it is critical to ensure that leading bodies have both outgoing and reserved members, both cheerful and sedate members, and both tough and mild members, and that members of such temperaments are compatible with each other. Since members differ from each other in the family background, growing experience and character, they have different temperaments, which is important for a leading body. The optimization of leading bodies is in the final analysis a process of allocating personnel properly; only when each member can exert his/her ability, favorable factors are there, while unfavorable ones are by-passed. And when members have complementary advantages, a leading body can be more vigorous and have a higher overall quality.

4.3.3　Solidarity among the Leading Bodies

Solidarity is important for measuring and testing the quality and Party spirit of leading bodies and leading cadres; it is also an important factor in determining whether leading bodies can make a concerted effort. To promote solidarity in leading bodies, the Party should achieve two things: one is to pay heed to study, political awareness and integrity and the other is to uphold democratic-centralism.

Study, political awareness and integrity make up a basic requirement for leading cadres and an important guarantee for the building of leading bodies as well. By consciously studying hard and acquiring more knowledge, leading cadres at all levels will have a higher mental realm. With a strong political awareness, leading cadres can remain sober-minded in face of complex international and domestic situations, keep firm to the correct orientation, withstand all kinds of tests, and have the courage to advocate the truth and correct mistakes. With integrity, leading bodies can have a better image, healthy political activities, harmonious relations among members and more ability for solving inner problems, remove factors not good for the solidarity, and lay a foundation for lasting cooperation.

Democratic-centralism, particularly collective leadership, is the institutional guarantee for the building of leading bodies. The chief leaders of leading bodies in Party committees and governments should be broad-minded, democratic in work style, respect other people, be good at pooling the wisdom of members, have the courage to assume responsibilities, and be able to unite members who have different views to work together. Members of leading bodies should perform their duties according to collective decisions and division of labor while being concerned with the overall work of leading bodies and take an active part in collective leadership. Leading bodies should promote the Party spirit, the sense of overall situation and the sense of principle, and call on members to respect, support and understand each other.

4.4 Reform on the Cadre and Personnel System

The cadre and personnel system is a generic term for the rules and regulations of the Party and government on the cadre and personnel work. Its reform is an important part of political restructuring, as well as the fundamental solution to building a contingent of high-caliber cadres and training a large number of outstanding personnel. Since the 1990s, with the advancement of economic restructuring and political restructuring, the central authority has treated the reform of the cadre and personnel system as a priority. In June 2000, the General Office of the CPC Central Committee had distributed "The Outline on Deepening the Reform of the Cadre and Personnel System", raising the overall objective, principles, emphases in work and basic requirements for the reform of the cadre and personnel system. In September 2001, at the Sixth Plenary Session of the 15th Central Committee, the CPC had adopted "The Decision of the Central Committee of the Communist Party of China on Strengthening and Improving the Party's Style of Work." In the Decision, the CPC had made it an important task of the improvement of Party style to "adhere to merit-based appointment of cadres and oppose unhealthy practices", and proposed to accelerate the reform of the cadre and personnel system, improve institutions, and select people with the criterion of work style and select those with a fine style. In the report to the 16th National Congress and another document titled "The Decision of the

Central Committee of the Communist Party of China on the Enhancement of the Party's Governance Capability" adopted at the Fourth Plenary Session of the 16th Central Committee, the need to deepen the reform of the cadre and personnel system has been reiterated and concrete requirements have been raised.

In recent years, local Party organizations have made active efforts in deepening the reform of the cadre and personnel system and made initial achievements. The achievements are: the retirement system for cadres has been established and improved, laying a foundation for abolishing the system of life-long tenure in leading posts; a new system for layered and classified cadre management has taken place, and a system of civil servants has been established and improved; the single appointment system was changed, and several other rules were put into practice, including appointment by election, appointment by designation, appointment by examination and appointment by invitation; the procedures for selecting and appointing cadres are more strict and standard. Generally the participation of the masses has increased and the cadre management work has been more standardized. Cadre evaluation systems have become more advanced: the regular evaluation system, with annual evaluation, evaluation during the term and evaluation at the end of the term was established (For leading Party and government bodies and leading cadres). And the assessment results are considered in the appointment of cadres, gradually solving the problem that cadres are often promoted but not demoted. Since the State Council has issued "The Interim Regulations on National Civil Servants", the system of civil servants has been gradually set up. In April 2005, the Standing Committee of the 10th National People's Congress deliberated on and approved the Civil Servant Law of the People's Republic of China at its 15th meeting. It marked that the system of civil servants in China has formally taken on the legal road, and it was a significant step for the reform of the cadre and personnel system.

The general objective for the reform of the cadre and personnel system for the present is to create an environment for appointing cadres which realizes openness, equality, competition and merit-based selection. Also, a cadre management mechanism with effective incentives has been set up and a supervision structure with complete laws and strict discipline has been established. The cadre and personnel management work should move to more democratic, scientific and law-based style. For all these aims it is projected to build a set of cadre and personnel institutions by 2010 that conforms to the general policies. Below, I will comment on the aspects necessary to achieve success in this sphere.

4.4.1 The System of Selecting and Appointing Cadres

The system of selecting and appointing cadres is a generic term for the principles, procedures and methods applied in the process of selecting, admitting, appointing and removing cadres; it is the major content of the cadre and personnel system, and also the key for setting up a mechanism for appointing cadres under which outstanding personnel can show themselves. What kind of cadres should be appointed? What kind of cadres should not? How to select and appoint cadres? These questions not only play an important guiding role, but also have a direct bearing on whether the Party will correct unhealthy tendencies in appointing cadres. The best solution to these problems is to develop inner-party democracy, follow the mass line, and enable Party members and ordinary people to have more right to know, to participate in, to choose and to supervise the selection and appointment of cadres; in another expression, to launch a "sunshine project" for cadre appointment.

The party should reform the ways of nomination and broaden the channels for the selection and appointment of cadres by transforming the practice of nomination mainly by leading bodies and leading cadres into a recommendation by corresponding Party organizations and leaders and self-recommendation.

The procedures for selecting and appointing cadres should be strictly followed, such as: democratic recommendation, observation by the corresponding Party organization, discussion and decisions by the corresponding Party committee, public announcement before appointment, and examination and approval by the next higher Party organization. We should continue reforming the ways of observing candidates, randomly determine the candidate to be observed instead of monitoring by leaders, change single-candidate system, change monitored observation into multiple-candidate, non-directional observation, and solicit opinions from the department of Party committees, Party members and the masses. We should strictly practice the voting system in Party committees, avoiding temporary motions and preventing decision-making by a few people.

The Party should push the open selection of leading cadres. In accordance with the notice of the Organization Department of the Central Committee "On Open Selection of Leading Cadres" released in March 1999, we should intensify our efforts in this regard, correctly understand the sphere of application of open selection, clarify the posts and requirements involved in open selection, standardize and improve relevant procedures and methods, strengthen the organization work of examinations and make the examinations more scientific, increase the proportion of openly selected leading cadres among newly selected ones, and make the work of open selection more effective.

We should continue promoting competition for posts in Party and government organs. In accordance with "The Opinions on Promoting Competition for Posts in Party and Government Organs" issued in July 1998, we should establish a competitive mechanism that is conducive for cadres to improve themselves.

4.4.2 System of Assessing Leading Party and Government Cadres

The cadre assessment system is a system under which organization and personnel departments make regular observations and appraisals on cadres' ideology and moral character, attitude to work, work capacity, performance and other aspects; it is an important part of cadre management and an important measure for strengthening the building of the ranks of cadres. A scientific cadre assessment system can help us distinguish and employ better cadres and plays a guiding role for adjusting cadres' value orientation, improving their work style and encouraging them to serve the people in a down-to-earth manner, and is an important approach to solving the problem of cadres unwilling to work at lower levels and to setting up a strict mechanism of reward, punishment and elimination.

We should work out scientific standards for cadres' performance evaluation and strictly carry out the procedures for such evaluation. We should improve the ways of assessing cadres' performance by combining qualitative assessment with quantitative assessment, assessment in normal times with assessment at regular intervals, and assessment by Party organizations with the assessment participated by the masses. Evaluate cadres' performance in an objective, fair and realistic way, correctly apply the evaluation results in the reward and punishment, or promotion and demotion of cadres, and set up a reasonable incentive mechanism. The Party should clarify the standards for identifying unqualified cadres, and deal with those having been identified after assessment. We should connect the cadre assessment system with the system of cadre removal, resignation and demotion, make faster adjustments for those unqualified cadres, and further unclog the flowing of cadres.

4.4.3 Life-Long Tenure Issues

The history of international communist movement and that of the CPC show that almost all communist parties around the world are unable to solve the problem of life-long tenure in leading posts, which provides institutional loopholes for highly centralized power and arbitrary decision-making by individuals. In November 1979, Deng Xiaoping had pointed out at a senior cadres' meeting, "The important thing is to establish a retirement system…It's not a question of slighting anybody, but of addressing a major problem that affects the prosperity and vitality of our Party and our state."[1] In February 1982, the CPC Central Committee issued the Decision of the Central Committee: "On Establishing a Retirement System for Veteran

---

[1] *Selected Works of Deng Xiaoping*, Volume 2, p.226.

Cadres". Following this, the CPC Central Committee and the State Council had issued a number of documents and gradually expanded the retirement system. At the 12th and 13th National congresses, the CPC had set up central and local advisory boards, an important, transitional organizational measure for the succession of the old by the new. By 1992, the retirement system was established, and the succession of the old by the new had achieved the expected progress. Therefore, the CPC had decided to give up establishing advisory boards. In this period, Deng Xiaoping had retired from leading posts, setting a good example for the Party. It was significant for the Party to abolish the system of life-long tenure in leading posts which could not be solved for a long time.

To abolish the system of life-long tenure in leading posts, we should make efforts in ideology and institutions. George Washington, the first president of the United States, had served two consecutive terms and then did not run for election of the third term, setting a good example. The 2,000-year feudalism in China has resulted in a deep-rooted thought which highly values official titles. To solve this problem, it is necessary to create a relaxed social environment, while leading cadres should be broad-minded, adapt to the Party's cause and the overall situation, and take a proper attitude towards retirement. Institutionally, it means to adopt a system of fixed tenures for leading Party and government cadres. In June 2006, the General Office of the CPC Central Committee had distributed "The Interim Provisions on Fixed Tenures in Leading Party and Government Posts", the first regulatory document of its type in the history of the CPC. The document had explicitly stated, "The tenure of leading Party and government posts lasts five years, and during the tenure cadres should remain as stable as possible; any cadre who has served two consecutive terms at the same post shall not be recommended, nominated or appointed to the same post; any cadre who has served 15 years or longer in leading posts at the same level shall not be recommended, nominated or appointed to leading posts at the same level." This document was important for a Marxist Party to abolish the de facto system of life-long tenure in leading posts.

4.4.4 Cadre Transfer System

The cadre transfer system is a system under which organization or personnel departments transfer cadres from one post to another and from one place to another in a planned way, and it is an important system for cadre management. In April 1999, approved by the CPC Central Committee, the General Office distributed "The Interim Provisions on the Work of Transferring Leading Party and Government Cadres." Based on this Interim Provisions, it had also distributed "The Regulations on the Work of Transferring Leading Party and Government Cadres" in June 2006, explicitly stating the targets, scope, methods, organization and implementation, discipline and supporting measures of this work. By promoting the cadre transfer system, it is possible to promote the rational flow of human resources and optimize the structure of leading bodies, and meanwhile enable cadres to broaden their horizon, become more competent, accumulate experience and enhance the art of leadership and help them to break away from the relationship network. In the cadre transfer system, it necessary to pay attention to the scope and intensity of transfers, and transfer cadres in a planned and step-by-step manner between different areas, between different departments, between local and central departments, and between the Party and government organs and state-owned enterprises or people's organizations. The Party should put emphasis on transferring chief leaders in Party committees and governments and leading cadres in critical departments or critical posts, intensify the cooperation between central organs and local organs, and promote job rotation among middle-ranking cadres in Party and government organs. Moreover, it is also necessary to intensify the cadre transfer work among Party committees, people's congresses, governments and the CPPCC. The Party should combine this system with the system of fixed tenures and the challenge system.

4.4.5 Standard Organizational Structures

Over the years, the highly centralized leadership system that came into being under the planned economy has resulted in over-staffing and several other drawbacks. After the Reform and Opening-Up policies were set, the organizational structure of governments has been adjusted, the division of functions and powers has been rationalized, and the over-staffing was cut down in several reforms, helping the transformation of government functions. At present there is a general consensus that the organizational setup of Party and government organs should be standardized. Party leaders have also emphasized to improve the structure of standing committees of Party committees; strictly control the number of leading posts in Party and government organs, and push more Party and government leaders to take posts in the other system; solve the problem of overlapping functions, and remove or merge Party or government departments that have the same or similar functions. At the same time, it is necessary to cut down the number of leading posts in people's congresses and the CPPCC. I think, these measures are important not only for building a contingent of high-caliber cadres, but also for reforming and improving the Party's style of leadership and enhancing its governance capability.

4.4.6 The Mechanism for Supervising the Selection and Appointment

To establish and improve a mechanism for supervising the work of selecting and appointing cadres, it is necessary to think on several aspects, including working out rules and regulations for the selection and appointment of cadres. Also ensure that these rules and regulations are strictly carried out, establish a system of regular examination and supervision of this work, and broaden the channels to enable more Party members and the masses to participate in overseeing this work. It is necessary to prevent and correct unhealthy tendencies in the selection and appointment of cadres. In December 2000, the Organization Department of the CPC Central Committee had distributed "Several Opinions on Strengthening the Supervision over Cadres in Organization Departments (for Trial Implementation)", which had defined the requirements for organization departments on how to conduct supervision. In July 2002, the CPC Central Committee had distributed "The

Regulations on the Work of Selecting and Appointing Leading Party and Government Cadres", which had defined the requirements for discipline inspection or supervision organs on how to conduct supervision and how to improve the supervision system and promote work discipline. In July 2003, the CPC Central Committee had distributed "The Measures for the Supervision and Inspection of the Work of Selecting and Appointing Leading Party and Government Cadres (for Trial Implementation)", providing supplementary measures for the above documents and further improving the system for supervising the work of selecting and appointing leading cadres. Discipline inspection or supervision organs should supervise and inspect the work of selecting and appointing cadres according to relevant regulations. And it is necessary to establish a joint conference system for organization or personnel departments and discipline inspection or supervision departments, so that they can exchange information and offer suggestions on how to strengthen the supervision over the work of selecting and appointing cadres.

4.5 The Strategy of Competent Personnel

In December 2003, the CPC Central Committee and the State Council had issued "The Decision on Further Enhancing the Development of Human Resources", expounding on the significance of the personnel strategy under new historical conditions: "To guide personnel work with the important thought of Three Represents, take development as the aim of the work, establish a scientific outlook on competent personnel, strengthen capability building of human resources, work to build three contingents of Party and government personnel, of managerial personnel in enterprises and of technical professionals, push forward structural adjustment of human resources, and make innovations in mechanisms for personnel work and optimize the environment for this work." I think, this is a difficult problem that we should concentrate on and solve.

4.5.1 Scientific Outlook on Competent Personnel

In the modern world, competition in comprehensive national strength of a country is in the final analysis the competition of competent personnel. What kind of people are competent personnel? There is no standard definition about this concept in the international community. In ancient China, the criteria included integrity, ability and knowledge. *The Contemporary Chinese Dictionary* explains: "person of ability and integrity; person who has some expertise." *Ci Yuan (Etymology)* explains: "one's ability and talent; person of talent and learning; one's character and appearance." In 1982, the State Council had approved "The Notice of the State Planning Commission on the Arrangement of Long-Term Planning," which had defined the concept of competent personnel as people with diploma of technical secondary school or above and people with a professional title of technician or equivalent or above. "The Decision on Further Enhancing the Development of Human Resources" had proposed a new definition: People who have certain knowledge or skill, are able to engage in innovative work, work for the socialist material progress, political civilization progress and cultural and ideological progress and make positive contributions to the great cause of building socialism with Chinese characteristics are competent personnel that the Party and state require. In the new definition, integrity, knowledge, ability and performance become major criteria for judging competent personnel, changing the old criteria of diploma and professional title.

To establish a scientific outlook on competent personnel, it is necessary to establish an idea that human resources are the primary resource and give full play to the basic, strategic and decisive role of human resources in economic and social development, and establish an idea that everyone could become a useful and capable person.

For a long time in the past, the Party had incorporated the development of human resources into the building of the ranks of cadres, but recently this approach was changed as incorporating cadres into the development of human resources. I think it is an important change in the concept of human resources as well as in the pattern of human resources management.

4.5.2 Building the Three Contingents

There are abundant and various types of competent personnel, so are the approaches to and methods of discovering, training and employing them. Party and government personnel, managerial personnel in enterprises and technical professionals are the pillars of the human resources in China and termed as the three contingents. The Party should pay attention to developing both international and domestic resources, focus on training, attracting and making good use of competent personnel, increase the number of competent personnel, improve the personnel structure, enhance the qualities of human resources, and attach special importance to the training of highly skilled and inter-disciplinary personnel, personnel with professional, technological and managerial knowledge and personnel understanding international practices and able to communicate in foreign languages. The three contingents share something in common but have different features; we should build them according to the law of human resource development and employ different methods. Something in common means we should help the three contingents of competent personnel to improve their qualities by study and practice. For the training of Party and government personnel, we should concentrate on improving their ideological attainment and tempering them in grassroots organizations, particularly in hard and complex working environments. For managerial personnel in enterprises, we should temper them in the market and enable them to learn and apply the rules of market economy and means of modern management. For technical professionals, we should train them to master high-grade, high-precision and advanced technology and research methods, in a spirit of devotion to science, enhance their innovative ability, and train them to apply research results.

4.5.3 Evaluating and Employing Competent Personnel

The mechanism for evaluating and employing competent personnel plays a significant guiding role in the personnel work and has a direct bearing on the qualities of people to be trained. It is necessary to set up a scientific system for evaluating various personnel based on their performance considering their integrity, knowledge, ability and other indicators. And we should establish different ways of evaluation. For example, it is critical to pay more attention to the opinions of the people when evaluating Party and government personnel, and in an economic enterprise the recognition of the cadre in the market is an important criterion, and when evaluating technical professionals, the recognition by society and the respective circles is critical. We should overcome unhealthy tendencies of overstressing diploma, seniority while under-rating ability and performance; remove institutional barriers hindering the flow of trained people; improve a personnel mechanism under which competent personnel could be employed; and create a social environment that encourages and supports personnel to make achievements.

The goals of the Party and state need a large number of competent personnel and open up better perspectives for training these people. We should implement the strategy of reinvigorating the country with competent personnel as a major and urgent task of the Party and state, enhance qualities of personnel in all aspects and extensively develop human resources, so as to provide organizational and personnel support to the new project of Party building.

Chapter 5

Building a Solid Membership System in a Marxist Party

Party members are the cells of Party and subjects of Party activities; the general characteristics of its members have a direct bearing on the qualities of the Party. In this sense, to build a healthy Party membership structure is a basic project of Marxist party building. Building a membership with high qualities, reasonable structure and proper size caters for the requirements of maintaining the Party's vanguard nature.

5.1 Vanguard Nature of Party Members

The vanguard nature of a Marxist party is demonstrated by its nature, goal, program, line, guiding ideology, objectives, principles and policies, organizational principle, style of work, and cadres' capabilities. Party members' overall quality and other aspects of the Party, demonstrated by its whole structure or by its individual Party members, are the essential part of a Party's vanguard nature. If the vanguard nature of a Party's members reflects the general qualities of the Party, then it may be reasonable to take Party members as the starting point in order to enhance the vanguard nature of that Party. Thus it is quite natural that proletarian parties take measures and safeguard the purity and vanguard nature of their membership.

5.1.1 Strengthening the Party Membership

The power and roles of Marxist parties rather depend on the quality of their membership, not the quantity. Hence, historically proletarian leaders have laid more emphasis on quality. When founding the first proletarian party in the world—the Communist League, Marx and Engels had also emphasized the vanguard nature of party members as one of the major issues for preserving the proletarian nature and accomplishment of the historical mission. In his efforts to build a new-type of a proletarian party in Russia, Lenin had also advocated a high quality of party membership as a key factor in the revolutionary cause. He had commented, "We should strive to raise the status and the significance of a Party member higher, higher, and still higher."[1] He also said, "We do not need fictitious Party members even given as a gift."[2]

The people usually view the Party through Party members around them. If Party members are of high quality and play an exemplary role, they will have a good image among the people and help to improve the Party's prestige and establish close ties with the people, and finally lead the people to carry out the Party's line, principles and policies. During the years of revolutionary wars, members risked a lot to join the CPC; Party membership meant sacrifice and devotion. We can conclude that most of those applying to join the Party at that time were outstanding people and could withstand tests. Moreover, the ruthless environment, just like waves, washed out scum and laggers. Liu Shaoqi called this mechanism a "natural and objective

---

[1] *Collected Works of Vladimir Lenin* (2nd Chinese edition), Volume 7, p.272.
[2] *Collected Works of Vladimir Lenin* (3rd Chinese edition), Volume 4, p.51.

qualification."[1] After the CPC assumed power, Party membership brought no danger but advantages, and the Party had to face the risk that a lot of spectators would probably slip into the Party and erode its membership with the thoughts or ideologies of exploiting classes. After New China was founded in 1949, its membership saw a sharp increase. When the Seventh National Congress was held in 1945, the CPC had a membership of 1.21 million, which grew to 5 million in the first half of 1950; in 1949 alone, 1.4 million new members had joined the Party. To purify the Party ideologically, organizationally and in the style of work, strengthen education on Party members and rectify primary organizations, the Central Committee held the First National Meeting of Organization Work from March to April in 1951. At the meeting, Liu Shaoqi delivered a speech titled "Eight Qualifications for Communist Party Members" and made a report titled "Strive for Higher Qualifications for Party Members." He expounded on the significance and urgency to enhance the qualifications of Party membership in light of the changes in the Party's status, working environment and its tasks. On May 4, 1957, when meeting the new ambassador of Bulgaria to China, Zhou Enlai said that a too big party was dangerous, because it would reduce communists to ordinary people and thus cannot function as a vanguard.[2] Later, although the Party took many measures, it was still quite difficult to manage such a big party with a huge membership. Particularly during the Cultural Revolution period some heads of the rebel faction and some violence-doers managed to become Party members, degenerating the membership. Shortly after the Cultural Revolution was ended, Deng Xiaoping had raised the question of qualifying Party members. He pointed out, "That's why we say that as we go about restoring our Party's fine traditions and style of work; we now face a problem about the qualifications of Party members. The question of whether a communist meets the requirements for the Party membership applies not only to new Party members but also to a certain number of veterans."[3] As

---

[1] *Selected Works of Liu Shaoqi*, Volume II, p.68. Beijing: People's Press, 1985.

[2] *Zhou Enlai Chronology (1949-1976)*, Volume II, p.40. Beijing: Central Party Literature Press, 1997.

[3] *Selected Works of Deng Xiaoping* (2nd edition), Volume 2, p.269.

it comes to the new century, the Party faces new challenges in building a strong membership, and has explored new ways of educating and managing Party members in light of changing situations and tasks. On November 7, 2004, the Central Committee distributed a campaign document "Opinions on Carrying out Party-Wide Campaign to Educate Party Members to Preserve Their Vanguard Nature Mainly by Putting the Important Thought of Three Represents into Practice." And, from January 5 to 6, 2005, a working session about the campaign was held. As planned by the Central Committee, the campaign was carried out from January 2005 to the first half of 2006, through one and a half years. This was an important strategic decision that the Party made after summarizing historical experiences and scientifically analyzing the international and domestic situations in the new period of the new century, its tasks and realities of its membership, as well as an inevitable need of consolidating its status as the ruling party, strengthening its governance capability and fulfilling its mission.

5.1.2 Requirement of the New Realities

The CPC is the ruling party of the largest socialist country in the world with nearly 75 million members, which is extremely rare in the history of political parties. Its membership is gaining new characteristics under new historical conditions:

The number of Party members has grown remarkably. When founded in 1921, the CPC only had a membership of over 50; in 1945 when its Seventh National Congress was held, its membership was 1.21 million; in 1949 when New China founded, its membership was over 4.48 million, accounting for 0.8 percent of the national population; in 1956 when the Eighth National Congress was held, its membership was 10.73 million, accounting for 1.6 percent of the national population; in 1978 when the reform and opening-up were just launched, its membership was 36.98 million. According to statistics provided by the Information Management Center under the Organization Department of the Central Committee, by the end of 2005, the CPC had a membership of over 70.80 million, accounting for 5.3 percent of the national population. In 2005 alone, 2.47 million new members had joined the Party; young and student members saw a remarkable increase in their total number: among new members, 1.98 million were under the age of 35, accounting for 80.1 percent of the total new members, while 734,000 were students, increasing by five percentage points.[1]

The structure of membership becomes plural. By the date of joining the Party, less than 2 percent members had joined the Party before New China was founded while over 98 percent joined the Party after this event. By gender, female members total 13.573 million, accounting for 19.2 percent of the total membership, a rather low proportion. By nationality, ethnic minority members total 4.516 million, accounting for 6.4 percent of the membership. By age, members at and under the age of 35 total 16.304 million, accounting for 23 percent of the total; members aged from 36 to 50, 38.193 million, 54 percent; members at and above 60, 16.313 million, 23 percent. By profession, workers total 7.959 million (including 1.424 million working in non-public sectors of the economy), accounting for 11.2 percent of the membership; farmers, herdsmen and fishermen, 22.639 million, 32 percent; office cadres, 19.155 million, 27.1 percent; servicemen and policemen, 1.559 million, 2.2 percent; students, 1.289 million, 1.8 percent; managerial staff and professional technicians from non-public sectors of the economy, 1.316 million, 1.9 percent; individual laborers and freelance professionals, 3.61 million, 5.1 percent; retirees, 13.283 million, 18.8 percent.[2]

The educational attainment of members has seen an increase. In 1949, members with college degree or above only accounted for 0.32 percent of the total, while illiterates and members with primary-school education made up 96.66 percent. In 1978, the former group accounted for 2.89 percent. In 2000, the latter group only accounted for 22.4 percent. By the end of 2005, members with high-school education or above totaled 41.087 million, accounting for 58 percent of the total; among them, members with college degree or above totaled 20.568 million, accounting for 29 percent of the

---

[1] "From 50-strong to 70.80 Million in 85 Years", *People's Daily*, Section 5, July 1, 2006.
[2] *Ibid.*

total.[1]

Party members seem ideologically more active than before. As the Party membership becomes younger and members' educational attainment increases, Party members' consciousness of democracy keeps growing. Meanwhile, the plural social life, particularly the development of the Internet has provided more sources of information, and brought about several changes to Party members' mode of thinking. It is generally observed that, they no longer simply accept and follow others as before; instead, they could think independently, and have stronger analysis ability and better judgment qualities.

In general, the mainstream of the Party membership could play an exemplary role and make contributions. Among national model workers and winners of May 1 awards, Party members account for more than 85 percent; and when fighting floods and providing disaster relief in 1998 and fighting against SARS disease in 2003, some Party members have sacrificed their lives or died on duty, and these phenomena naturally credit the Party.

Party building scholars have generally commented that there are some problems among Party members that cannot be ignored. Some members do not meet qualifications prescribed in the Constitution of the Party, and some members cannot adapt to new situation or fulfill the new tasks. Scholars offer more concrete ideas: "Some Party members are not firm in their ideal or belief or lack confidence in socialism, and have crises of belief or confidence to varying degrees. Some have an unclear understanding of the Party's program and thus get strayed in worldview, outlook of life or values; while some minority is affected by mammonism, hedonism and ultra-individualism, and has a weak sense of devotion, thus only thinks of themselves, haggles over individual fame and interests whereas they are indifferent to the collective, public and others. Some are undisciplined and do not earnestly fulfill their duties as Party members, and they are unwilling to take part in Party activities or do not pay membership dues on time; some pay no attention to Party spirit, which provides soil for goody-goody doctrine

---

[1] "From 50-strong to 70.80 Million in 85 Years", *People's Daily*, Section 5, July 1, 2006.

and liberalism, and they spread complaints or hearsay information; some do not like to persuade people to join mass incidents and even do not take an active part themselves; some lack the pioneering spirit, keep to outdated or conservative ideas and are not competent, and consequently they cannot play an exemplary role in production, work, study and social life; a small number of members are ideologically and politically degenerated, thus some members indeed violate the Party discipline or the country's laws. In recent years, the number of cases involving violations of laws and Party discipline has kept growing. From 2000 to 2003, the Party has employed disciplinary measures against 288,000 Party members or cadres who were involved in economic misbehavior. In 2006, discipline inspection commissions at all levels of the Party have studied 123,489 cases, and applied disciplinary measures against 97,260 members.

Many reasons were suggested for the above problems: international environment, domestic environment, lax control and inadequate education by Party organizations, personal reasons, some concrete difficulties or contradictions involving personal interests, etc.

To enforce the important thought of Three Represents and preserve the Party's vanguard nature, every Party member needs to preserve his/her vanguard nature; as long as every member is a vanguard, can the Party become the vanguard and shoulder the new mission in the new century. All above cases indicate that raising the overall quality of Party members becomes a prominent problem under new historical conditions.

5.2 Qualifications for the Party Membership

The qualifications for the Party membership are basic requirements that a Marxist Party raises for its members based on its nature, program and historical mission; requirements are criteria and norms measuring whether Party members are qualified. These qualifications are generally demonstrated in Articles 1, 2, 3, 4 of the Party's Constitution, covering minimum requirement for membership, basic requirements for membership, and Party members' duties and rights. Keeping to qualifications for membership is the primary issue for building a strong Party membership, and the key for preserving the vanguard nature of Party members.

5.2.1 The Qualifications Are Improved in Practice

Qualifications for membership always attract close attention from proletarian parties and revolutionary leaders. When founding the Communist League, Marx and Engels drew out the conditions of membership, which were also qualifications for League membership: a way of life and activity which corresponds to the aim of the League; revolutionary energy and zeal in publicity; acknowledgment of communism; abstention from participation in any anti-communist political or nationalist association and notification of participation in any kind of association to the superior authority; subordination to the decisions of the League; observance of secrecy concerning the existence of all League affairs; and unanimous admission into a Party community. When founding a new-type Russian proletarian party, Lenin had designed rigorous qualifications for the membership of Bolshevik Party. In July 1903, at the Second Congress of the RSDLP, Lenin had waged a fierce struggle with Martov and other people on what kind of people could join the party and whether a member should join one of the party organizations. Martov and others held that a member did not have to join or work in one of the party organizations while Lenin had opposed to that view, because he believed that only when a member joins and works actively in one of the party organizations, can a Marxist party truly become an advanced, organized force of the proletariat, rather than an amorphous, lax group. Finally, Lenin's opinion was approved at the congress and this principle was written into the Constitution of the Party.

For the unique conditions of China and that of the Party work, the CPC had also paid a special attention to qualifications for its membership. Soon after the CPC was founded, Mao Zedong had proposed to recruit new members from among "true comrades" who held a firm belief in Marxism. The Constitution of the CPC adopted at the First National Congress prescribed clearly in Article 4: Anyone, regardless of gender and nationality, that accepts the Party's program and policies and is willing to become a loyal member, can be admitted as recommended by a Party member. But before joining the Party, he should sever all ties with parties or groups that attempt to oppose our Party's program.[1] In December 1929, "Resolution of Gutian Conference" for the first time prescribed the "conditions of the admission of new Party members": (1) no error in political ideas (including class consciousness); (2) loyalty; (3) possession of the spirit of sacrifice and ability to work actively; (4) no thought of getting rich; (5) abstention from opium and gambling. In October 1938, at the Sixth Plenary Session of the Sixth Central Committee, Mao Zedong had proposed that, a Party member should be a model in 11 aspects: in fighting bravely; in obeying orders; in observing discipline; in political activities; in contributing to inner-party unity and solidarity; in carrying out anti-Japanese tasks; in coordinating relations between parties of the united front; in being clean and honest, using no friends or relatives, working hard without asking for payment; in seeking truth from facts; in being foresighted and sagacious in research activities. In May 1939, Chen Yun, who was the Secretary of the Secretariat of the Central Committee and Head of the Organization Department of that organ, had written a document "How to Be a Communist Party Member", in which he had raised six qualifications for the Party membership: struggling for communism all one's life; putting the interests of the revolution above everything else; observance of Party discipline and of secrets of the Party; carrying out the Party's resolutions in spite of all setbacks; being a model for the masses; study activity. In 1945, the CPC had adopted a new Constitution at its Seventh National Congress, which included for the first time the four duties and four rights of Party members in addition to qualifications for membership. After the Party assumed the ruling position, it had demanded higher requirements for its members. In 1951, Liu Shaoqi had written the "Eight Qualifications for Communist Party Members." In 1956, the

---

[1] Archives Bureau of the CPC Central Committee, *Selected Documents of the CPC Central Committee*, Volume 1, p.3.

Constitution adopted at the Eight National Congress of the Party had defined the "Ten duties and Seven rights" for Party members. But the Constitutions adopted at the Ninth and Tenth National congresses during the Cultural Revolution had replaced Party members' duties and rights with "Five Criteria for Successors" which contained some elements of "left" ideological errors. The new Constitution adopted at the 12th National Congress in 1982 had reviewed those "left" errors, and restored the articles about Party members' duties and rights, at the same time had added new contents in light of the new period. In this Constitution, Article 2 had defined the basic requirements for membership of the ruling party. The Constitutions adopted at the 14th, 15th and 16th National congresses had all supplemented the 1982 Constitution with new necessary contents, and generally improved the qualifications for the Party membership.

5.2.2 Minimum Qualifications for the Party Membership

The minimum qualifications for the Party membership refer to the identity and basic qualifications that a new applicant should meet. As prescribed in the Party's Constitution, "Any Chinese worker, farmer, serviceman, intellectual or any advanced element of other social strata who has reached the age of 18 and who accepts the Party's program and Constitution and is willing to join and work actively in one of the Party organizations, carry out the Party's resolutions and pay membership dues regularly may apply for membership in the Communist Party of China." This article defines those who can apply for membership in the Party. The minimum qualifications include:

About the age: Constitutions adopted at the Second, Third and Fourth National congresses had not set a limit to the age for applicants. In 1927, the "Resolution on the Third Amendment to the Constitution of the CPC" in Article had proposed the following phrase: "Any Party member should have reached the age of 18." It was the first time that the Party had set a limit to the age for applicants, and later it had continued to apply it after the Seventh National Congress. The reason that the Parties make the age of 18 as the entry barrier is that generally speaking, a person reaching the age of 18 becomes an adult, and then has better political judgment and is able to determine his/her political belief and ideal. In legal terms, a person reaching the age of 18 is believed to have the capacity for act. Naturally only adults can join a political organization like the CPC. In the revolutionary war period, the CPC was not so strict with the age; but today it does not allow any minor to join its ranks.

About the social origin: The CPC is an advanced political party with the working class as its class basis, which determines that the Party should recruit members from among workers, farmers, servicemen and intellectuals. But, a Marxist party does not refuse advanced elements of other social strata. Since the founding of New China, great changes have taken place in economic structure as well as in social structure. There is a trend that classes become simpler while strata in them are more diversified. To adapt to such changes, the CPC changed stipulations about the social origin of its members in its Constitutions and documents. The Constitution adopted at the Eighth National Congress of the Party in 1956 had prescribed, "Any Chinese citizen who works and does not exploit the labor of others and who accepts the Party's program and Constitution and joins and works in one of the Party organizations, carries out the Party's resolutions and pays membership dues regularly may become a member of the Communist Party of China." No fundamental changes were made to the article about an applicant's social origin in Constitutions adopted at in the Ninth, Tenth and 11th National congresses. To adapt to new class relations, the Constitution adopted at the 12th National Congress in 1982, had amended "poor and lower-middle farmers" in the previous Constitution as "farmers" and had changed "may join" into "may apply for (membership of the Party)". The Constitutions adopted at the 14th and 15th National congresses continued to use this formulation. But the Constitution adopted at the 16th National Congress had offered a new expression, amending the wording "other revolutionary elements" as "advanced elements from other social strata."

Other social strata refer to the strata other than workers, farmers, servicemen, intellectuals and cadres, and are mainly entrepreneurs and technicians at privately owned high-tech enterprises, managerial staff employed by foreign enterprises, individuals engaging in small-scale business, private entrepreneurs, employees of intermediary agencies, and freelance professionals. Thus, I suggest that his amendment better conforms to changes in the social structure of the society.

These strata were permitted and had emerged after the reform and opening-up were launched, and later were promoted by Party policies. In 2001, Jiang Zemin, in his speech at the 80th Anniversary of the Founding of the CPC, had used a term calling them "builders of socialism". Later, the Central Committee has continued to use this term in its documents.

Among scholars, generally there is no big dispute about recruiting advanced elements from among the majority of other social strata. The controversy is about whether to admit private entrepreneurs into the Party. I would like to offer the reader an analysis on this issue. I suggest not be too direct or absolute about this problem. We cannot simply equal people of other social strata with private entrepreneurs, or simply reduce the admission of advanced elements of other social strata to the admission of private entrepreneurs. There should be a correct understanding of private entrepreneurs. The private sector of economy had grown after the reform and opening-up policy was launched, and is now one of the important components among the diverse economic forms of the country; hence private entrepreneurs have become a relatively independent social stratum. But on the other hand today's private entrepreneurs have not the same social origins with those capitalists in the 1950s, and should not be regarded as capitalists.

Naturally, it is regarded as both a major theoretical problem and a serious realistic problem as to whether to admit private entrepreneurs into the Party. Before August 1989, there was controversy in the theoretical circles whether private entrepreneurs could be admitted into the Party, and the Party had no document commenting about this problem. But, in August 1989, the "Notice of the Central Committee of the Communist Party of China on Strengthening Party Building" had for the first time commented on this issue as: "The private sector of the economy is a supplement to the socialist economy with public ownership. Private entrepreneurs' legitimate business and rights and interests should be protected. Our Party is the vanguard of the working class. Private entrepreneurs in fact exploit workers, and thus cannot be admitted into the Party." The Notice also pointed out, "Our Party is the vanguard of the working class, not a party for all people. Its nature should never be vague."[1] For those cadres and intellectuals who used to be Party members but had chosen to become private entrepreneurs, the Notice also said, "In addition to abiding by national policies and laws, when running their businesses and paying tax according to laws and regulations, private entrepreneurs who have joined the Party should uphold the Party's ideal and program, fulfill their duties, and consciously accept oversight by Party organizations; and when distributing their income, they should invest their due income as managers and the majority of after-tax profit in production so as to increase the wealth of society and help to develop public undertakings; they should treat workers as their equals and respect their legitimate rights and interests. Those who fail to do so cannot be Party members any longer."[2] Based on this Notice, the CPC had advocated the principle of not admitting private entrepreneurs. For rather a long time, the CPC had closed its door to private entrepreneurs. There were several major reasons. Private enterprises at that time were not so big, and there were just few high-tech ones. The Party had to go through a study process before it had a clear understanding of the nature of private enterprises and the social origin of private entrepreneurs. Moreover, it can be suggested that the 1989 political rebel and its consequences were also a factor in decision making. The Party had probably prioritized to maintain a stable and unified political environment.

In 2001, Jiang Zemin had delivered a speech at the 80th Anniversary of the Founding of the CPC, in which he had pointed out, "The main criteria to admit a person into the Party are whether he or she works wholeheartedly for the implementation of the Party's line and program and

---

[1] The Party Literature Research Center of the CPC Central Committee, *Selected Important Documents since the 13th National Congress of the Communist Party of China*, Volume 2, p.598. Beijing: People's Press, 1991.

[2] *Ibid.*

meets the requirements for the Party membership. The basic components and backbone of the Party are those from workers, farmers, intellectuals, servicemen and cadres. At the same time, it is also necessary to accept those outstanding elements from other sectors of society who have subscribed to the Party's program and Constitution, worked for the Party's line and program wholeheartedly, and have proved to meet the requirements for the Party membership through a long period of tests."[1] This was a brand new definition for the criteria for the Party membership under new historical circumstances. Yang Chaoying, a famous Party building scholar had offered the following ideas on this change: "We should view the Party criteria from the angle of history. Simply regarding previous limitations wrong is not an attitude out of historical materialism. We should understand "other social strata" and "advanced elements of other social strata" defined in the Constitution adopted at the 16th National Congress of the CPC and at the same time we should recruit Party members mainly from among workers, farmers, intellectuals, servicemen and cadres, thus expanding the basic components and backbone of the Party. ....Statistics show that from 1993 to 2002, the proportion of members from the stratum of private entrepreneurs has grown year by year, 13.1 percent in 1993, 17.1 percent in 1995, and 29.9 percent in 2002; but 90 percent of them had joined the Party before starting private businesses.[2]

About basic belief and organizational discipline: The Party Constitution states that a person "who accepts the Party's program and Constitution and is willing to join and work actively in one of the Party organizations, carry out the Party's resolutions and pay membership dues regularly may apply for membership in the Communist Party of China." That means the Party members should have a firm belief in communism, consciously observe the Party discipline and strictly act upon the Party's Constitution and regulations.

---

[1] *Selected Works of Jiang Zemin*, Volume 3, p.286.

[2] Yang Chaoying, "Party Building Reaps Fruit in Non-public Enterprises", *Daily of Chinese People's Political Consultative Conference*, B1, July 2, 2004.

5.2.3 Membership of the CPC as the Ruling Party

Article 2 of the Party Constitution states: "Members of the Communist Party of China are vanguard fighters of the Chinese working class imbued with communist consciousness. Members of the Communist Party of China should serve the people wholeheartedly, dedicate their whole lives to the realization of communism, and be ready to make any personal sacrifices. Members of the Communist Party of China are at all times ordinary members of the working people. Communist Party members should not seek any personal gain or privileges, although the relevant laws and policies provide them with personal benefits and job-related functions and powers." This article was added at the 12th National Congress in 1982 and had set basic requirements for members of the CPC as the ruling party.

Different from the revolutionary war period, naturally the biggest test for the CPC as the ruling party is the governance test, thus also a test for its members is how to establish a correct worldview, outlook of life, values, and correct outlooks on power issue, their individual interests and status. I suggest the membership of a Marxist party should be in essence to possess the belief and values and devotion for the cause of the liberation of mankind.

Communist consciousness is a kind of political belief, a kind of ideology and an ideological level, which requires that Party members should make the realization of communism their lifelong goal, show all good merits reflecting the Party's vanguard nature when struggling for this cause, such as selflessness and wholehearted devotion to public duty, and gain a thorough revolutionary spirit and serious scientific attitude.

"Serving the people wholeheartedly" is the only purpose of Communist Party members, which demands that they regard this purpose as the starting point and goal of all their words and deeds and always give top priority to the people's interests. For the CPC as the ruling party, the biggest danger is severance from the masses. Every Party member should bear in mind the fundamental purpose of serving the people wholeheartedly and that the Party is built for the public and exercises state power for the people, thus do something practical and good for the people and maintain close ties with the people.

"Members of the CPC are at all times ordinary members of the working people." It is an essential characteristic of Party members, demanding that they maintain original merits as working people and stay in union with the masses. Power is a double-edged sword; it can be used to serve the people and to seek personal gains. The position of the Party as the ruling party should not be the ground and offer conditions in which Party members could seek personal gains; and in particular, leading cadres should be self-disciplined and never use power to seek profits for themselves or their families.

5.2.4 Specific Requirements for Party Members

Specific requirements for Communist Party members refer to the eight duties prescribed in Article 3 and "Eight Rights" prescribed in Article 4 of the Constitution. The duties refer to the obligations to Party organizations and the cause of the Party that Party members should fulfill: covering study, politics, ethics, discipline, and style of work. They are formulated in detail as rules governing Party members' actions.

Constitutions before the Seventh National Congress of the Party had no special articles about Party members' duties, but had only defined some specific requirements. The Constitution adopted at the Seventh National Congress had formulated four duties; the Constitution adopted at the Eighth National Congress in 1956 had set ten duties for Party members; the Constitution adopted at the 12th National Congress in 1982 had prescribed eight duties; while the Constitutions adopted at the 14th, 15th and 16th National congresses included eight duties and added some new contents in them. The present Constitution of the Communist Party of China embodies specific duties for Party members, which reflect new and higher requirements for Party members reflecting the spirit of the times.

I would like to comment on the "Eight duties of Party members" which cover four aspects. The four aspects include:

Study: It is understood as Party members should conscientiously study

Marxism-Leninism, Mao Zedong Thought, Deng Xiaoping Theory and the important thought of Three Represents, study the Scientific Outlook on Development, study the Party's line, principles, policies and resolutions, acquire essential knowledge concerning the Party, obtain general, scientific, legal and professional knowledge and work diligently to enhance their ability to serve the people.

Politics and work: Party members should implement the Party's basic line, principles and policies, take the lead in reform, opening-up and socialist modernization, encourage the people to work hard for economic development and social progress and play an exemplary and vanguard role in production, work, study and social activities. Meanwhile, Party members should adhere to the principle that the interests of the Party and the people stand above everything else, subordinating their personal interests to the interests of the Party and the people, being the first to bear hardships and the last to enjoy comforts, working selflessly for the public interests and working to contribute more.

Organizational discipline: It means that the Party members should conscientiously observe the Party discipline, abide by the laws and regulations of the state in an exemplary way, rigorously guard secrets of the Party and state, execute the Party's decisions, and accept any job and actively fulfill any task assigned to them by the Party. Party members should uphold the Party's solidarity and unity, be loyal to and honest with the Party, combine their words with deeds, firmly oppose all factions and small-clique activities and oppose double-dealing and scheming of any kind.

Ethics and style of work: Party members should earnestly engage in criticism and self-criticism, boldly expose and correct shortcomings and mistakes in work and resolutely combat corruption and other negative phenomena. Party members should maintain close ties with the masses, disseminate the Party's views among them, consult with them when problems arise, keep the Party informed about their views and demands in good time and defend their legitimate interests. Party members should promote new socialist ways and customs, take the lead in practicing the socialist maxims of honor and disgrace, and advocate communist ethics. Party members should step forward and fight bravely in times of difficulty or danger, should dare to make any sacrifice to defend the interests of the country and the people.

The rights refer to the power and interests that Party members could practice as prescribed in the Constitution. Articles in this regard have been improved with the changes in circumstances and the development of the Party itself. In previous Constitutions, the one with the first formal statement about Party members' rights was adopted at the Seventh National Congress of the Party, including four rights. The Constitution adopted at the Eighth National Congress in 1956 had increased the number to seven. The Constitution adopted at the 12th National Congress had prescribed eight rights, which are also valid at present. But to develop inner-party democracy and protect Party members' rights, the Central Committee had released the "Regulations of the Communist Party of China on Guaranteeing Members' Rights" (for Trial Implementation) on January 7, 1995, and officially enacted it on September 22, 2004, after nine years of trial implementation. The Regulations includes explicit and more concrete provisions about Party members' rights based on the Constitution and better criteria for protecting Party members' rights, and prescribes responsibilities for Party organizations and leading cadres at all levels in this regard and requirements for accountability.

According to Article 4 of the Constitution and the related Regulations, Party members' rights are mainly the rights to know, to participate, to choose, to supervise, and to appeal. The rights cover three aspects:

First, the rights to take part in daily activities of the Party, including the rights to attend relevant Party meetings, to read relevant Party documents, to benefit from the Party's education and training, to participate in the discussion of questions concerning the Party's policies or theories, and to make suggestions and proposals regarding the work of the Party.

Second, the rights to oversee Party organizations and other members, including the rights to criticize, to present information or charges against any Party organization or member violating discipline or the law to the Party in a responsible way, to demand disciplinary measures against such a member, or to call for dismissal or replacement of any incompetent cadre.

Third, the rights to safeguard individual political rights and interests, including the rights to participate in voting and elections and to stand for election, to defend oneself, bear witness or argue on the behalf of others, and to make reservations, and to put forward any request, appeal, or complaint to higher Party organizations.

Party members' rights reflect their position as major players within the Party. It is an indispensable condition for developing inner-party democracy to protect Party members' rights. No Party organization, up to and including the Central Committee, has the right to deprive any Party member of the above-mentioned rights. All above mean that effective measures should be practiced to protect Party members' rights, including punishing any behaviors encroaching on Party members' rights and calling into account those responsible according to laws and regulations.

As Marx and Engels had pointed out at the "General Rules of the International Working Men's Association", "no rights without duties, no duties without rights."[1] It means that, the duties and rights of Party members are correlated and interdependent. On the one hand, each is conditional for the other. Party members can only enjoy rights on the prerequisite of having fulfilled their duties; they are restricted by duties, and cannot enjoy rights without fulfilling duties. Similarly, when Party members fulfill duties, the rights they practice constitute a condition and a guarantee; if unable to enjoy rights, generally they can hardly fulfill duties. On the other hand, the two supplement each other. That is to say, the two are not opposite, but promote each other. If Party members can earnestly fulfill duties, they will have a stronger sense of responsibility for the cause and work of the Party and a stronger capability of participating in and discussing state affairs, and subsequently will be able to better exercise democratic rights and bring into full play the initiative and creativity. If the rights are respected, Party members will have a stronger sense of pride and honor and a stronger internal impetus, and thus will be stricter with themselves and earnestly fulfill all the

---

[1] *Marx & Engels Selected Works* (2nd Chinese edition), Volume 2, p.610.

duties.

Generally, other class parties are comparatively lax political groups, usually without rigorous rights and duties; whereas proletarian parties emphasize the unity of rights and duties, which is determined by their nature and reflects their vanguard nature. Experience and lessons from several proletarian parties have proved that since members' rights were not guaranteed, these parties have lost their vitality. Party building scholars generally agree that: in the current situation of the Party, members are relatively weak in light of the criteria for the vanguard nature and the exemplary role, which, to a great extent, has something to do with their failure to earnestly fulfill duties and failure to correctly exercise rights. Some members only tend to enjoy rights, and are unwilling to fulfill duties, undertake tasks assigned by Party organizations or to act within the requirements of Party discipline. Also some members have a weak sense of rights and democracy, do not understand or respect their due rights, do not know how to exercise their rights, do not actively fight against behaviors encroaching on their rights, and do not care about the Party's work and activities. Some Party organizations underline duties but undermine rights, asking Party members to fulfill duties but ignoring their rights and even inhibit inner-party democracy. Naturally, all the above practices are contrary to the Constitution of the Party and should be correctly rectified.

5.2.5 The Vanguard Nature Is Historical and Concrete

Under different historical circumstances, the Marxist parties have different tasks, thus should have different requirements for its members. Naturally, each period in a Party's history presents some unique characteristics. Marxists should reflect the characteristics of the time when adhering to the qualifications for Party members and preserve their vanguard nature.

The document "Opinions of the CCCPC on Carrying out Party-wide Campaign to Educate Party Members to Preserve Their Vanguard Nature" distributed on November 7, 2004, had raised "4+1" requirements for Party members: holding fast to ideals and beliefs, upholding the Party's purpose, strengthening the consciousness of the Party, carrying forward the fine traditions, and plus solving practical problems. The requirements were then summarized as: studying conscientiously, holding fast to beliefs, taking into consideration the overall situation, truly caring for the people, striving to make progress, forging ahead in a pioneering spirit, working hard on one's post, and making selfless devotion. On January 14, 2005, General Secretary Hu Jintao of the CPC had made an important speech on this issue, emphasizing six points. His proposals were formulated as follows: first, holding fast to ideals and beliefs, and always working hard for the building of socialism with Chinese characteristics; second, keeping studying diligently, and enhancing the capability of practicing the important thought of Three Represents; third, upholding the Party's fundamental purpose, and always bearing in mind the fundamental principle that the Party is built for the public and that it exercises state power for the people; fourth, working hard, and cautiously and conscientiously making achievements at work; fifth, observing the Party discipline, and safeguarding the Party's solidarity and unity in practice; and sixth, adhering to the "Two Shoulds" and retaining the political qualities of Communist Party members.

I should also note that requirements for each Party member should be based on his social origin, profession, position and educational attainment. There should be a consensus and a combination on specific requirements that are based on the Constitution and CCCPC regulations' general guidance with those notions which reflect the spirit of the times and characteristics of different social groups and which conform to the reality of each profession. These above integrated, should constitute the criteria for evaluating Party members and standards of their behaviors. In practice, the basic principles should be combined with specific requirements for Party members, and also overall requirements should be combined with their specific service requirements. Thus individuality of each member should also be kept in mind with a standpoint of development and dialectic.

University students constitute a special group among Party members, and generally expected to do better in meeting the qualifications and preserving their vanguard nature. The current Party Constitution formulates that Communist youth organization attached to the Party is the "shock force" in Party's political activities. On May 4, 1998, Jiang Zemin had delivered a speech at the centenary of the founding of Peking University, and had raised four requirements for university students and other young people. Those four requirements were: acquiring scientific knowledge while strengthening ideological attainment; learning from books while delving into social practice; trying to realize individual value while serving the country and the people; establishing a lofty ideal while working hard for it. These were hopes and ideal requirements for university students and other young people. This was indeed a good example considering the distinctive characteristics of the time and based on the realities of this group.

The four points in essence were also consistent with the general qualifications for Party members. University students are generally special being part of the youth, while those being Party members are leaders among university students and they should bear in mind the Party's purpose, be firm in their beliefs, study hard, be modest and prudent, be strict with themselves, take the overall situation into account, be ready to shoulder heavy tasks, look at the large picture while starting from the small one, and play an exemplary role in study, work and life.

5.2.6 The Cultivation of Party Spirit

In July 1939, Liu Shaoqi had written "How to be a Good Communist" in which he had expounded on the necessity why Party members should cultivate and temper themselves and had proposed the contents and correct ways to do so. That work had indeed offered a systematic theory in this regard. He had proposed that the Party members should engage in all-round self-cultivation: "engage in self-cultivation in the Marxist-Leninist theory; self-cultivation in applying the Marxist-Leninist stand, viewpoint and method to the study and handling of all problems; self-cultivation in proletarian ideology and morality; self-cultivation in upholding unity in the

Party, practicing criticism and self-criticism and observing discipline; self-cultivation in developing the style of hard work and persistent struggle; self-cultivation in building close ties with the masses; self-cultivation in various branches of scientific knowledge, etc."[1] In June 1941, he had written his work: *The Class Nature of People*, explaining what Party spirit is. He pointed out, "Communists' Party spirit is the highest and collective expression of the class nature of proletarians, the highest expression of the nature of proletarians, and the highest and collective expression of the interests of proletarians. Communists' efforts to cultivate and temper Party spirit are a process to remold their nature. Communists should develop all the great, progressive characteristics of the proletariat to the highest level. Every Party member should remold himself to obtain all these good merits. This is a remolding of their nature."[2]

According to Liu Shaoqi, Party spirit referred to concrete manifestations of the class nature and vanguard nature of proletarian parties demonstrated by their members. In his words: "It demands that Party members have a high level of proletarian consciousness, and remold themselves in accordance with all the good merits of the proletariat, including: taking scientific theories as the guide to action, taking communism as the objective, serving the people wholeheartedly, having a strong sense of organization and discipline, safeguarding the Party's solidarity and unity, maintaining close ties with the masses, and courageously carrying out criticism and self-criticism. Communists' Party spirit integrates the class nature and vanguard nature of the proletariat with scientific and practical aspects of Marxism."

Party spirit is historical and dynamic and it possesses distinctive characteristics of the time. That means, its basic principles keep unchanged, but its contents and forms of expression evolve with the progress of time. Under new historical conditions, communists' Party spirit is demonstrated in holding high the great banners of the Party ideologies, putting them into

---

[1] *Selected Works of Liu Shaoqi*, Volume I, p.109.

[2] The Party Literature Research Center of the CPC Central Committee and Party School of the CPC Central Committee, *On Party Building by Liu Shaoqi*, p.225. Beijing: Central Party Literature Press, 1991.

practice, devoting to reform and opening-up and socialist modernization, serving the public, making selfless contributions, and working hard for building a moderately prosperous society in all respects.

In a Marxist party, to cultivate and temper the Party spirit is a long and hard progress that combines theory with practice and integrates the remolding of the subjective world with the changes of the objective world. Party members should constantly overcome anything incompatible with Party spirit by theoretical study and practice, thus upgrading their ideological and moral levels.

5.3　Training Activists and Recruiting New Members

Generally, Party building scholars suggest as: to enhance the quality of Party membership and preserve the vanguard nature of Party members, the first thing is to strictly control "the entrance gate" of the Party and do a good job in training activists who apply for Party membership and in recruiting new members. Interpreting the Constitution of the Communist Party of China and the notions in the document "the Rules of the Communist Party of China on the Work of Recruiting New Members (for Trial Implementation) distributed by the Organization Department of the CCCPC; I would like to offer the following aspects:

Basic policy aspect in recruiting new members: The basic policy for recruiting new members refers to the basic principle that the Marxist party formulates for the recruitment of new members in a given period based on its political tasks, situation of its membership and its organizational basis in this period; it is important for guiding the work of recruiting new members. In the past, the CPC had also formulated different policies. For example, in the new-democratic revolution period, a policy of "absorbing intellectuals in a great number" and "boldly admitting new members while keeping bad elements outside" was agreed. In the early period after New China was founded, the Party had formulated another policy of "admitting new members actively and prudently." In June 1988, in the nationwide organizational meeting the Party had decided a new basic policy for this work in the new period as: "comply with qualifications, guarantee quality, improve structure and recruit prudently." In August 1989, "the Notice of the Central Committee on Strengthening Party Building" had further clarified this policy. In September 1994 at its Fourth Plenary Session of the 14th Central Committee, the CPC had officially approved the document "Decision of the Central Committee on Several Important Issues about Strengthening Party Building", which had reaffirmed the previous basic policy. This policy can be interpreted as an extension and development of the policy in the 1950s ("admitting new members actively and prudently").

The above document had defined the basic requirements as follows: "To recruit new members in the new period, we should strictly comply with the qualifications for Party membership prescribed in the Constitution and give priority to the quality of Party members, and at the same time gradually improve the structure of and the quality of membership and the Party's combat effectiveness in all respects. To be specific, to comply with the qualifications demands that we recruit new members according to the qualifications prescribed in the Constitution and absorb true advanced elements, but we shall not degrade the qualifications or even set up new ones. To guarantee quality demands that we take effective measures at work and be strict in the entry qualifications, ensuring that every new member is a vanguard of the Chinese working class with communist consciousness. To improve structure requires that we formulate and carry out working programs in this regard; to give macro-guidance, making the age structure, educational structure, occupational structure and geographical distribution of Party members more reasonable. To recruit prudently demands that we adhere to the principle of individual admission without being rash or focusing on the quantity or closing the door."

To carry out the basic policy for recruiting new Party members in the new period, I suggest the relations below should be correctly handled:

First, the relationship between quantity and quality: In a populous country, we cannot build the Party into a mass Marxist party without a certain quantity of members; but on the other side the Party's vanguard nature would not be demonstrated without quality. In a Marxist party these two sides form a dialectical unity. Between the two, the quality plays a dominant role, while the quantity is premised on guaranteed quality. What proportion should the Party membership be compared with the national population? There are different opinions on this issue. At present, the CPC membership makes up about 5.3 percent of the national population. Some scholars hold that the proportion shall not exceed five percent; otherwise, it would cause problems.

Second, the relationship between the focus and the general: The Party has reiterated many times in its documents and organizational meetings that it should recruit Party members mainly from among workers, farmers, intellectuals, servicemen and cadres, thus expanding the basic components and backbone of the Party, and on the other side quicken the efforts to recruit members from those in the forefront of production and work and from among prominent intellectuals and young people. Recruitment work with focus on the latter groups is considered an important measure for improving the structure of membership, solving the problem of the Party's weak influence in some areas, strengthening the Party's ties with the working class, and increasing the Party's influence among young intellectuals. But, I think in the recruitment work the focus should not overly emphasized, on the other side general people should not be ignored. The focus and the general should be combined with prominence given to the former.

Third, the relationship between training and recruitment: It needs a process to train an ordinary person into an advanced element of the working class. In this process, the subjective interacts with the objective while the internal cause interacts with the external cause. Over many years, the Party has adhered to the principle that an individual should join the Party on a voluntary basis. But this does not mean that Party organizations should do nothing but wait till non-party people come to them. For the issue of training and recruiting new members, the Marxist party should overcome wrong practices in which Party organizations wait "natural maturity" of applicants or focus on recruitment while neglecting training; and should take initiative to work better in this regard.

Training activists who apply for party membership: A good and practical job in training, educating and observing the activists who apply for Party membership should be the routine organization work of the Party. Party organizations should, by publicizing the Party's political line and carrying out careful and in-depth ideological and political education, deepen the Communist Youth League (CYL) members' and non-Party people's understanding of the Party, orient and inspire them to apply for Party membership and to get closer to Party organizations, and thus expand the ranks of the activists. To be specific, Party organizations should design and carry out plans to educate activists on basic theories, basic line, fine traditions and style of work of the Party, and also help them to have a correct reasoning for joining the Party.

Party organizations should observe an activist on a regular basis, and make him/her the target for recruitment after collecting opinions from the leading Party members' group concerned. After further information is gathered from the activist's liaison and the masses inside and outside the Party, Party branch committees should approve the application. For a targeted applicant, Party organizations should make a careful political examination and then prepare a comprehensive document covering eight aspects: the applicant's political quality; reason for joining the Party; occupational performance; attitude and performance in social activities; attitude to learning, academic record and professional attainment; accurate description of the applicant's shortcomings; results of the political examination; the training process and major reasons for admitting the applicant into the Party.

As the Party's reputation keeps growing, the number of activists who apply for Party membership grows as well. In 2005, 17.67 million people applied for Party membership, among whom, 13.37 million were under the age of 35, accounting for 75.7 percent of the total. Therefore, the training of these people seems a very heavy task.

Complying with the procedures of recruitment: Strict fulfillment of the procedures for admission is an important measure for guaranteeing the quality of Party members. The purpose is to organizationally ensure that qualified advanced elements are admitted into the Party.

The current Constitution prescribes: "An applicant for Party membership should fill out an application form and be recommended by two full Party members; the application should be accepted at a general membership meeting of the Party branch concerned and approved by the next higher Party organization; the applicant should undergo observation for a probationary period before being granted full membership; and a probationary Party member should take an admission oath in front of the Party flag."

Article 5 of the Constitution states: "New Party members should be admitted through a Party branch, and the principle of individual admission should be adhered to." The principle was established by the Party during the revolutionary wars, and has been proven in many years of practice an important principle for guaranteeing the quality of Party members. This principle demands that Party branches should fulfill all the procedures and admit new members individually, rather than in groups.

When a voting is held in the meeting of the Party branch concerned, the applicant may also vote for himself/herself and Party members who recommend the applicant shall not abstain from the vote. The applicant can only be approved when he/she gets more than half of the votes from Party members with the right to vote. General Party branches of independent organizations under direct leadership of Party committees above the county level, and general Party branches of large industrial enterprises and branches for universities and colleges, can examine and approve applicants for Party membership only after they are authorized by Party committees above the county level.

Article 5 of the Constitution also states: "Under special circumstances, the Central Committee of the Party or the Party committee of a province, autonomous region or municipality directly under the Central Government may admit new Party members directly." This procedure was practiced in some cases. Similar formulations had appeared in Article 5 of the Constitution adopted at the Fifth National Congress, at the Eighth National

Congress, and in the Constitutions adopted at the 12th, 14th and 15th National congresses. As recorded in relevant documents, from the Second to the Eighth National Congress of the CPC, the Central Committee had admitted 11 members directly: Yang Du, Ye Ting, Zhou Taofen, Xu Fanting, Zhao Shoushan, Fan Mingshu, Guo Moruo, Li Youran, Zhao Bosheng, Dong Zhentang and Xu Guangping. After the 12th National Congress, the Central Committee directly admitted three members: Zhuang Xiquan (former vice-chairman of the Chinese People's Political Consultative Conference), Tao Zhiyue (former chairman of All-China Federation of Returned Overseas Chinese), and Dong Qiwu (former high-ranking officer of the Kuomintang and former deputy commander of Xinjiang Military Command of the Chinese People's Liberation Army). Soong Ching Ling, former honorary president of the People's Republic of China, was also directly admitted by the Central Committee.

Granting full membership to probationary members: The observation and education of probationary members is also an important aspect for guaranteeing the quality of Party members. After going through necessary procedures and approved by the next higher Party organization, an applicant becomes a probationary Party member and thus obtains membership. The probationary period of a probationary member is one year, which shall never be ended ahead of time. Probationary members have the same duties as full members. They enjoy the rights of full members except those of participating in voting and elections and standing for election. During the probationary period, probationary members should accept education and observation of Party organizations and temper themselves in inner-party activities.

Upon the expiration of the probationary period of a probationary member, the Party branch concerned should promptly discuss whether he/she is qualified for full membership. A probationary member who conscientiously performs his/her duties and is qualified for full membership shall be granted full membership as scheduled. The Party standing of a member begins from the day he/she is granted full membership on the expiration of the probationary period. If a probationary member is not fully qualified for full membership and further observation and education are needed, the probationary period may be extended, but by no more than one year. If a probationary member fails to perform his/her duties and is found to be unqualified for full membership, his/her probationary membership shall be annulled. Any decision to grant a probationary member full membership, extend a probationary period, or annul a probationary membership should be made through discussion held by the general membership meeting of the Party branch concerned and approved by the next higher Party organization.

In real life, there is often such a negative phenomenon. Some people lower the standards for themselves after becoming probationary members and no longer strive to make progress; on the other hand; some Party organizations also loosen the education and observation of these people but grant them full membership as long as they do not make serious mistakes. I think these practices to some extent affect the quality of Party membership and have a negative influence among the masses.

Any Party member under the age of 28 can both be a member of the Party and the CYL (Communist Youth League). The Constitution of CYL stipulates that CYL members can hold their CYL membership after joining the Party, until the age of 28. Young Party members with CYL membership should take an active part in CYL activities; when Party and CYL activities are held at the same time, they should usually take part in Party activities, or in CYL activities with the approval of the Party organization concerned.

5.4 Educating and Managing Party Members

The education and management work aiming Party members refers to the activities that Party organizations carry out in accordance with the Constitution and Central Committee regulations to make Party members conscientiously fulfill duties and properly exercise rights. It is an important part of the Party's organization work, and its aim is to preserve the vanguard nature of Party members and enable them to better play an exemplary role.

In June 2006, the General Office of the Central Committee has distributed four documents about the permanent mechanism of preserving the vanguard nature of Party members: Opinions on Strengthening Regular Education of Party Members, Opinions on Doing a Good Job among Party Members in Maintaining Close Ties with and Serving the People, Opinions on Strengthening and Improving the Management of Floating Party Members, and Opinions on Establishing and Improving a System in which Local Party Committees and Departmental Party Groups Are Accountable for Primary-Level Party Building. In fact these four documents are a summary of the experience; the CPC accumulated in the latest party-wide campaign to educate Party members and they aim to offer a permanent mechanism for education and management work. Below I would like to review these mechanisms.

5.4.1 Improving the Education and Management

The education and management of Party members is a routine of Party work and a quite heavy work. It is more difficult than the recruitment of new members, and the Party should always keep educating and strengthening management of Party members, whether new or old, ordinary ones or leading cadres. And it is a long process, and cannot be achieved in one step but should be developed in several stages. Over the years, the Party has invested great efforts in this respect, it can be said that some achievements were reached. But most Party building scholars have admitted that these efforts could not fully or properly respond to the changes in the environment and to changes in the ideology of Party members. Problems areas are defined as: Political contents are overemphasized while comprehensive knowledge is neglected in the education; some educational contents are too much and too extensive; the educational methods are simple and outdated; and formalism is quite widespread. Thus education often gets half the result with double effort, and even evokes bad feelings among members. Therefore, we should explore a new approach to the education of Party members on the basis of summarizing previous experience. Below, I will summarize general suggestions on education.

A more planned education: Over a long period in the Party history, the education had mainly centered on political tasks of the Party, and thus possessed a character of "movement" or "campaign" and a random nature. It was a usual phenomenon that the work for a given stage was not finished but another work was started for the next stage. This practice had generally caused frustration in the primary-level Party organizations and members. Of course, it is necessary to educate Party members through certain periods, but such periodic programs should not be arranged so frequently. Many scholars emphasize the significance of educating in daily works.

Scientific content: The education should cover not only ideological and political aspects but also comprehensive knowledge. The contents should be designed in a scientific way and in accordance with the current situation and tasks facing the Party and considering the realities of the industries and occupations of Party members. The world today is in an era of knowledge explosion, and science and technology progresses with each passing day. If people do not learn hard, they will lag behind. Party organizations should work hard and provide an atmosphere to turn the CPC into a learning party, turn China into a learning society, and turn Party members into learning members. The education contents should include: major ideologies such as Marxism-Leninism, Mao Zedong Thought, Deng Xiaoping Theory, the important thought of Three Represents, the Scientific Outlook on Development, the building of a harmonious socialist society, and the socialist outlook on honor and disgrace; basic knowledge of the Party and its Constitution; the line, principle and policies of the Party, the current situation, tasks and national conditions; the common ideal of socialism in China and lofty ideal of communism; patriotism, collectivism and socialist ideologies; the fine traditions, style of work, and discipline of the Party on efforts to combat corruption and build a clean government; knowledge of market economy, legal knowledge, scientific and cultural knowledge, and professional skills. The world today is in an era of knowledge explosion, and science and technology progress with each passing day. If not learning hard, we will lag behind. Party organizations should work hard and provide a platform with the aim to turn the CPC into a learning party, turn China into a learning society, and turn Party members into learning members. They should help Party members develop into inter-disciplinary professionals, enabling them to play greater roles.

Modernized education methods: With the emergence of advanced modern media tools and diverse sources of information, the Party should adopt them. Traditional ways of education such as holding meetings, distributing documents, listening to reports and reading newspapers are no more so effective. Branches should combine traditional educational methods with modern ones and make full use of the Internet, newspapers and periodicals, broadcasting, television and video-tapes, in a quicker, more convenient, more direct and lively way. Instead of the previous method in which leaders or education workers transferred knowledge into Party members, a new method characterized by self-education should be developed which is more effective and practical.

Institutionalization of the management: The management and the education of Party members supplement each other; education can enhance their consciousness while management can strengthen the supervision over them, combining self-discipline with discipline by others and thus forming a permanent mechanism whereby Party members can preserve their high qualities. The management of Party members should be more institutionalized. For example, the system of "three meetings and one class" (general membership meeting, branch committee meeting, leading members' group meeting, and Party class) should be keenly practiced. The others which have proved to be effective: democratic appraisal system of members, the system of double regular organizational activities, and the system of democratic meetings, should be more improved. Scholars also suggest new systems such as inner-party supervision system, a realistic award, and incentive system for Party members.

Putting people first in education and management: An important content of Marxist historical materialism is to promote overall and free development of each human being. Putting people first is the essence and core of the Scientific Outlook on Development policy. Related to Party affairs, putting people first is to respect, care and love Party members and give play to the major role of Party members. Each Party member has two identities, occupational and political. Under the conditions of market economy, individual party members also face new problems, get confused and have to deal with many practical problems, just like ordinary people. Party organizations should give special care and support to old members who joined the Party before the founding of new China, members who work in hard environment, members who are laid-off and members who lead a hard life. Party organizations at all levels, while leading their members to maintain close ties with and serve the masses, should do a good job in caring, support Party members, and give practical help to them.

5.4.2 Education and Management of Floating Members

A floating Party member refers to a member who cannot take part in regular activities of the Party organization where his/her formal membership credentials reside for rather a long time due to the changes of occupation or residence. Under the socialist market economy, the industrial structure has been adjusted and the personnel system has been reformed, thus people are in transformation from state employees to social men. A direct result is that there appear more floating Party members, which adds to the difficulty of educating and managing Party members. At present, floating Party members have four characteristics. First, the number grows sharply. Statistics show that by the end of 2003, there were over 1.2 million floating Party members—today 2.3 million—which are still in contact with Party organizations, and the number continues to grow. Second, the occupational structure is diversifying, including migrant workers, laid-off and then re-employed workers, the self-employed, unemployed university graduates, unemployed veterans, intellectuals moving around, and people going abroad for business or personal affairs. Third, the average age of members is decreasing. Most of the floating Party members are young, and many are educated and have professional skills. They are in the prime ages of their life and thus possess advantages in fierce social competition. Fourth, these floating Party members are widely distributed in different sectors. They can adapt themselves to the economy with diverse forms of ownership. Floating members are found in every sector of society and in every trade and profession. Most of them work in non-public (private) sectors of economy while a few work in state-owned enterprises and public institutions. All above realities suggest that appropriate methods should be developed to arrange a regular management system and regular organizational activities for them.

5.4.3 Treatment of the Unqualified Party Members

Here, unqualified Party members have special connotations. They are mainly Party members who lack revolutionary will, fail to fulfill membership duties, are not qualified for membership, and do not play the exemplary role, but they are a different category from corrupt members punished with Party disciplinary measures. Although they have not violated Party discipline and state laws, they do not act like Party members. There are a small number of unqualified members within the Party, but they have a bad influence, making the ranks of our Party lax and impairing the image of the Party.

The Party holds that a qualified person can join the Party on a voluntary basis and any Party member has the freedom to withdraw from the Party. Article 9 of its Constitution explains how to deal with this issue. When a Party member asks to withdraw, the Party branch concerned shall, after discussion by its general membership meeting, remove his/her name from the Party rolls, make this removal public and report it to the next higher Party organization for the record. When a Party member who commits serious mistakes asks to withdraw, he/she shall be expelled from the Party, instead of withdrawing. For unqualified Party members, the Party should follow the policy of "sticking to qualifications, mainly relying on educating, making differential treatment, and taking comprehensive measures" and prudently and properly handle their cases, either persuading them to withdraw or expelling them from the Party. A Party member who fails to take part in regular Party activities, pay membership dues or fails to do the work assigned by the Party for six successive months without good reason is regarded as having given up membership. According to the current Constitution, general membership meeting of the Party branch decides on the removal of such a person's name from the Party rolls and reports it to the next higher Party organization for approval.

Statistics show that from 1989 to June 2001, the CPC took measures against 473,000 unqualified members in total employing democratic appraisal methods[1]; in 2005, the Party took organizational measures against 44,700. Scholars generally suggest that the Party should take severer measures against unqualified members to safeguard the purity of member structure. They suggest Party organizations at all levels should adapt themselves to the new situation and new tasks, constantly enhance Party members' consciousness of their vanguard nature, and stimulate their internal motivation for self-education and self-improvement.

---

[1] *People's Daily*, Section 4, June 29, 2001.

Chapter 6

Building the Primary Organizations of the Party

In terms of organizational system, the primary organizations of the Party constitute the base of its entire organizational system. A Party is made up of a number of members, but it is not a simple addition of members but an organized troop. A Marxist party is a unified whole organized in accordance with the principle of democratic-centralism, which is an important reason for its combat effectiveness. From top to bottom, the Party's organizational system is divided into three closely related basic sub-systems: central, local and primary.

A Marxist party has its unique organizational form and structural setup based on its class nature, worldview, ideal and objectives. Representing the interests of a minority, the capitalists, bourgeois parties generally believe in an idealistic, historical viewpoint of heroes and advocate elitist politics, and since a long period of history, they don't have appropriate primary organizations, or, they do not need to rely on the key role of primary organizations and rank-and-file members. Contrary to bourgeois parties, Marxist parties believe they should represent the interests of the working class and the broad masses, and thus attach importance to the building of primary organizations and regard it as symbol of and reliable guarantee for their success.

6.1 Marxist Parties and Primary Organizations

The founders of Marxist parties have always valued the role of primary organizations highly. As early as the Communist League was founded, Marx and Engels had designed a systematic structural setup from bottom to top as: communities, circles, leading circles, the Central Authority and the Congress, ensuring the entirety and unity of the League. In the organizational structure of Marxist parties, communities are the organizations at the grassroots level. In August 1847, when the Brussels Community and Brussels Circle were set up, Marx was elected secretary of the Community and member of the circle committee, presiding over the work of the community and circle. In November 1847 at its Second Congress, the Communist League approved the "Draft Rules of the Communist League" (See Appendix 1) by Marx, Engels and other people, which had presented an explicit formulation on the "organizational structure of the League". It is interesting that a special independent chapter was devoted to "the Community" as the primary organization. After the failure of the European Revolution, the Communist League had suffered a big damage; Marx and other leaders had returned to London and set up a new Central Authority. In March 1850, Marx and Engels summarized the experience and lessons of previous struggles in the "Address of the Central Committee to the Communist League," saying that the League "should work for the creation of an independent organization of the workers' party, both secret and open and separate from legalist democratic intellectuals, and the League should aim to make everyone of its communes (community) a center and nucleus of workers' associations in which the position and interests of the proletariat can be discussed free from bourgeois influence."[1]

In the process of setting up a Marxist party in Russia, Lenin had also paid keen attention to the issue. In the debate against the leaders of the Socialist (Social) Democratic Party in the Second International, he pointed out that if Party branches were not set up and they were not consolidated by basic-primary organizations in the factories, mines or railway units, a firm organizational system would not be there. To organize and mobilize the broad workers and masses, "a strong illegal organization of the Party Centers, systematic illegal publications and—most important of all—local and particularly factory Party groups, led by advanced members of the workers themselves, living in direct contact with the masses: such is the foundation on which we were building, and have built, a hard and solid core of a revolutionary and Social-Democratic working-class movement."[2] And he also pointed out that every Party branch should become a "base for agitation, propaganda and practical organizational work unit among the masses."[3]

The reasons that Marxist parties pay much attention to the building of primary organizations are as follows: First, in terms of class nature, every Marxist party is a part of the working class, a vanguard organization through which the working class and the broad masses strive for complete emancipation of themselves, and a faithful representative of the interests of the working class and the broad masses. To build such an organization, Party members should become masters of the Party; on the other side, to ensure members' position as masters and give play to their role, the Party should build itself as a powerful union through its primary organizations. Second, in terms of worldview, historical materialism and dialectical materialism are two basic philosophical grounds on which Marxist parties observe and analyze the past, present and future of the human history. Marxists always believe that history is ultimately created by the people, and the emancipation of mankind

---

[1] *Marx & Engels Selected Works* (2nd Chinese edition), Volume 1, p.369.

[2] *Collected Works of Vladimir Lenin* (2nd Chinese edition), Volume 17, p.4. Beijing: People's Press, 1988.

[3] *Ibid.*, p.338.

is not endowed by the savior, gods or emperors, but achieved by the people themselves under the correct leadership of Marxist parties with active efforts and hard struggle of its members. In the process of realizing their ultimate cause, primary Party organizations play a key role in organizing Party members and the masses. Third, in terms of objectives, the ultimate goal of Marxist parties is to overthrow the rule of the exploiting classes, realize the dictatorship of the proletariat, eliminate exploitation, eliminate differences and realize communism. To achieve this goal, it requires persistent struggle by many generations of the people, a dozen or even several dozens; it needs enthusiasm and creativity, power and wisdom of all communists; it relies on Marxist parties who can unite all the forces that can be united with and mobilize all the positive factors that can be mobilized.

From the above, we can see that it is a unique characteristic of the building of Marxist parties and a component of Marxist Theory of Party Building to attach great importance to the building of primary organizations, which is also a key issue in the practice of building Marxist parties.

As a Marxist party, the CPC has, in the long process of its practice, has thus established its own theory on the building of primary Party organizations.

The CPC was a result of Marxism and Leninism integrating with the Chinese labor movement, and came into being as influenced by the October Revolution of Russia and the May Fourth Movement of China and with the help of the Communist International led by Lenin. In the early days after the Party was founded, it only had two levels of organizations—Central Committee and local committees—due to its small membership. The first Constitution of the Communist Party of China adopted at the Second National Congress of the Party for the first time set forth the organizational structure in Article 4: "In all villages, factories, railway organs, mines, barracks, schools and other organs, three to five Party members should form a group with an elected group leader. The group is subordinated to the local Party branch. (If there is no local branch, the district executive committee can designate a nearby branch as—or make itself—the superior of the group; if there is no district executive committee, then the group is under direct administration of the Central Executive Committee.) When there are two groups or more in one or two integrated organs, the local executive committee should appoint several individuals as cadres of each group. Each group is a basic unit of the Party's organizational system, through which the Party trains Party members and organize activities; and all Party members should join a group." The "group" mentioned here was later renamed "branch"; it is the basic primary organization of the Party and the first level unit through which Party members participate in the inner-party life, and it shoulders the direct responsibility of educating and training Party members. In January 1925, the CPC approved the "Resolution on the Organizational Issue" at its Fourth National Congress, which, for the first time, made clear the expression of its basic cell—"Party branch": "The basic organizations of our Party should be branch organizations with industry and organization as unit. For small handicraftsmen and those people engaging in business and commerce who cannot be organized into branches with organization as unit, we can organize them based on region." At this Congress, the CPC had adopted the Second Amendment to the Constitution of the Communist Party of China, which stated, "Three Party members or more should form a branch." In June 1927, the Party adopted the Third Amendment to the Constitution stating: "a branch is the basic organization of the Party" and "is the organization through which the Party has direct contact with the masses" and also formulated the six specific tasks and norms for its activities.

After the failure of the Great Revolution (1924-1927), the CPC was forced to take a tough road of leading the Chinese revolution—independently—without a class alliance. In respect of the building of primary organizations, leaders' collective of the first generation, with Mao Zedong as their representative, made creative exploration in light of actual conditions of revolution and Party building. In the autumn of 1927, when the troops of the Autumn Harvest Rising marched to the middle section of Luoxiao Mountains across the boundary between Hunan and Jiangxi, Mao Zedong re-organized the troops in Sanwan, and stated for the first time that the Party should establish branches on a company basis to reinforce absolute leadership of the party over the army. In November 1928, he pointed out in a report to the Central Committee: "The Party branch is organized on a company basis; this is an important reason why the Red Army has been able to carry on such arduous fighting without falling apart."[1] During the War of Resistance against Japan (1937-1945), Chen Yun had written an article in June 1939 titled "Party Branches", in which he said that "the branches are the grass-root organizations as well as the most basic organizations of the Party" and "are the core with which the Party unites with the masses."[2] "Party branches should not only organizationally assume the role of leadership core and fortress, but also play such a role in reality."[3] In May 1945, Liu Shaoqi had devoted a special part to the basic (primary) organizations of the Party in the report to the Seventh National Congress of the Party about amending the Party Constitution, and proposed: "a Party branch is a working unit of the Party among the masses of the people, and it is a bridge between the masses of the people and the leading bodies of the Party"[4] and had termed it as "fortress."[5] "Bridge" and "fortress" have been used to describe Party branches until today.

After the CPC became the ruling party, its primary organizations have spread across the country. It became an important part of Party building to reinforce primary Party organizations. In September 1956, the CPC made new rules about the setup of primary organizations at its Eighth National Congress, classifying primary organizations into three levels from bottom to top: branch, general branch and primary Party committee. In the report on the revision of the Party Constitution, Deng Xiaoping had underlined the significance of building primary Party organizations: "primary organizations

[1] *Selected Works of Mao Zedong* (2nd Chinese edition), Volume 1, pp.65-66.
[2] *Selected Works of Chen Yun* (2nd Chinese edition), Volume 1, p.145. Beijing: People's Press, 1995.
[3] *Ibid.*, p.147.
[4] The Party Literature Research Center of the CPC Central Committee and Party School of the CPC Central Committee, *On Party Building by Liu Shaoqi*, p.450.
[5] *Ibid.*, p.488.

form the basic links between the Party and the masses, and an important political task of the Party's leading bodies is to constantly check and help them improve their work."[1]

In view of new requirements and new tasks for the building of primary Party organizations in Reform period after 1978, Deng Xiaoping had warned the whole Party: "If, when faced with concrete problems, a Party organization in a production team, factory, workshop or section can follow the mass line, consult its rank and file, offer good advice, call on their Party members to lead by offering examples and thus really solve the problems, then such a Party organization is making valuable contributions to the four modernizations task."[2] The Constitution adopted at the 12th National Congress of the Party set forth eight basic tasks for Party branches in light of new requirements and new tasks for the building of primary Party organizations in the new period. After the Fourth Plenary Session of the 13th Central Committee of the Party was held in 1989, the Party's third generation of the central collective leadership, with Jiang Zemin at the core, had also paid great attention to this issue.

6.2 Primary Organizations: Foundation for a Militant Party

In September 1994, at its Fourth Plenary Session of the 14th Central Committee, the CPC has adopted the Decision of the Central Committee; "On Several Important Issues about Strengthening Party Building," which pointed out: "The primary organizations of the Party constitute its foundation for doing all its work and building up its combat effectiveness, and undertake important responsibilities of maintaining direct ties with the masses, publicizing its line, principles and policies among them, organizing and uniting with them, and carrying out its line, principles and

---

[1] *Selected Works of Deng Xiaoping* (2nd edition), Volume 1, p.253.
[2] *Selected Works of Deng Xiaoping* (2nd edition), Volume 2, p.280.

policies at the grassroots level."[1] The new Constitution adopted at the 16th National Congress of the Party stipulates in Article 31: "The primary Party organizations are militant bastions of the Party in the basic units of society, where all the Party's work proceeds and they serve as the foundation of its fighting capacity."

Below, I would like to analyze the position and functions of the building of primary Party organizations in Marxist parties:

First, as I have stated above, in terms of organizational system, the primary organizations of the Party constitute the base of its entire organizational system. From top to bottom, the Party's organizational system is divided into three closely related basic sub-systems: central, local and primary. The central organizations of the Party make up its core and are its leading bodies; the local organizations are the intermediate links between central and primary organizations; and the primary organizations are the base of the whole organizational system, through which the Party organizes its members and makes itself a strong force. In August 1989, at the National Meeting of Heads in Charge of Organizational Work, Jiang Zemin had commented, "Where do the Party's combat effectiveness and power lie? I think it is first demonstrated by nearly three million primary Party organizations in their function as fortresses. Otherwise, there could be no leadership of the Central Committee? If all the primary organizations are played down, I believe that the General Secretary would certainly become a 'leader alienated from the people.' Therefore, we should never be vague on this principle matter... Finally, without the fighting capacity of all the primary Party organizations, our Party's combat effectiveness would be empty. Where is the source of the power? Primary organizations."[2]

Second, in terms of coordinated development of the Marxist Party,

[1] The Party Literature Research Center of the CPC Central Committee, *Selected Important Documents since the 14th National Congress of the Communist Party of China*, Volume 2, p.965.

[2] The Party Literature Research Center of the CPC Central Committee, *Selected Important Documents since the 13th National Congress of the Communist Party of China*, Volume 2, pp.582-583. Beijing: People's Press, 1991.

the primary organizations are the sources for the growth of the Party. Party building is a comprehensive project, and the building of the primary Party organizations is the infrastructure of this project. Building primary organizations demands a lot of hard, careful and realistic work. With regard to coordinated development, the primary organizations of the Party shoulder an important task of recruiting, educating, managing and supervising Party members. Since the primary organizations are in close contact—or part of—basic social units, they can find, select and train political activists and recruit new members. In this way, they are the basis on which the Party keeps absorbing newcomers and expands itself. They are the branches or schools where Party members are educated and trained; the primary organizations undertake a task of educating and managing Party members, and help improving the quality of the membership and the combat effectiveness of the Party.

Third, in terms of being strict with Party membership, the primary organizations undertake a high-level responsibility. For a ruling Marxist party, the changes in social position and economic circumstances usually bring about corruption, degradation and other bad phenomena. To combat such phenomena, the primary organizations are duty-bound. As stipulated in the Constitution of the Party, "Every Party member, irrespective of position, should be organized into a branch, cell or other specific unit of the Party to participate in the regular activities of the Party organization and accept oversight by the masses inside and outside the Party. Leading Party cadres should attend democratic meetings held by the Party committee or leading Party members' group. There shall be no privileged Party members who do not participate in the regular activities of the Party organization and do not accept oversight by the masses inside and outside the Party." The primary organizations are one of the subjects of inner-party oversight. For the Party to exercise self-discipline, first the primary organizations should do a good job in managing members under their administration. To be strict with party members, first the primary organizations should do a good job in managing, educating and supervising members under their administration, particularly those at leading positions, in strict accordance with Party regulations and rules. Therefore, the key for achieving better results in being strict with Party members is to build the primary organizations well.

Fourth, in terms of work division, the primary organizations are the executors of all the work of the Party. It needs unified understanding, coordination and action of the Party to implement the Party's line, principles and policies. When coordinating and sharing the Party work, the central organizations are responsible for making decisions in a macrocosmic sense and making overall arrangements; the local organizations are responsible for conveying the guiding principles of the Central Committee and making specific plans; and the primary organizations are responsible for leading and mobilizing all Party members and the masses to carry out the tasks formulated by superior organizations. All the Party work should be finally carried out by the primary organizations. Thus without them, the Party work would be an empty talk indeed.

Fifth, in terms of the Party-mass relationship, the primary organizations are bridges through which the Party maintains close ties with the masses. As the primary organizations are set up at the grassroots level of society and close to the masses, the Party can maintain close ties with the masses through them. The primary organizations are not only cells of the Party, but windows through which the masses learn about the Party. The primary organizations should spread and carry out the Party's principles and policies among the masses, while keep leading and decision-making bodies of the Party informed of the desires, demands and opinions of the masses in good time, so as to ensure that decisions that the Party makes are scientific and oriented towards the masses. At the same time, the primary organizations can do good, practical things for the masses, and help build up the Party's prestige among the masses by their cadres demonstrating high working capabilities and good style of work.

Sixth, in terms of governance capability, the primary organizations are important for the Party to constantly improve its art of leadership and governance capability. A Marxist party, based on its philosophical stand, always trusts and relies on the masses; on their wisdom, power and competence; this relationship is also valid for members and non-party people. Since genuine knowledge only comes from practice and practice refers to masses, social activities, the achievements and experience from practice are the source of the Party's capacity and leadership wisdom. Party can summarize experience of the masses and pool their wisdom in a timely manner through the primary organizations.

6.3 Organizational Setup and Tasks of Primary Organizations

The structure, organizational setup and activity model of the primary organizations are developed in the long practice of Marxist Party building, as they have a direct bearing on the functioning of the organizations.

6.3.1 Organizational Structure of Primary Organizations

In different historical periods and in different societies, Marxist parties have different structures for their primary organizations, but the basic principles are the same. First is the principle of production or work, which means that a primary organization should be set up nearby the production units or work units of Party members. Second is the principle of number, which means that the level of a primary organization should be determined by the number of its members. In the era of non-monopoly capitalism when Marx and Engels lived, large-scale social production drove thousands of people from scattered villages into capitalist factories, the division of labor in the production process and living together had strengthened interpersonal relationship between industrial workers, and the spread of advanced ideas enabled them to have the consciousness of class identity, thus when early Marxist parties were establishing their primary organizations, they had naturally adopted the principles of production and number. Such two principles of setting up primary organizations have been proven effective in the building and development of Marxist parties. Of course, later such methods were applied not only in urban areas and enterprises, but also in rural areas and other primary organizations of society.

Although in the age of revolution, traditional agriculture was dominant in the Chinese society, modern industries made their way in cities of China and industrial workers thus had made up the class basis for the CPC. After the CPC was founded, it borrowed experience from the building of the Bolshevik and set up its primary organizations at the grassroots level, such as in enterprises, villages and army troops, in accordance with the principles of production and number. In February 1922, the CPC set up the first branch of industrial workers at Anyuan Mine and Zhuping Railway; in the autumn of 1924, it set up the first army branch at Huangpu Military Academy; in June 1925, it set up the first rural branch in Shaoshan. In May 1945, in his report on the revision of the Party Constitution, Liu Shaoqi made the following summary: "As provided in the Party Constitution, the basic organizations of our Party is formed on the basis of production units or work units, this is one of our Party's organizational principles, which places the basis of our Party organizations in the cells of the social organism."[1]

After the CPC had assumed power, it still set up and developed primary organizations across the country based on the principles of production and number. During the reform and opening-up, particularly during the establishment and improvement of the socialist market economy, profound changes have taken place and are taking place in the economic structure, mode of economic operation and organizational form of social population in China. But the principles and basic activity model of primary organizations of the Party have remained to this day. Since such principle and model demand that Party organizations be set up at the grassroots level of society, the primary organizations can maintain close ties between the Party and the masses to the utmost extent, expand the Party's mass foundation, and increase the Party's influence in the whole society.

At present, the primary organizations of the Party refer to Party organizations that are set up by grassroots-level units under the county

---

[1] Liu Shaoqi, *On Party Building*, p.488.

level according to the Constitution. Vertically, they are in three levels: primary committee, committee of a general branch and branch committee; horizontally, they are formed in enterprises, rural areas, government organs, schools, research institutes, communities, social organizations, companies of the People's Liberation Army and other basic units, where there are at least three full Party members.

The primary organizations of the Party are set up mainly based on the principle of production or work, that is, nearby the production units or work units of Party members. In other words, the primary organizations are set up according to the nature and characteristics of the industry or trade that Party members are engaged in, and according to the number of Party members. Generally, in a primary organization with over 50 members, a committee of a general Party branch can be set up with approval by the higher Party committee, and several branches can be set up under the committee of general Party branch. In a primary organization with over 100 members, a primary Party committee can be set up with approval by the higher Party committee, and several committees of general branches and Party branches can be set up under the primary committee.

As stipulated in the present Constitution of the Party, the leading bodies of the primary Party organizations include the primary Party committees, committees of general Party branches and committees of Party branches— from top to bottom—A primary Party committee is elected by a general membership meeting or a meeting of delegates, while the committee of a general Party branch or a Party branch is elected by a general membership meeting. Results of the election of a secretary and deputy secretaries of a primary committee, general branch committee or branch committee of the Party shall be reported to the next higher Party organization for approval.

For the term of the leadership of the primary organizations, there were no written rules in the new-democratic revolution period as the Party was long trapped in ruthless wars and its primary organizations had often changed. After the CPC had assumed power, the Constitution adopted at the Eighth National Congress had stipulated that a primary Party committee, general Party branch committee or Party branch committee should be elected for a term of one year. According to the Constitution adopted at the Ninth National Congress of the Party, "Every primary Party organization should be re-elected every year; under special circumstances, the reelection can be held ahead of schedule or postponed." The Constitution adopted at the Tenth National Congress of the Party said, "Branches and general branches of the Party are re-elected every year, while primary committees are re-elected every two years. Under special circumstances, the re-election can be held ahead of schedule or postponed." After the Reform and Opening-up policies were carried out, the Party adopted a new Constitution at its 12th National Congress in 1982, saying that "a primary committee is elected for a term of three years, while a general Party branch committees or a Party branch committees is elected for a term of two years." The Constitution adopted at the 14th National Congress of the Party said, "a primary committee is elected for a term of three or four years, while a general Party branch committees or a Party branch committees is elected for a term of two or three years." The Constitution adopted at the 16th National Congress of the Party in 2002 states: "a primary committee is elected for a term of three to five years, while a general Party branch committees or a Party branch committees is elected for a term of two or three years." The changes show that the term of the primary Party organizations have become longer. There are several major reasons. After the CPC became the ruling party, its membership has expanded with the fast growing national population; After the Reform and Opening-up policies were carried out, the rapid development of social and economic life has led to a stronger social mobility and social volatility of Party members. The wider spread of the system of democratic election at self-governing primary organizations requires that Party organizations be relatively stable. Moreover, on the vast land of China, the conditions are different and primary Party organizations in different places differ in size; a simple and uniform stipulation on the term is considered inappropriate for the building of leadership and the consistency and stability of the work.

Among all the primary organizations, the most bottom Party branches are the most basic organizations and fortresses at the grass-roots level of society, and thus are the emphasis of Party building at the primary level. As prescribed in the Constitution, Party branches should be formed in basic units where there are at least three full Party members. The establishment of a Party branch is subject to approval of the higher Party committee. Members of a Party branch committee are elected by a general membership meeting for a term of two years. The number of members is determined as the work requires and based on the number of Party members: appropriately three to five, and no more than seven. A Party branch committee usually consists of a secretary, a deputy secretary, and commissaries in charge of organization, publicity, discipline inspection, the youth and confidentiality. A Party branch with less than 10 members usually does not have a committee, but a secretary, and a deputy secretary and when necessary; both the secretary and deputy secretary are directly elected by a general membership meeting. When there is a vacancy in a Party branch committee, a general membership meeting should be held in good time to elect a candidate. When the general membership meeting of a Party branch is not in session, the Party branch committee is responsible for daily work. The secretary and deputy secretary preside over the routine work of the branch. A Party branch committee should carry out resolutions approved at the general membership meeting and report to it its work at regular intervals.

To more effectively carry out Party building, usually there are Party groups working under a Party branch. Party groups are not primary-level organizations of the Party, but part of Party branches. A Party branch committee divides the branch into Party groups in accordance with the number and distribution of its members and as party work requires. In the establishment of Party groups; production unit and party work are the main consideration, and the division is the same as administrative division. A Party group should include at least three people, among whom at least one should be full Party member. Under the leadership of a Party branch, Party groups are responsible for managing and organizing Party members and directing their daily activities.

6.3.2 Main Duties of Primary Organizations

The main duties of the primary Party organizations usually include: to disseminate and carry out the Party's line, principles and policies; organize Party members to study political theories and acquire general, scientific and professional knowledge; educate, manage and oversee Party members; admit and recruit new Party members; maintain close ties with the masses; and oversee Party members and leading cadres. Since the Party has different tasks and missions in a given period, its general objectives vary in different periods and so do the main tasks of primary organizations. After the CPC became the ruling party, the Constitutions adopted at the Ninth and Tenth National congresses included five articles about the tasks while 12th National Congress had agreed on eight articles. The Constitution adopted at the 16th National Congress has maintained the basic content of the eight articles though some adjustment was made in the wording (See Appendix 2).

6.4 Improving the Building of Primary Party Organizations

The building of the primary organizations occupies a very important position in the building of the organizational system of the Marxist Party. For a ruling Marxist party, it is a basic project helping to preserve the Party's vanguard nature, improving its governance capability and consolidating its ruling position. In the Reform and Opening-up period, Party building scholars have often commented on the urgency of improvements. Below I will present the reader the Party's recent efforts on this issue.

6.4.1 Recent Efforts for Improving Primary Party Organizations

After the Fourth Plenary Session of the13th Central Committee of the Party in 1989, central collective leadership, with Jiang Zemin at the core, had paid more attention to the building of primary organizations of the Party. At the 14th National Congress, the CPC raised the objective of establishing and improving socialist market economy. In the face of new situation, the

CPC had adopted the "Decision of the Central Committee of the Communist Party of China on Several Important Issues about Strengthening Party Building," presenting an explicit guideline for strengthening and improving the building of the primary organizations: "First, concentrate on the Party's basic line, serve the central task, and evaluate the work of primary Party organizations by how much actual results they have achieved in fulfilling their tasks. Second, study new conditions and solve new problems with the spirit of reform, make use of present successful experience for innovation and creation, and improve the activities and work style of primary organizations. Third, be strict in inner-party activities, strictly enforce Party discipline, foster healthy trends, fight against bad practices, maintain the vanguard nature and purity of Party members, and increase the ability of primary organizations in solving their own contradictions. Fourth, set foot on routine work, make feasible long-term plans, and work hard to solve current conspicuous problems."[1]

The report to the 15th National Congress of the Party had concisely summarized and reiterated this guideline. And on the same line of development, the report to the 16th National Congress of the Party made a further summary of the guideline for the building of primary Party organizations.

The new elaboration in the 16th Congress gave an emphasis on the important thought of Three Represents, as a guide in the Party work. The Constitution adopted at this Congress also included new contents about establishing primary Party organizations in communities, social organizations and intermediary spheres, and expanded the coverage of the organizations and work of the Party. It had extended the term for primary committees; and had given more detailed definitions on the duties of different primary organizations. At the Fourth Plenary Session of the 16th Central Committee, the Party approved "the Decision of the Central Committee of the Communist Party of China on Strengthening the Governance Capability of the Party." In

---

[1] The Party Literature Research Center of the CPC Central Committee, *Selected Important Documents since the 14th National Congress of the Communist Party of China*, Volume 2, pp.966-967.

the third part of this document, there was a clear emphasis: "to base ourselves on the building of primary organizations and membership of the Party"; in the ninth part, it made special arrangements for strengthening and improving the building of its primary organizations and placed special emphasis on "caring and protecting Party members and cadres at the grassroots level" and "improving Party workers group and bringing into full play their function." All the above changes tried to reflect the new requirements in the new historical period.

Over a decade, the Central Committee has made considerable efforts in this regard including abundant measures. A special teleconference meeting was held on the building of primary organizations in rural areas; many scholarly and political articles were published; several million cadres were sent to counties and villages to rectify weak, lax or lagging Party branches and branches in impoverished villages, and trained in rotation rural Party members and cadres. And intensified efforts to build the leadership of state-owned enterprises, actively promoted the cadre and personnel system reform, improved the system of enterprise leadership to meet the needs of modern enterprise system, and attached importance to Party building in enterprises that had stopped production, closed down or gone bankruptcy. More attention was given to Party building in non-public (private) enterprises, too. Useful explorations were started in the working mechanism, organizational form and working methods of Party building in neighborhood units and communities, successful results were achieved in recruiting new members from young intellectuals, and in the ideological and political education of college students.

Statistics show that by the end of 2005, there were 3,520,000 primary Party organizations around China, including 170,000 primary Party committees, 210,000 committees of general Party branches and 3,140,000 Party branches from bottom to top. The number was a big increase compared with 190,000 in 1949, 2,100,000 in 1978, and 3,452,000 in 2003. In particular, the coverage of the primary Party organizations increased in new economic entities, new social organizations, urban neighborhoods and townships. Among the 98,000 non-public (private) enterprises that had over 50 employees and met the requirements for the establishment of Party organizations, 97.9 percent saw Party organizations established. Among 9,000 private non-enterprise entities with required conditions, 8,000 saw Party organizations established, accounting for 88.9 percent of the total. Among 6,000 urban neighborhoods, there were 180,000 primary Party organizations, 30 for each neighborhood on average; among 36,000 townships, there were 1,102,000 primary organizations, 31 for each township on average.[1] These primary organizations are believed to make up rich resources for the Party's ruling position, the organizational foundation for its leadership and governance, as well as an important foundation for the socialist state power.

6.4.2 Latest Measures for Improving the Building of Primary Party Organizations

Over the years, although the Party has underlined the significance of the building of its primary organizations, the work is still stagnant in some organizations due to the rapid changes in social structure, brought about by the economic restructuring. In rural areas, the abolition of the people's commune system, the spread of the household based contract responsibility system and the emergence of township enterprises and the tertiary industry have naturally increased the movement of rural population. Consequently, the former mode of educating, managing and overseeing Party members could no longer be applied, and regular, organized publicity and mobilization activities are unable to be carried out among the masses. In urban areas, enterprises enjoy increasing autonomy in management since the end of 1970s and the reform of the business management system since the early 1980s have also resulted in important changes. Thus some primary organizations could not adapt themselves to these new situations. In the meantime, with the emancipation of minds and the implementation of the opening-up policy, some Party members and cadres could not keep pace with the times and have changed mentally. Moreover, in the middle and late 1980s, the work of the

---

[1] Zhang Shouhua, "Expand and Demonstrate Vitality", *People's Daily*, Section 5, June 1, 2006.

primary Party organizations was weakened. Consequently some primary organizations become weak and lax, and some had even disintegrated; some cadres of the primary organizations had given up honest and upright conducts and divorced themselves from the masses. Some Party members degrading to a weaker sense of Party spirit and could not play an exemplary role among the masses; and in some rural primary organizations, cadres had become too old and their educational level were not sufficient, and thus were unable to lead the masses to a new direction; some Party branches had been controlled by family clans and become a tool in their struggle for power and wealth.

These new unhealthy phenomena had alarmed the Party and the scholars. And Jiang Zemin had made a warning-like evaluation on the issue: "An unstable foundation will shake the whole ground. As it comes to the new century, old problems have not been completely resolved yet but on the other side new problems are cropping up. How to adapt to the adjustment of economic structure, the development of diverse sectors of the economy and the diversification of employment, and make the primary organizations of the Party more rational and more scientific? How to adapt to the diversification of people's interests, needs and mindsets, and do a good job in ideological and political work with focus? How to adapt to the characteristics of different groups of Party members, and improve the operational model of the primary organizations? How to solve the problem of irrational age structure and relatively backward educational structure of Party cadres, and build up the ranks of high-caliber part-time and full-time Party cadres?" After this comment, research and efforts had become more energetic.

I would like to review the latest efforts made to solve the above problems; the primary organizations of the Party are widely distributed in all the regions, industries and social spheres; and also they are at different levels, hence have different tasks and functions. For this reason, we cannot offer just one method for the building of all the primary organizations, as we done in the past. In the past the Chinese society was quite in-complex and in a unitary pattern.

First, the efforts in building the primary organizations in rural areas:

Agriculture is the foundation of the national economy, farmers make up the overwhelming majority of the Chinese population, and the rural development has a bearing on the overall situation of the reform, development and stability of China—the issues of agriculture, farmers and countryside constitute a key to the building of a moderately prosperous society in all respects. Naturally, it was significant to strengthen and improving the building of the primary organizations in rural areas. In February 1999, the Central Committee had issued "the Regulations of the Communist Party of China on the Work of Rural Primary Organizations," raising clear and specific requirements for rural primary organizations with regard to the organizational setup, responsibilities and tasks, economic development, development of socialist culture and ethics, the building of the contingent of cadres and leadership, the building of the ranks of Party members and other aspects. The regulations embodied a general guideline demanding rural primary organizations to conscientiously carry out the Party's rural policy and play a leading role in deepening the rural reform, developing the rural economy in all aspects, promoting cultural and ideological progress, leading farmers in striving for a moderately prosperous life, and achieving common prosperity and common progress. And in September 2003, the General Office of the Central Committee circulated a document "the Opinions on Deepening Party Building Activities at the Village, Township and County Levels in Rural Areas," adjusting the objective and requirements for the building of rural primary organizations. The "Opinions" document had set forth five requirements for village and township Party organizations as: good leadership, good ranks of Party members and cadres, good working mechanism, good performance in building a moderately prosperous life, and good response from farmers; it also included work plans aiming to improve those Party organizations.

At present, in accordance with the overall requirements of the "new socialist countryside project", the Party focuses to consolidate the achievements in the educational campaign and set up an effective mechanism that enables primary organizations to educate cadres regularly which will also benefit the farmers in the long run. The key is to build up village-level administrative organizations with village Party committees at the core, so that there are healthy village Party branches and committees leading village affairs, stronger village-level collective economy and standardized rules for democratic management.

Second, the efforts in building primary Party organizations in state-owned and collective enterprises: State-owned enterprises constitute the pillars of the national economy, a major source of the financial revenue of the country, and an important expression of the socialist public ownership, also the basic force enabling the economy of China to take part in international competition and cooperation. Under the new situation, the invigoration of state-owned enterprises is a major issue for China to establish and improve the socialist market economy and consolidate the socialist system. The Party Constitution clearly states the function and tasks of the primary organizations in state-owned enterprises. In January 1997, the Central Committee had issued "the Notice of the Central Committee of the Communist Party of China on further Strengthening and Improving Party Building in State-owned Enterprises," setting forth explicit requirements for the work of Party building in state-owned enterprises from nine aspects and proposing overall arrangements. In a state-owned or collective enterprise, the primary Party organization acts as the political nucleus and works for the operation of the enterprise. The primary Party organization guarantees and oversees the implementation of the principles and policies of the Party and the state in these enterprises and supports the board of shareholders, board of directors, board of supervisors and manager (factory director) through their operations. It relies on the workers and office staff, and also supports the work of the congresses of representatives of workers and office staff and participates in making final decisions on major questions of the enterprise. It works to improve its own organization and provides leadership over ideological and political work, efforts for cultural and ethical progress, the trade unions, the Communist Youth League and other mass organizations.

Third, the efforts in building primary Party organizations in neighborhoods and communities: The primary organizations in neighborhoods and communities are the Party's organizations at the grassroots level in urban areas. With the deepening reform of the political and economic systems in urban areas, the primary Party organizations in neighborhoods and communities are playing a bigger role in social service and social management. Moreover in urban areas, new economic entities have emerged in large numbers and various intermediary social organizations have developed rapidly, bringing about new problems for the building of the primary Party organizations in neighborhoods and communities. From 1999 to 2002, the Organization Department of the Central Committee has organized three special meetings to study the improvements on this work, focusing on Shanghai, Nanjing, Shenyang and Beijing urban areas.

Fourth, the efforts in building primary organizations in social organizations and intermediaries: In the new period, social organizations and intermediaries have developed rapidly in China, with a large number of employees. Thus the work of Party building in these entities becomes a new topic of grassroots Party building. In February 1998, the Organization Department of the Central Committee and the Ministry of Civil Affairs had issued "the Notice on Some Problems of Establishing Party Organizations in Social Organizations." And, in July 2000, the Organization Department of the Central Committee had circulated a document: "the Opinions on Strengthening Party Building in Social Organizations." These documents all embody clear requirements for the work of Party building in social organizations and intermediaries.

Fifth, the efforts in building primary Party organizations in non-public economic institutions: Non-public economic institutions mainly refer to foreign and private enterprises. Foreign enterprises include Chinese-foreign joint ventures, Chinese-foreign contractual enterprises and wholly foreign-owned enterprises, they are termed as: enterprises with three kinds of capital. Non-public sectors of the economy are products of the reform and opening-up policies. The work of Party building in these entities is a major and brand-new topic for the Party in the new period. In September 2000, the Organization Department of the Central Committee has circulated the document "the Opinions on Strengthening Party Building in Self-employed, Private and other Non-public Sectors of the Economy (for Trial Implementation), explicitly stating the significance, urgency, guideline and principles of the building of primary Party organizations in non-public economic institutions", and the position, functions and powers of Party organizations in them. The CPC further explained major tasks of the primary organizations in non-public economic institutions in its report to the 16th National Congress and correspondingly in the new Party Constitution (2002) as: In a non-public economic institution, the primary Party organization carries out the Party's principles and policies, guides and oversees the enterprise in observing the laws and regulations of the state, exercises leadership over the trade union, the Communist Youth League organization and other mass organizations, rallies the workers and office staff around it, safeguards the legitimate rights and interests of all quarters (parties in the enterprise) and stimulates the healthy development of the enterprise.

Sixth, the efforts of Party building in Party and government organs, schools, research institutes, cultural organizations and other public institutions: The primary Party organizations in Party and government organs include Party committees and subordinate general branches and branches. These Party organizations are set up in different departments of Party and government organs at different levels. The functions and powers of Party and government organs determine that their primary Party organizations have the following characteristics. First, in this sphere there are few non-Party people. Second, their members and cadres take part in the formulation and implementation of Party and state policies, and thus they have a big influence. Third, their members and cadres hold different powers, posing an arduous task for the building of a fine Party culture and a clean and honest government. In this sense, the primary organizations in Party and government organs are special and important. In March 1998, the Central Committee circulated a document "the Working Rules for Primary Organizations of the Communist Party of China and State Organs," providing institutional and standard grounds for Party building in these organs. In March 1996, it issued another document titled "the Working Rules of the Communist Party of China for Primary Organizations in General Institutions of Higher Learning, and re-establishing the "principal accountability system under the leadership of the Party committee." The document had emphasized the position of Party committees as the leadership core in institutions of higher learning, and demanded that the primary Party organizations in these institutions reinforce and improve moral education and train builders of and successors to the cause of socialism with lofty ideals, moral integrity, good education and a strong sense of discipline.

Chapter 7

Party's Work Style

The work style of the Marxist party includes its image, political outlook, nature, purpose, program and line, and constitutes an important symbol reflecting its vanguard nature. Establishment of the work style of the Marxist party is an important component of Party building and thus runs through the Party's whole life. For a ruling Marxist party, the work style, a critical issue and an important part both of Party building and of the development of socialist culture and ethics in the society, has a bearing on the ruling position of the Party, state power and social stability.

7.1 Improvement of the Party's Work Style

Every political party in the world has its own work style demonstrating its nature. But due to the differences in social environment, cultural background, historical traditions, class stand and political attitude, some parties improve their work style consciously while some form their own style unconsciously. Marxist parties have gradually brought into being a systematic theory of the improvement of the work style during the long practice of party building, and explore ways to employ this theory.

7.1.1 Scientific Concept of the Party's Work Style

Non-Marxist parties seldom use the concept of party style. The scientific concept of the Party's work style is unique to proletarian parties. Engels was the first to use the word "style" in inner-party activities and party building when he criticized the "flattering" and "gaudy" style of opportunists like Bakunin. After the victory of the October Revolution, Lenin used the word "style" for many times to criticize bureaucracy, isolation from the masses and dilatory style of work in Soviet state organs. Although Marx, Engels and Lenin did not raise an explicit concept of the Party's work style, they had advocated and upheld the spirits of pragmatism, criticism and self-criticism, respect for and close ties with the masses, laying a theoretical foundation for the formation of the work style of proletarian parties.

It was the Chinese communists, with Mao Zedong as their representative, who raised the scientific concept of the Party's work style, made a comprehensive and systematic exposition on it and included "the improvement of the Party's work style" as an important component of Marxist party building. In December 1929, in the "Resolution of Gutian Conference," the CPC had analyzed the relations between the three components: the improvement of ideology and work style and the Party's line, marking an initial progress in conceptualizing the improvement of the work style. In the 1930s, the Party had started to solve the problem of work style in Party building in the Soviet Area. In 1942, the Party had started the first Party-wide Rectification Movement in Yan'an headquarters. During this movement, Mao Zedong had written many articles, including "Reform our Study," "Rectifying the Party's Style of Work" and "Opposing Stereotyped Party Writing," making in-depth expositions on the scientific concept of the Party's work style and the contents of and approaches to the improvement of the work style, hence bringing into being a complete concept of the improvement of the work style. In February 1942, in his "Rectifying the Party's Style of Work," Mao Zedong had first raised the scientific concept of the Party's work style: "Fight subjectivism in order to rectify the style of study, fight sectarianism in order to rectify the style in Party relations, and fight Party stereotypes in order to rectify the style of writing." He had also pointed out: "The style of study and the style of writing are also the Party's style of work."[1] I think these works mark Mao's contributions to the Marxist Theory of Party Building.

After Mao had raised the scientific concept of the Party's work style, as a matter of fact, for a long period theoreticians did not carry a research work on this concept. In the 1950s, Yang Xianzhen, a renowned theoretician of the Party, had explained the concept from the perspective of philosophy and the relationship between it and the worldview. In the 1980s, Huang Kecheng, then permanent secretary of the Central Commission for Discipline Inspection of the CPC, had summarized the various forms of the Party's work style from ideology, politics, work and life of Party members at a symposium. In the meantime, some theorists have also offered different definitions from different aspects. It was not until the late 1980s that people had reached a consensus on it.

According to statements of revolutionary leaders and achievements of Party building theorists, we can make this definition: the Party's work style, or style of work, is the consistent attitude and behavior that the whole Party, including organizations at all levels and individual members, shows in ideology, politics, organization, work, life and other aspects. It is an important reflection and outward expression of the Party's nature, purpose, program and line. It reflects the overall outlook of the Party, and is a comprehensive issue relating to all aspects of Party building. The Party's work style originates from ideology, comes into being in practice, and shows itself in action of both Party organizations at all levels and every Party member. It showcases the mode of thinking, political stand, organizational principle, attitude of work, lifestyle and moral norms of a political party. In this sense, the Party's work style bears on its image.

7.1.2 Characteristics of the Party's Work Style

To understand the scientific connotations of the Party's work style, we

---

[1] *Selected Works of Mao Zedong* (2nd Chinese edition), Volume 3, p.812.

should understand its general characteristics. To summarize, the Party's work style is characteristic of externality, consistency, group, diversity and times.

Externality means that the Party's work style expresses itself by means of tangible words and acts, instead of pure ideas or concepts. The people can see, feel, come to know and understand the style in visual ways.

Consistency means that the Party's work style is a long-term, consistent act that exists and functions in a rather long time, instead of at some special time and at some place.

The group feature means that the Party's work style is demonstrated in some act of the majority or a certain number of members and the act can become a common practice within the Party; it is an expression of group style, not of individual act.

Diversity means that the Party's work style can be found in every aspect of the activities of Party members and organizations at all levels in diverse forms.

The close connection with the times means that the concrete forms of expression of the Party's work style and the focus of the improvement of the style develop and change catering to objective, historical conditions and the changes of the times.

7.1.3 Essence of the Party's Work Style

The essence of the Party's work style is the relationship between the Party and the people. We can grasp it from the following aspects.

The Party's work style is the most direct approach through which the people can come to know the Party. According to the general law of cognition, people first acquire perceptual knowledge and then conceptual knowledge of a phenomenon in its process. The Party's work style is an outward expression of the Party that people can perceive most easily; the people come to know the Party from its words and acts, first having a general impression by means of direct observation and then having a comprehensive understanding with conceptual knowledge.

The Party's work style has a direct bearing on the people's attitude to the Party. The reason that the people have chosen the CPC from among all the parties in China, is that they are affected and moved by the Party's fine style of work, come to know the correctness of the Party' program and line and the fairness of the Party's cause, and personally feel that the Party truly represents their interests. The fine work style of the Party has a cohesive power, unites the masses around the Party, and makes the masses trust, support and follow the Party. But unhealthy tendencies and corruption within the Party result in the masses' distrust in the Party and even great disappointment and wavering.

One of the primary purposes of the improvement of the Party's work style is to strengthen the ties between the Party and the masses. The relationship between a proletarian party and the masses has been always part of the Marxist Theory of Party Building. Macroscopically, the issue of the Party's work style is an issue of the relationship between the Party and the masses. Marxist Party stresses the improvement of its work style, so as to preserve its nature as the vanguard of the working class and maintain close ties with the masses.

After reaching a certain consensus in theoretical circles, the CPC had issued the document on "Decision of the Central Committee of the CPC on Strengthening and Improving the Party's Style of Work" at the Sixth Plenary Session of the 15th Central Committee in 2001, pointing out: "The core of strengthening and improving the Party's style of work is to maintain flesh-and-blood ties with the masses."[1] I think this was a precise summary of the essence of the Party's work style.

7.1.4 Rules Governing the Improvement of the Party's Work Style

Like all other systems, the Party's work style also has certain rules governing its development. From the 80-plus-year history of the Party, I can

[1] The Party Literature Research Center of the CPC Central Committee, *Selected Important Documents since the 15th National Congress of the Communist Party of China*, Volume 2, p.1998. Beijing: People's Press, 2003.

summarize the following rules.

First, the Party's work style is closely connected with its political line. The political line determines the work style, while the style has a direct influence on the formulation and implementation of the political line; the two supplement each other. Therefore, I suggest Marxists should understand and handle the issue of the Party's work style from the perspective of political line.

Second, the Party's work style is closely connected with Party spirit and worldview. The Party spirit is the inherent foundation of the work style, while the style is a natural and outward expression of Party spirit; between the two is the relationship between essence and phenomenon. The worldview is the basis of Party spirit which is the soul of the work style; the worldview determines Party spirit which determines the work style; in origin, the Party's work style is an issue of worldview, an issue of Party spirit. Such inherent and inevitable linkages between the three decide that Marxists should handle the issue of the Party's work style from the perspective of worldview and Party spirit.

Third, social mentality influences the development of the Party's work style. A positive social mentality can promote the consolidation and development of fine style of work, while a negative one can encourage evil trends within the Party. The Party's work style is closely connected with social morality, thus determines that comprehensive measures are necessary.

A correct understanding of the Marxist Theory of the Improvement of the Party's Work Style, including the scientific concept, characteristics and essence of the style and general rules of its development, can help to view and analyze problems of the Party's work style in an objective, comprehensive manner and with a historical approach and as a developing system.

7.2 Why Work Style Is Vital?

The Party's work style is closely connected with its life, and thus occupies a very important position in Party building. In the era of revolutionary wars, the Party's work style had a direct bearing on its survival, development and expansion. After the CPC had assumed power, it is more vital to the survival of the Party and the future of the state. The CPC experienced a dramatic change from an oppressed, encircled and suppressed Marxist party to the ruling party position. Would it degenerate after taking power? This problem is raised for communists around the world and the international communist movement. The 100-plus-year history of the communist movement have proved that this problem could possibly occur. It is not an abstract and theoretical problem, but a critical and practical problem.

After the CPC had assumed power, it has maintained the flesh-and-blood ties with the masses. The Party's nature, purpose and historical tasks require to establish a fine image among the people. In the early period after New China was founded, the Party had launched "the Party consolidation campaign and the movement against three evils (corruption, waste and bureaucracy)", enhancing the improvement of its work style to a height that it influenced the regime consolidation and new successes for the revolutionary cause. The whole Party ranks were called to maintain the fine style of: being modest and prudent, plain living and hard struggle, and were warned against sugar-coated bullets from the bourgeoisie. However, due to imperfect democratic practices of the Party and state and the impact of feudal and bourgeois ideas, unhealthy tendencies, such as divorce from the reality and the masses, subjectivism, bureaucracy and sectarianism, had grown and developed within the Party, which had finally resulted in the big error of the Cultural Revolution. During the Cultural Revolution, the Party's work style and social morality was destroyed while unhealthy tendencies prevailed, weakening the Party's fighting capacity. After the Third Plenary Session of the 11th Central Committee of the Party in 1978, the second generation of the central collective leadership, with Deng Xiaoping at the core, had attached great importance to the improvement of the Party's work style. In November 1980, at the third symposium on "the implementation of the Several Rules of Inner-Party Activities," Chen Yun, then first secretary of the Central

Commission for Discipline Inspection of the Party, had pointed out: "The work style of the ruling party is an issue vital to the survival of the Party. For this reason, we should always concentrate our efforts on the issue of the Party's work style."[1] This conclusion immediately won agreement from other top leaders including Deng Xiaoping and soon became a common view of the whole Party. In June 1981, the CPC had approved an important evaluation document on the history of the CPC titled as: "the Decision on Several Historical Problems of the Party since the Founding of New China" at the Sixth Plenary Session of its 11th Central Committee. This document had also affirmed Chen Yun's conclusion thus the elevated "improvement of the work style" to one of basic tasks of party building. In October 1987, the CPC reiterated this view at its 13th National Congress, and regarded it as a new progress that the Party had made in developing theory of scientific socialism since the Third Plenary Session of the 11th Central Committee. Afterwards, Jiang Zemin, core leader of the third generation, had made an evaluation on the 1989 political turmoil in China and on the facts that some big established parties of the world had collapsed or transformed due to degeneration and corruption: "Corruption is a virus damaging the health of the Party and state organs. If we let down our guard and let it spread, it will destroy our Party, our people's political power, and our cause of socialist modernization."[2] His statement had also increased the awareness on the issue.

I think, to be specific, the improvement of the work style is significant for two reasons.

First, the Party's work style affects the formulation and implementation of its correct line. On the one hand, the Party's line, principles and policies are closely connected with its work style. To lead the socialist modernization drive to success, the Party should first depend on correct line and policies, and second on its fine style of work. A fine style of work is the prerequisite to the formulation of the Party's line, principles and policies. Only with the

---

[1] *Selected Works of Chen Yun* (2ⁿᵈ Chinese edition), Volume 3, p.273. Beijing: People's Press, 1995.

[2] *Selected Works of Jiang Zemin*, Volume 1, p.319.

fine work style, can the Party combine Marxist theories with Chinese realities and work out the line, principles and policies that keep with the objective laws and reflect the interests, wishes and demands of the people. On the other hand, the Party's work style directly influences the implementation of its line, principles and policies. The Party relies on its members and cadres to carry out its correct line, principles and policies, to influence and motivate the people and to turn the line, principles and policies into conscious acts of the masses. History has proven that whether a Party's line, principles and policies are correct or not, determining the work style, which, in turn, has a far-reaching influence on the formulation and implementation of the line, principles and policies.

Second, the style of a Party has a direct bearing on the realization of its leadership. The Party's leadership quality is the fundamental guarantee for the success of the cause of the proletariat. The Party realizes its leadership not by power, position and administrative orders, but by employing its correct line, principles and policies to guide the masses, employing effective ideological and organizational work to unite with the masses, and employing the fine style of work and the exemplary role of Party members to motivate the masses. A bad style of work would weaken the Party's vanguard nature and creativity, art of leadership and governance, and its capability of fighting corruption and guarding against degeneration and risks. According to the *Analects of Confucius*, "If the ruler himself is upright, all will go well even though he does not give orders. But if he himself is not upright, even though he gives orders, they will not be obeyed." In this sense, the Party's leadership is demonstrated in the efforts to carry forward its fine traditions and style of work and give play to the exemplary role of Party members.

Thus we can see that the Party's work style effects the will of the people and the destiny of the Party and state. The improvement of the Party's work styles is an issue of universality in Party building. We, Marxists should understand its position and function from the strategic perspective, and do a good job in this regard.

7.3 The Fine Traditions and Work Style of the Party

The fine traditions and work style of the Party refer to the noble characters, virtues and spirit that the CPC had cultivated and fostered in its long practice of revolution, construction and reform periods. They include **the three major styles**—integrating theory with practice, forging close ties with the masses, practicing criticism and self criticism—and the style of being modest and prudent, plain living and hard struggle. The fine traditions and work style of the Party are determined by its nature and purpose, reflect its essence, characteristics and the principle of Party spirit for Party members, and constitute the mainstream of the Party's style of work. The Party's high prestige among all the ethnic groups of China was established on the basis of its fine traditions and style of work to a great extent. To strengthen and improve the Party's work style, it is natural that the fine traditions and style of the Party should be inherited and carried forward.

7.3.1 The Role of the Chinese Communists

The fine traditions and work style of the Party were not innate or intuitive in the world; they came into being in the Party's practice of revolution, construction and reform as the results of the Party's efforts in integrating Marxism and Leninism with China's realities and absorbing the traditional culture of the Chinese nation with a critical view. Communists have absorbed the two: both Marxist theories and the rich contents of the traditional Chinese culture, like the hard work of several generations of Chinese communists. I believe, the Chinese nation is a nation stressing moral qualities. In ancient China, there were words like *fengsu* (custom), *fengyi* (bearing), *fenghua* (morals and manners) and *fengji* (morals), either referring to some custom coming into being over a long period, or the bearing of a person or style of a group, or reforming and educating others with good characters, or that people act according to the same law. The Chinese people, since old times, had believed in the idea of integrating morality and politics: cultivating oneself, putting your family in order, running the local government well, and bringing peace to the entire country; and upheld that "uprightness comes first among the 100 virtues" (from *Shi Shuo Xin Yu*, or *New Anecdotes of Social Talk*, by Liu Yiqing), and that "a gentleman is ashamed if his word do not match his actions" (from the *Analects of Confucius*); and scrupulously abided by the norms of "self-surrender" and "using virtue and practicing benevolence" (from *Meng Zi*, or *Mencius*). As the inheritors of the advanced culture of the Chinese nation, the Chinese communists have absorbed and made good use of the above cream in their practice, thus brought into being a unique style.

And, Mao Zedong had made the summary of the Party's fine traditions and style of work during the new-democratic revolution period. In April 1945 when the Party was approaching to the final victory of the Anti-Japanese War and seized the opportunity to decide on the future of China, Mao Zedong had summarized the 24-year experience of the Party in his report to the Seventh National Congress, titled "On Coalition Government." He had pointed out: "Armed with Marxist-Leninist theory, the Communist Party of China has brought a new style of work to the Chinese people, a style of work which essentially entails integrating theory with practice, forging close links with the masses and practicing self-criticism."[1] He regarded these three styles as remarkable signs distinguishing the CPC from all the other parties, and asked all the Party members to carry them forward. In March 1949, at the Second Plenary Session of the Seventh Central Committee of the Party on the eve of the victory of the Chinese people's revolution, Mao Zedong had warned the whole Party: "To win countrywide victory is only the first step in a long march of ten thousand *li* (trans. kilometer) The Chinese revolution is great, but the road after the revolution will be longer, the work greater and more arduous. This should be made clear now in the Party. The comrades should be taught to remain modest, prudent and free from arrogance and rashness in their style of work. The comrades should be taught to preserve the style of plain living and hard struggle."[2]

---

[1] *Selected Works of Mao Zedong* (2nd Chinese edition), Volume 3, pp.1093-1094.
[2] *Selected Works of Mao Zedong* (2nd Chinese edition), Volume 4, pp.1438-1439.

7.3.2 Contents of the Fine Traditions and Work Style of the Party

The fine traditions and work style of the Party include several aspects, which I would like to overview below.

First, the style of integrating theory with practice:

The CPC is a proletarian party which was founded according to Marxist theories and style. The integration of theory and practice is a characteristic and trait of the Party and reflects the spirit of it. If Marxism-Leninism, Mao Zedong Thought, Deng Xiaoping Theory and the important thought of Three Represents were not integrated with reality, they would become dead dogmas. To carry forward the style of integrating theory with practice demands that: Marxists should study realistic problems under the guidance of scientific theories and bring into being new theories which conform to reality, and they should test, measure and develop the truth in practice.

Second, the style of maintaining close ties with the masses:

One thing that distinguishes the Party from all the other parties is that it maintains close ties with the broad masses, serves the people wholeheartedly, does not divorce itself from the masses, continuously takes the people's interests into consideration, and is accountable to the people and the leading organs of the Party. To carry forward the style of maintaining close ties with the masses, Marxists should adhere to the Party's mass line as a fundamental line, do all the work for the masses, rely on the masses, and start from the masses and go to the masses.

Third, the style of criticism and self-criticism:

Criticism and self-criticism are two weapons that ensure the healthy development of the Party and at the same time enhance its fighting capacity. Mao Zedong had employed an analogy to explain the issue: "cleaning the house, washing the face and looking into the mirror to examine himself with the method of criticism and self-criticism". To carry forward the style of criticism and self-criticism, Marxists should fight against two wrong tendencies. One is undermining principles and failing to criticize shortcomings, mistakes and bad phenomena within the Party. The other is being simple, rude, subjective, or arbitrary when criticizing others. At present,

I think in China Marxists should concentrate their efforts on opposing the first tendency. To make correct use of the weapons of criticism and self-criticism, people who criticize should say all that they know without reserve, while being realistic and paying attention to the effects of the critic; people who are criticized should correct mistakes if they have made any and guard against them if they have not, listen to others' opinions with an open mind, and be bold enough to correct any shortcoming or mistakes. Criticism and self-criticism are two methods for solving contradictions within the Party and among the people and for realizing democracy, and are good for developing inner-Party democracy and implementing democratic-centralism.

Fourth, the style of remaining modest, prudent and free from arrogance and rashness:

Remaining modest, prudent and free from arrogance and rashness is a true quality of the communists. To carry forward this style, Marxists should adopt a correct attitude towards previous achievements; always remain cautious and conscientious, work diligently, keep forging ahead, and advance with the times; guard against arrogance after several successes, or complacence and conservatism, and instead, be sober-minded, be mindful of potential dangers, not be conceited, never slacken efforts, and stay away from stagnation.

Fifth, the style of plain living and hard struggle:

Plain living and hard struggle is a style of work and life unique to communists. It reflects how the communists blaze new trails with keen determination and never yield in spite of repeated setbacks in order to realize the Party's political program and line. It is a strong spiritual support for the Chinese nation to rely on and develop itself, for the country to advance and progress, and for the Party to flourish. To carry forward the style of plain living and hard struggle, we Marxists should be earnest and down-to-earth, work with utmost concentration, not fear from difficulties and be diligent and thrifty, on the other hand we should criticize unhealthy practices such as anxiety for quick success and instant benefits, love of pleasure, resting on one's laurels, extravagance and waste.

I think, the fine traditions and work style of the CPC make up the spiritual wealth of both: the Party and the Chinese nation, and a valuable tool for the Party to achieve success in future, and an heirloom for the Party, which should be handed down from generation to generation.

7.3.3 New Connotations on the Party's Fine Traditions

The work style of the Marxist party should reflect the characteristic of the times; the fine traditions and work style of the Party are always connected with the theme and spirit of a certain epoch. That is to say, the essence does not change, but the forms of expression change with the change of epochs. In January 1995, Jiang Zemin had delivered a speech at the Fifth Plenary Meeting of the Central Commission for Discipline Inspection of the Party. He had compared the relationship between revolution, construction and reform periods, and their relations with inheriting fine traditions and had also emphasized innovations: "In the long process of revolution and construction, our Party has brought into being and developed a whole set of fine traditions and style of work. They make up our political advantage and the heirloom for us to run the Party and state; we shall never discard them at any time, or we will suffer big setbacks... We should not only inherit and carry on all the fine traditions and style of work of the Party, but also enrich, develop and carry them forward in combination with new practice, thus enabling them to play a better role."[1] Under new historical conditions and in light of new practice, we Marxists should still place the three famous styles and **Two Shoulds** at the core of the Party style, but on the other hand explore and innovate new styles, such as orienting towards the world trends based on national conditions, reforming with keen determination and making great efforts in development, being high-spirited, hardworking and promising, forging ahead and having the courage to make innovations, being rigorous, pragmatic and accountable, working selflessly for the public interest and bearing in mind the overall interests, democracy and equality, unity and harmony, being honest and upright and working hard for the people, observing disciplines

---

[1] Jiang Zemin, *On Party Building*, p.171.

and obeying laws. Thus we could add new connotations to the Party's fine traditions reflecting the spirit of the epoch.

Moreover, we should also explore new ideas and new methods for the education on the Party's fine traditions under the new situation. Naturally, it is quite improbable for the young people of today to have a good grasp of the Party's fine traditions due to the lack of direct personal experience. The old, stereotyped methods can hardly be accepted. We should educate young people on the Party's fine traditions from a more open perspective and with methods closer to their ideas; combine such education with the education for all-round development; combine their educational orientation with policy orientation; advocate positive and healthy mainstream values; and create a fine social environment.

7.4 The Requirement of "Eight Do's and Eight Don'ts"

In September 2001, at the Sixth Plenary Session of the 15th Central Committee, the Party had approved "the Decision of the Central Committee of the Communist Party of China on Strengthening and Improving the Party's Style of Work," the first one of its type adopted at a central meeting in the history of the Party. The Decision had made an in-depth exposition on the significance and urgency of the improvement of the Party's work style and proposed overall arrangements on this work, raising eight requirements of "eight do's and eight don'ts" as follows: (1) emancipate the mind and seek truth from facts; do not stick to old ways and make no progress; (2) combine theory with practice; do not copy mechanically or take to book worship; (3) keep close ties with the people; do not go in for formalism and bureaucracy; (4) adhere to the principle of democratic-centralism; do not act arbitrarily or stay feeble and lax; (5) abide by Party discipline; do not pursue liberalism; (6) be honest and upright; do not abuse power for personal gains; (7) work hard; do not indulge in hedonism; (8) appoint people on their merits; do not resort to malpractice in personnel placement.

The resolution had also made an additional evaluation: "to strengthen and improve the Party's work style, we need to concentrate on solve problems of the styles of: ideology, work, leadership, study and life style." This resolution had generally received a positive response among the Party building scholars.

7.4.1 Bureaucracy, Formalism and Other Unhealthy Tendencies

Contrary to the fine traditions and style of work of the Party, unhealthy tendencies within the Party refer to problems that are bad and of the greatest concern to the people in a certain period and certain scope. To be simple, they are attitudes or behaviors of some Party organizations or members conflicting with the Party's nature and purpose. These tendencies include: appointment of people by favoritism, forming cliques, abuse of power for personal gains, offering or accepting bribes, and demoralization. I think, the masses are most unsatisfied with and resent most with bureaucracy and formalism.

Bureaucracy is generally a style of work and leadership when some Party organizations or cadres become alienated from reality and the masses, do not concern about the people's interests, or give orders instead of making genuine investigations. To be specific, the style expresses itself as arrogance, abuse of power, ossification, sticking to established practice, overstaffing, inefficiency, and irresponsibility, etc. In May 1963, in an essay titled "Oppose Bureaucracy" Zhou Enlai had listed 20 practices of bureaucracy and called it "a political disease which mostly occur in the leading organs."[1] We can see that those practices of bureaucracy that Zhou Enlai criticized still exist today to varying degrees, and have even developed in some aspects.

Formalism refers to a style of work with which some Party organizations or cadres only stress forms instead of practical effects. The style expresses itself as overstatement, empty talk, polite formulations, untrue statements, ambition for great achievements, falsification and exaggeration, lip service, launching vanity projects, waste of money and manpower, etc.

We observe that bureaucracy and formalism severely damage the images

---

[1] *Selected Works of Zhou Enlai*, Volume 2, p.418. Beijing: People's Press, 1984.

of the Party and the government, disturb the implementation of the Party's line, principles and politics, and infringe upon the immediate interests of the masses. Naturally hard efforts are necessary to rectify them.

7.4.2 Improving the Style of Leading Cadres

The key point in the improvement of the Party's work style is to improve the style of leading cadres. To rectify the styles prevalent among the people, we should first rectify the Party's style; to rectify the Party's style, we should first rectify the style of leading cadres, which is of vital importance to the improvement of the Party's work style. Leading cadres have a strong influence on the Party's work style, and it is natural that the people and rank-and-file Party members place high hopes on them. In January 2007, General Secretary Hu Jintao had delivered an important speech at the Seventh Plenary Meeting of the Central Commission for Discipline Inspection of the CPC. In the speech, he had demanded that the Party should intensify the efforts in improving the style of leading cadres in all respects under the new situation. He had advocated a good style from eight aspects: to study hard and put into practice what has been learned; to bear the masses in mind and serve them; to pay real attention to doing solid work and strive for actual effects; to struggle hard and lead a plain living; to take the interests of the whole into account and strictly enforce orders and bans; to develop a democratic style of work and work together in harmony; to use power impartially and perform official duties honestly; to lead a moral, healthy life.

Unhealthy and corrupt practices often take place among leading cadres of the Party. The reasons are as follows. First, leading cadres are at the posts of leadership and have power and influence, which makes it convenient for some corrupt people to abuse power for personal gains. Second, the socialist market economy enables some people to get rich first, and thus some leading cadres can also be eager to become rich overnight. Some brazenly embezzle state money, breaking the law and violating discipline; some trade power for money in economic activities. Third, since China is now in a period of institutional transition, the institutions for supervising and restraining leading cadres are not perfect yet, leaving some loopholes for some people to exploit for personal gains under the cloak of economic development.

How to do a good job in improving the style of leading cadres has become a pressing problem in the improvement of the Party's work style. To solve the problem at the roots, Marxists need to pay attention both to ideological and institutional aspects. The leading cadres should be educated with correct world outlooks on: life, values, power, interests, and status, and should be reminded of the Party's purpose: serving the people and the idea that "power is a test, duty and motive," I think thus their ideological and ethical standards could be improved. Advanced standard rules, mechanisms and institutions are necessary to select and employ cadres and restrain leaders' behaviors, so as to bring into being a powerful supervision and restraint mechanism and thus prevent abuse of power. Leading cadres need good family environment to support them in performing official duties honestly. Some leading cadres have a good style, because their families support them. Some indeed make mistakes, because their spouse, children or relatives go beyond their bounds. For this reason, the education of leading cadres' families is also an important issue.

7.5 Anti-Corruption and the Party

To resolutely fight against and prevent corruption is a serious political struggle that bears on the very subsistence of the Party and state, a major political task for the whole Party members. Marxists should fully understand the longevity and complexity of the issue under the new circumstances, and keep deepening the anti-corruption campaign.

7.5.1 Major Expressions of Corruption

Originally, corruption means decay of a matter, by rot or oxidation. In Party activities and social life, it mainly refers to the behaviors of some Party and state staff who abuse public power for personal gains. In a broad sense, it refers to behaviors of some powerful people in society who break state laws or violate norms of conduct and abuse public power and resources for the interests of individuals or small groups while infringing upon the public interests and the people's interests, such as bad practices in some departments or industries and business bribery. In a narrow sense, it refers to behaviors of some Party members, especially some leading cadres, who break state laws or violate Party discipline and abuse power for unlawful interests of themselves, their families or cliques; such behaviors include the abuse and misuse of power, such as embezzlement, bribery and dereliction of duty.

From the above, we can see that corruption could spread to a wider range than the Party space since it could occur in various spheres of the whole society; and moreover, corruption is more serious compared with unhealthy tendencies; people involved in corruption discard state laws and/ or violate the Party discipline; naturally they should be investigated and punished.

At present, major manifestations of corruption are as follows:

Politically, some Party members take a pragmatic attitude toward the Party's line, principles and policies, or seem approving them in public but oppose them in private spheres, even some express their views—contrary to the Party's decisions—in public sphere. Some Party members are keen on producing and spreading political rumors and spreading political views of liberalism.

In the sphere of economy, embezzlement and bribery are two major demonstrations. Some leading cadres of Party and government organs take advantage of their positions and embezzle state property and trade their power for money. Some organs forget the dividing line between officials and businessmen and confuse the functions of governments with those of enterprises, and exploit loopholes in the Reform process for individual gains. Some judicial organs take bribes and commit illegalities for the benefit of friends. Some staff in the administrative or law-enforcing authorities charge unreasonable fees, arbitrarily force donations arbitrarily or impose arbitrary fines.

Ideologically, wavering in beliefs is its main manifestation of corruption.

Thus some party members doubt or even negate the socialist system, praise all the Western values indiscriminately while overlooking Chinese thoughts and culture without a solid analysis. Some Party members believe in individualism and also worship money.

Organizationally, appointment of people by favoritism prevails. Some leading Party cadres appoint people by personal preferences and relationships, violating the organizational discipline rules. Some try to get their children or relatives promoted or appointed by all means or through influence. Some use their positions to curry favor or even ask for, buy and sell official titles. Some Party members falsify their educational career to get a higher professional title. Some leading cadres provide fake materials to get promoted.

In life, extravagance is a major expression. Some organizations squander public funds by offering expensive banquets, giving presents as souvenirs, cash gifts, securities, travel tickets in China and further to foreign countries. Some departments or organizations hold various kinds of unnecessary celebrations. Some cadres use public money to set up above-standard office buildings, buy imported limousines or decorate cadres' residences. And a very few Party members and cadres become corrupt and degenerate, taking or trafficking drugs, gambling or going whoring.

7.5.2 Root Causes of Corruption

Corruption is a historical phenomenon and in essence is a product of the exploiting system and the exploiting classes. The socialist system under the leadership of the CPC is incompatible with any corruption. But various phenomena of corruption still exist in socialist China; there are many complicated causes, including economical, political, social, historical, ideological and cultural factors.

The first root cause is the influence of remnants of the feudal thought. China has a long history of feudalism, and now still sees the remnants of feudalism and other impacts of the exploiting classes. Some feudal views, such as the "special privilege" mentality, sense of hierarchy and patriarchal concept, are quite deep-rooted in China. New China was established in a semi-colonial and semi-feudal society; but feudal views have not disappeared with the overturn of feudalism and the establishment of the socialist system. Remnants of the feudal thoughts somehow find their ways into political activities of the Party, and their impact on Party members and cadres should not be underestimated. Although the Party has done a lot, it has not yet eliminated all these remnants. Under the new situation of reform and opening-up, the dregs of society, such as some old ideas, conventions and customs, have emerged again; the "special privilege" mentality, sense of hierarchy and nepotism are recently being replaced by abuse of power for personal gains, bureaucracy, appointment of people by favoritism, patriarchal system, abuse of the position for personal privileges, relationship network, etc. which become sources of corruption and naturally they cannot be eradicated in the short run.

The second root cause is the influence of decadent bourgeois ideas and lifestyle. After the Third Plenary Session of the 11th Central Committee of the Party in 1978, China had adopted a basic national policy of Reform and Opening-up, borrowing and utilizing all achievements of modern civilization from other countries in the world, including developed capitalist countries; in this process, decadent capitalist items have got a chance to step into China. In the Reform and Opening-up period, some people cannot withstand the test when practicing the ruling positions: they relax and ignore remolding their world outlook, and forget the Party's purpose of serving the people wholeheartedly; when faced with money and material stuff, they forget their integrity, seek ease and comfort and pursue pleasure. Thus money worship, hedonism and ultra-individualism prevail. These decadent ideas and values work together, challenging and eroding people's minds, and causing chaos in theory and ideology. This is also an important cause of corruption.

The third root cause is the imperfect institutional system. China is now at the primary stage of socialism, and it needs to go through a hard period of institutional transition before an advanced socialist market economic system is established. During the transformation from planned economy to the socialist market economy, both the drawbacks of the old system and the imperfect and incomplete components of the new system manifest themselves in loopholes and the old and the new system conflict each other and cause some cracks to pass through and also during the transformation work naturally many things cannot be controlled as desired and there occurs some weak points; thus gives an opportunity for some speculators and corrupt elements.

For example, in the early stage of market economy, the government had practiced a double-track system for pricing (real cost prices of the new and the subsidized prices of the old system were practiced side by side); as a result, "official-run business" and "bureaucrat speculators" had become popular. In this transitional period cadres had profited a lot by trading the power of approving prices and allocating purchase quotas. After the transition the natural innate contradictions of market economy manifest themselves, such as the contradiction between the drive of individual enterprise interest and care for public interest of the majority, that between the exchange value and use value of commodities and that between commodity supply and demand. All these contradictions foster a profiteering attitude, money worship and fetishism and a strong desire for material stuff in some people, which are the economic causes of corruption.

The fourth root cause is a relaxation in ideological and political work and ethical and cultural development. In recent years, some Party members believe that it is a "pragmatic necessity" to concentrate on economic development while it is "about long term principles" to promote ideological and political, cultural and ethical progress; thereafter, they separate the linkages between the two and hold a wrong view that the efforts devoted to economy will promote the development of productive forces alone, while the efforts in ideological and political, cultural and ethical work have nothing to do with the development of productive forces. They neglect the dynamic interactive effect of the superstructure on economic base of the society. I think they concentrate on advancing material progress while neglecting ideological and cultural progress and this is a halfway and partial implementation of the principle of "addressing both issues and attaching sufficient importance to both" which was agreed on when the reforms were started. For some time, more importance was attached to material benefits instead of ideals, taking instead of giving, rights instead of obligations, enjoyment of ease and comfort instead of hard struggle, and to personal feelings instead of principles. A weak ideological and political work in the Party have certainly resulted in a lower ideological motivation and mental confusion among some Party members, thus they have become indiscriminate and lost their resistance capacity to decadent ideas.

The fifth root cause is the imperfect supervision mechanisms in the Party. At present, the Party adopts a supervision system under the leadership of Party committees at the same level. Although this system plays an important role and helps the discipline inspection commissions to fulfill their supervision functions and improve the Party's work style, there are still drawbacks in this system: the Party's supervision organs lack due authoritativeness. Under the present supervision system, a discipline inspection organ has to face the risk of getting the sack when supervising the Party committee at the same level and its members, particularly when dealing with the major leading cadres. Moreover, some supervision rules are only principles without detailed stipulations for enforcement, and cannot be concretely carried out in supervision; the higher position the cadre or organ is, the harder it is to supervise them.

The sixth root case is insufficient punishment of corrupt individuals. A severe punishment according to laws is an important measure for curbing and eradicating corruption. In recent years, the Party has dealt with many cases relating to corruptions; but in general, the efforts are not sufficient, and some leading cadres have even protected corrupt elements.

In summary, the reasons why corruption has spread at the current stage are complicated, covering objective and subjective reasons, historical and realistic ones, and institutional and personal ones. Marxist approach is necessary to analyze the reasons and try to find effective ways to prevent corruption.

7.5.3 Serious Impacts of Corruption

The spread of corruption erodes the Party's body, undermines its reputation, damages its relationship with the masses, hinders economic development, and affects social stability, shaking the foundation of the Party's governance.

First, corruption damages the Party's relationship with the masses, shaking the basis of the state regime. In the history, regime changes have emerged one after another; the most fundamental factor is the support of the people: with the support of the people, one can obtain state power, while without it, one will lose power. The Party had assumed power with the support of the people and rules the country with the support of the people; the flesh-and-blood ties with the people are the source of our Party's power. Corruption has the strongest "centrifugal force" and is the most unpopular among the people. It destroys the Party's relationship with the masses and hurt the people's feelings, eroding the foundation of the socialist regime. The spread of corruption also provides some Western countries with a leverage to westernize and disunite the country. Hostile forces at home and abroad make a big hue and publicity work about corruption in China; their vicious intentions are to exaggerate corruption of a few people into corruption of the Party, then totally repudiate the Party, win the mass support, and finally push for "peaceful evolution" from socialism back to capitalism.

Second, corruption obstructs the progress of the Reform policy, and affects economic development and social stability. Corruption destroys social productive forces, affects the macro-deployment of resources, results in the loss of state-owned assets, hinders normal economic operations, and widens the wealth gap in the society. The subjects of corruption adopt a power-seek-rent method and easily obtain a large amount of wealth, virtually depriving other people of the opportunity to acquire wealth by honest work and fair competition. As a result, a few corrupt individuals pocket the benefits of the reform while the broad masses are not able to share them, which, in turn, would provoke strong resentment among the public and destroy social stability.

Third, corruption causes moral decline and corrupts social values. Morality is a part of cultural values and foundation of social psychology cohering with a certain social structure and legitimates a social formation; thus it is an important means of safeguarding social stability. Individually, corruption is actually a moral degradation. It means that some leading cadres do not practice basic professional and social ethics, and are unqualified for leadership posts. These people's conducts—lacking ideals, mental confusion, imbalanced psychological behaviors, and even putting profit above everything and seek quick success and instant benefits—generate bad impacts on the public moral values and behaviors.

Finally, corruption is an unlawful act and degrades the society into a state of disorder. Over the three decades of Reform and Opening-up policy, China has made major progress in developing a socialist judicial system. However, the legislation still lags behind the actual social life, and moreover, there are still some spheres without sufficient legislation which could strictly enforce the law or prosecute unlawful acts. The corruption in civil service sphere and judicature is the severest corruption and a major reason for the spread of other kinds of corruption. As long as corruption exists, there will be no true equality before the laws and no true fairness and justice, let alone a new social, political and economic order.

7.5.4 Punishing and Preventing Corruption

Since the Third Plenary Session of the 11th Central Committee in 1978, the Party has summarized the experience and lessons of the anti-corruption campaign since the founding of New China, and worked hard in practice to explore effective ways of punishing and preventing corruption in the light of the characteristics of the new period. It has gradually established a new approach to fighting corruption, that is, to address both symptoms and root causes and take more comprehensive measures, to be prepared for protracted combat while on the other side try to achieve successes in each stage of the long process. This new gradual approach aims to mobilize the masses to create a positive public atmosphere and avoids the old practice of employing revolutionary mass movements, aims to rely on education and more on the legal system and supervision. Of course this does not mean old methods were unnecessary and will not be necessary in the future. As formulated in the report to the 16th National Congress of the Party: "strengthen education, develop democracy, improve the legal system, tighten supervision, make institutional innovation and incorporate anti-corruption in all our major policies and measures so as to prevent and tackle corruption at its source" is a realistic policy. I think this new approach is a summary of the Party's experience gained in the fight against corruption after assuming power and considering the new conditions of the Reform and Opening-up period. At present, I think it is necessary to concentrate on the following aspects to deepen the anti-corruption campaign:

First, to focus on the central task of economic development is the basis in progressing to contend with corruption. At the present, anti-corruption efforts are carried under the circumstances in which the focus of the Party and state work has been shifted from class struggles to socialist modernization. Therefore, naturally the importance of the anti-corruption efforts should be treated as a part at the overall level of socialist modernization; i.e. building socialism with Chinese characteristics. Over the three decades of reform and opening-up, the political leaders of the party have also warned that it would not be correct to depart from the central task of economic development when practicing anti-corruption efforts or lead them as a pure, independent political movement beyond economic development. I think, to combat the corruption phenomena with focus on economic development, we also need to place this issue in an important position since it effects the overall situation: neither interrupt economic development because of punishing corruption, nor let corruption freely spreading under the pretext of economic development.

Second, there should be a consensus and a higher confidence in the fight against corruption. During the transition to socialist market economy, the top leaders had resolutely demanded to fight against corruption and intensify the fight, showing their will and self-confidence. But some Party members, even leading cadres, do not have a clear understanding of its significance, lack confidence and are full of doubts, thus cannot perform against corruption in their sphere of duties. If such attitudes are not reversed, it will surely affect the advancement of the fight.

Third, the legal system should be perfected and efforts against corruption should be more standardized and law-based. Using judicial means to restrain Party and state organs and their staff is a radical cure for abuse of power and other criminal activities. The imperfect legal system is an important reason why corruption spreads and cannot be eradicated. To improve the legal system, legislation should be perfected, particularly in the sectors most likely to nurture corruption. Moreover, we need to ensure strict law enforcement and resolutely punish corruption. For exposed cases about corruption, especially major and key ones, a thorough investigation should be applied and those giving protection to the suspect and obstructing the case should be also seriously punished. To ensure strict law enforcement, also a contingent of highly qualified judicial personnel should be educated to institutionally ensure that the judicial and procuratorial organs are in a position to exercise adjudicative and procuratorial powers independently and impartially according to law.

Fourth, supervision institutions and the power restraint mechanism should be strengthened. Unrestrained power will certainly cause corruption; strengthening supervision is the key to preventing abuse of power. The fundamental way of preventing and punishing corruption is to restrain the power of cadres such as: establishing a checks and balances system, tour system, job rotation system and power decentralization system. Moreover, we should set up a restraint mechanism to supervise the process of using power, and formulate explicit and concrete procedures for using power. The public should be well informed in the whole process of fighting against corruption; results should be more open and transparent by promoting more people to supervise the process. I think, at present, to improve supervision institutionalization, the emphasis should be put on an advanced coordination between the supervision subjects: the Party, people's congresses, special government organs (Hong Kong, Macao); judicial organs, the Chinese

People's Political Consultative Conference and the non-Communist Parties. I also advocate promoting social supervision including media supervision and supervision by public opinion.

Fifth, we should be strict with Party members and address both symptoms and root causes of corruption. Addressing symptoms and root causes of corruption are two aspects of the fight against corruption, complementing and promoting each other. Addressing symptoms is to punish various behaviors of corruption and check rampant activities of corrupt individuals or entities. If they are punished, the people's trust and their confidence will be raised, creating a prerequisite to permanently cure corruption. Corruption is a chronic and stubborn disease and recurs again and again. Addressing root causes is to prevent and control corruption from its source; with this approach we can consolidate present achievements and progress to a permanent solutions. In January 2005, the Central Committee has released a document titled: "the Outline for Establishing and Improving a System for Preventing and Controlling Corruption with Emphasis on Education, Institutions and Supervision." This document was highly appreciated by scholars and the general public. At present, in line with this document anti-corruption efforts have become more vigorous, and suggested institutions are being established.

Sixth, I think to combat corruption, we should strategically get prepared for a protracted struggle, while tactically trying to achieve success in each stage. The causes of corruption are very complicated and involve wide and many spheres; thus it is difficult to achieve a total solution in the short run. In the early period of reform and opening-up, the Party had set a policy: "to achieve a fundamental turn for bettering a Party style, we need five years," which demonstrated the Party's determination, but thing have proved that it needs more time and the struggle is more complex. We should get prepared for a protracted struggle and make unremitting efforts. However, we should also have a sense of urgency and take effective measures to tackle corruption in each period based on its characteristics. I suggest that the two aspects above should be clearer.

In 1992, after the 14th National Congress of the Party, an important reform and campaign was implemented, which prohibited army troops, armed police and judicial and public security organs from engaging in business. Also group of major unhealthy cases were investigated and handled; economic entities run and administered by central Party and government organs were separated from these organs; fines and confiscation were managed in accordance with the principle of separating revenues from expenditures; judicial and public security personnel had voluntarily accepted collective education and rectification; also a joint action and special struggle against smuggling were carried out. I think this was a tactical success. After the 16th National Congress, the Central Committee has paid more attention to the fight against corruption, intensified the efforts to investigate and handle relevant cases, and earnestly carried out several special operations and another tactical success was achieved.

At present, we need to intensify the efforts in investigating and handling corruption-related cases. The emphasis should be put on cases involving leading Party and government organs, leading cadres and judicial organs, administrative and law-enforcing organs, management organs of economy and their staff. Special attention should be paid to cases about abuse of power for personal gains, such as embezzlement and bribery, and defalcation of public funds for speculating in the stock market or real estate industry; cases involving cadres from Party and government organs who take part in smuggling or support, connive at and even cover up for the manufacturing and sales of fake and forged commodities; and cases about dereliction of duty. We should handle both those cases involving a large number of individuals and a large amount of money and cases involving high-ranking cadres who have top power and a big influence.

Seventh, we should strengthen the Party's leadership, and depend on the leadership structures and their working mechanisms to fight against corruption. This concept was also raised at 15th National Congress of the Party: "We shall resolutely check corruption depending on Party committees exercising unified leadership, Party and government organs exerting concerted efforts, discipline inspection commissions organizing and coordinating this work, and other departments assuming their respective responsibilities, should rely on the support and participation of the masses." This was actually an emphasis on the leadership structures and on their working mechanisms. Leading cadres at all levels should fulfill two responsibilities: undertake the work of improving the Party's work style and building clean government in their sphere of jurisdiction; and on the other side fight against corruption together with economic development, cultural and ideological promotion and other work.

Eighth, I think, international exchange and cooperation on this issue is important and experience of foreign countries should be studied. At present, corruption has spread all over the world and is transnational and international. Governments of all countries are intensifying the fight against corruption domestically, while seeking international cooperation. Following this world trend, the CPC and the Chinese government should take part and make more contributions. On the one hand, we should learn from successful experience of other countries and regions, such as the civil service system of Singapore, the properties declaration system of the United States and the supervision system of Cuba on its party members and cadres. The UN Convention against Corruption, adopted on October 31, 2003 at the 58th UN General Assembly and came into effect on December 14, 2005, is the first formal and inclusive international document against corruption. In recent years, the discipline inspection, supervision and judicial organs have actively conducted international exchange and cooperation in this regard; they have established relations with more than 70 countries and regions, established stable cooperative channels with more than 30 countries and regions, and signed more than 50 treaties of judicial assistance, extradite and transferring extradited people with more than 40 countries and regions, and are discussing with some countries about agreements on the cooperation against corruption. China has held the Seventh International Anti-Corruption Conference, the Seventh Meeting of Asian Ombudsman Association, and the Fifth Regional Anti-Corruption Conference for Asia and the Pacific. It has also made major progress in working with the international community to arrest corrupt officials fleeing into China. China has arrested 596 suspects at large in 2003 and 614 in 2004. I think there is still much room to progress in international cooperation against corruption.

In summary, the deep-seated historical origins and present environment of corruption decide that the fight against corruption is a long, arduous and complicated process, and the whole task cannot be accomplished just in one stroke. The fight should be a systematic project, addressing both symptoms and root causes, initiating comprehensive measures and carrying the current work vigorously and energetically.

Institutional Improvement of the Party

As a general accepted definition by Party building scholars, an institution is a series of regulations or norms which influences human activity. And institutional improvement covers all aspects of Party building; it is a conveyer and an important guarantee of Party building. As a major theoretical and practical issue, the institutional improvement is playing a more and more important role in the building of the CPC. Institutional improvement is an inevitable need for the Party to establish and improve a permanent mechanism for preserving its vanguard nature and also to be strict with its members.

8.1 Institutions: Maturity of the Marxist Party

Every society, organization or party should have institutions. Institutions guarantee the orderly operation of society and social fairness and justice. I think they are of special significance for a ruling party.

8.1.1 Concept and Function of Institutions

The Chinese word *"zhidu"* had also appeared in ancient Chinese books. Traditionally, it refers to system, rules, regulations or charters that restrain people's acts. *The Contemporary Chinese Dictionary* lists two explanations: first, system, institution, rules or regulations that all the people should observe, such as work rules and regulations, and fiscal system; second, system or institution formed under certain historical conditions in the political, economic and cultural fields, such as socialist system or patriarchal clan system of feudalism.[1] The word covers a wide range. From the perspective of state and society, it may refer to the political or economic system of a country; but specifically, it may include the party system, system of representation, legislative system, judicial system, administrative system, election system, system of public finance, income distribution system, and social security system. The people's congress system, the system of multi-party cooperation and political consultation under the leadership of the CPC, and the regional ethnic autonomy system of China are all political institutions.

Institutions can bind, guide, encourage and punish people. A good institutional design usually can regulate behaviors, spread goodness and restrain evil. *The Convict Ships*, written by British historian Charles Bateson, recorded how British businessmen transported convicts to Australia from the 18th to 19th century. At first, the British government paid on the number of convicts embarking at each port. To earn more money, masters of private ships packed every ship with as many convicts as possible. The cramped space, poor nutrition and sanitary conditions resulted in a rather high death rate, which not only caused huge economic losses, but also aroused strong social criticism. How was this problem solved? The British government did

---

[1] Institute of Linguistics under Chinese Academy of Social Sciences, The 2002 Enlarged Edition of *The Contemporary Chinese Dictionary*, p.1622. Beijing: Commercial Press, 2002.

not give moral lessons to ask ship masters to be kind, nor did it send officials to supervise them; it worked out a simple and operable system, that is, the government paid ship masters not on the number of convicts embarking, but on the number of convicts disembarking in Australia. To ensure that convicts could survive the long life afloat, ship masters dared not to mistreat convicts any more. This system produced quick results as soon as it was put into effect. In 1793, three convict ships arrived in Australia, and it was the first time that the government paid on the number of convicts disembarking. Among 422 convicts on board, only one had died. Later the system was further developed, and bonus was paid if the convicts were in good health and no one died. Therefore, the death rate dropped to 1 to 1.5 percent. In fact the character of the ship masters had not changed, they were greedy as before and the government had achieved something without enforcing a special law or employing supervision. What the government did was to change the system of payment, and then the problem was solved. This example tells us that a bad institution can make a good person do evil while a good institution can make a bad person do good.

8.1.2 Institutional Improvement as a Mark of Maturity

The Party's institutions refer to a whole set of systems, regulations, rules and procedures established according to the Constitution of the Party, with democratic-centralism as the foundation and core. Institutional improvement is an indispensable component of Party building.

Looking back on the 80-plus years since its founding, we can find that the Party had gone through several twists and turns in terms of institutional improvement. After the Party was founded, the major task was to draw out a Party constitution and carry it out; there were no good institutions that the Party can adopt. In this period, several big errors took place within the Party, including Chen Duxiu's rightist line, Qu Qiubai and Li Lisan's leftist errors, Wang Ming's leftist and then rightist errors. There were various reasons for such big errors. The Party was still not mature enough in polities, but imperfect and incomplete institutional structure was also important.

The CPC's institutional improvement in its true sense had started after the Zunyi Conference. In September 1938, the Political Bureau of the CPC Central Committee decided to set up a central working organ for drafting rules, and Liu Shaoqi and a few other were responsible for drafting three inner-party regulations: The decision on the work rules and disciplines for the Central Committee; the decision on the work rules and disciplines for Party organizations and cadres at all levels; and the decision on interim organizations of Party committees at all levels. In November 1938, Liu Shaoqi had delivered the report on these three documents at the Sixth Plenary Session of the Sixth Central Committee of the Party, which were all adopted at this session. From then on, the Party's leadership and working systems, work rules and disciplines were officially established. In September 1942, the Political Bureau of the CPC Central Committee had issued "the Decision of the Central Committee of the Communist Party of China on Unifying the Party's Leadership in Anti-Japanese Base Areas and on Adjusting Relations among Organizations." During the War of Liberation (1945-1949), Mao Zedong had drafted the documents "On Setting up a System of Reports"; "On Strengthening the Party Committee System"; "Methods of Work Committees" and other documents, and had given giving explicit stipulations on the Party's style and methods of leadership. These were the Party's efforts in institutional improvement before assuming power.

After the CPC became the ruling party of China, it had adopted the old institutions from the years of revolutionary wars. After the three transformations were completed, the problems of old institutions unsuitable for Party building gradually came to the surface. Although the CPC paid some attention to its institutional improvement at the Eighth National Congress in 1956, it could not be able to reach a consensus within the Party, thus could not pay sufficient attention or take effective measures. In addition, hot political movements domestically and internationally had interrupted the Party's institutional improvement in theory and in practice. Consequently, the Party had strayed from democratic-centralism. Before the end of the Cultural Revolution, the Party had not been able to solve the problems in its leadership, organizational and working systems and it even discarded those systems that had been proven effective in the past. I think these were all bitter lessons of the Party building.

It was Deng Xiaoping who put the Party's institutional improvement at a very important position and attached great importance to it. In August 1980, he summarized the lessons of the Cultural Revolution in his article "On the Reform of the System of Party and State Leadership": "It is true that the errors we made in the past were partly attributable to the way of thinking and style of work of some leaders. But they were even more attributable to the problems in our organizational and working systems. If these systems are sound, they can place restraints on the actions of bad people; if they are unsound; they may hamper the efforts of good people or indeed, even in certain cases, may push them in the wrong direction. Even so great a man as Comrade Mao Zedong was influenced to a serious degree by certain unsound systems and institutions in the Party, which resulted in grave misfortunes for the Party, the state and himself.... There is a most profound lesson to be learned from this. I do not mean that the individuals concerned should not bear their share of responsibility in the mistakes, but rather I mean that the problems in the leadership and organizational **systems** are more fundamental, widespread and long-lasting, and that they have a greater effect on the overall interests of our country. This is a question that has a close bearing on whether our Party and state will change its political color; therefore the entire Party should pay attention to this issue."[1] He had thus given incisive exposition on the importance of institutional improvement.

I think if we make a comprehensive survey of the history of international communist movements, we will find out that the biggest lesson for the building of the ruling party in socialist countries is the lack of institutions. The Communist Party of the Soviet Union set up a highly centralized leadership system when Stalin was in power, besides there was a life tenure tradition in leading posts and individual decisions could be given on major problems. In 1943 a document of the CPC had suggested that the top leader

[1] *Selected Works of Deng Xiaoping* (2nd edition), Volume 2, p.333.

had the final say on every problem, initiating an institutional loophole for Mao Zedong's mistake in his later years. Deng Xiaoping believed that the problems in the Party and state activities, such as bureaucracy, patriarchal methods and privileges of various kinds, were partly attributable to the way of thinking and style of work of some leaders, but were more attributable to the problems in the organizational and working systems itself. He had pointed out: "Some serious problems which appeared in the past may arise again if the defects in our present systems are not eliminated. Only when these defects are resolutely removed through planned, systematic, and thorough reforms, will the people trust our leadership, our Party and socialism. Then our cause will truly have a future of boundless promise."[1] At the 13th National Congress, the CPC had solemnly advocated a new approach "to progress in the new road of Party building by relying on reform and institutional improvement rather than political movements."[2]

8.1.3 Strengthening Institutional Improvement

In his report to the 15th National Congress of the Party, Jiang Zemin had made an interesting comment: "education is the basis, the legal system is the guarantee, and supervision is the key." The tasks of the Party and the current situation of its institutional improvement work show that almost all the problems of Party building have something to do with imperfect institutions. For example, in terms of decision making, the thoughts on the rule of men formed during several thousand years under the feudal, autocratic rule can hardly be eradicated in a short time; these thoughts often have negative impacts on some cadres, who make decisions by power or personal will, instead of caring for the laws and regulations. Some cadres are used to decide things by racking their brains, and some put their personal opinions above Party organizations. Consequently, the Party work becomes subjective, random, disorderly and passive, and sometimes even a high price is paid for

---

[1] *Selected Works of Deng Xiaoping* (2nd edition), Volume 2, p.333.

[2] The Party Literature Research Center of the CPC Central Committee, *Selected Important Documents since the 13th National Congress of the Communist Party of China*, Volume 1, p.54.

that. To change such a situation, I think the remnants of old thoughts on the rule of men should be rooted out and the Party should set up and improve a sound decision-making system to institutionally ensure democratic and scientific decision making and avoid unnecessary mistakes. Here is another example. In the management of Party membership, some old ways of management are no more applicable under the new circumstances when Party members are more independent and their value orientation and behaviors are diversified, because these old ways usually neglect the evil qualities of humanity or emphasize self-discipline but neglect discipline by others, placing social relationship and interpersonal trust above institutions and discipline. As a result, violations of Party discipline and regulations or even state laws can occur one after another. Therefore, to strictly educate, manage and supervise Party members, there should be a correspondent system that is scientific and conforms to the Party's vanguard nature and the new socialist economy to keep a tight rein on Party members. Another example is about the improvement of the Party's work style and the building of clean government. Currently, many problems have been exposed, showing that there are too many institutional loopholes in those spheres. The three systems for leading cadres at county and department level and above—"income declaration system, gift registration system and reporting system on major matters"— have become a mere formality or not widespread. Thus there is a lack of sufficient evidence in determining some leading cadres' income and property. In spite of repeated prohibitions, unhealthy tendencies and corruption in the fields of land expropriation, construction work, medical care and health, and education fee, particularly business bribery, secret departmental coffer, unauthorized use of funds that violate the financial discipline still continue to exist. The reason is that institutions still have loopholes which are the breeding ground for corruption. Only by intensifying the efforts in institutional improvement, corruption could be reduced and prevented from the root and to the possible maximum extent.

I think there are some conspicuous problems now in the Party's institutional improvement: the attention paid is not sufficient, and the sense of institutions among Party members is not strong enough; some institutions are too general or broad and do not have enough details for implementation; institutions are not carried out to full extent, and the investigation and punishment of acts in violation of institutions are not intense enough. Consequently, there is no institution to observe or there are institutions but they are not observed, weakening the authoritativeness and positive effects of institutions.

The socialist market economy and the social transformation need a compatible legal system, demand further development of the legal system, and thus require further improvement in the Party's institutionalization. Therefore, strengthening institutional improvement is necessary for the Party to adapt to social transformation, develop its initiative to meet challenges, enhance its art of leadership and governance and increase its capability of fighting against corruption and guarding against degeneration and risks, as well as a fundamental guarantee for the Party to be strict with its members. In 2005, particularly after the experience accumulated in the campaign to educate Party members to preserve their vanguard nature, establishing a permanent mechanism was generally proposed for preserving Party members' vanguard nature and also a permanent mechanism for strengthening and improving Party building was emphasized. At the Sixth Plenary Meeting of Central Commission for Discipline Inspection held in January 2006, Hu Jintao had also underlined the Party's institutional improvement with the Constitution of the Communist Party of China at the core and demanded a constant enhancement on the quality and level of the institutional improvement.

8.2 Characteristics, Functions and Types of the Institutions

The institutions of a Marxist Party are the sum total of all the norms of conduct that Party members and organizations at all levels should observe. These institutions have their own characteristics and functions and can been categorized into several types.

8.2.1 Characteristics of Marxist Party Institutions

I think the institutions of a Marxist Party have four characteristics.

First, they are highly authoritative. The institutions of the Party reflect its general will; they are formulated by Party organs of power or authorized organs through certain strict procedures. Thus naturally these institutions should be highly authoritative. Compared with ideological education, institutions are more rigid.

Second, they are universally applicable. When formulated, the institutions of the Party become rules that all should observe and are binding upon Party organizations at all levels and all Party members. Within the Party's institutional framework, all Party organizations and members enjoy the same rights and fulfill the same duties. Any individual or organization that violates the institutions should be investigated and dealt with.

Third, they are relatively stable. The institutions of the Party are rules that are relatively stable in a given period or rather a long time, and no member shall change them at random. Even when the objective circumstances change and it is necessary to revise or improve the institutions, this change should be done by certain organs through certain procedures. These institutions should be not changed whenever the leadership changes, or whenever the leaders change their views or shift the focus of their attention. Therefore, the institutions of the Party should be more stable and more reliable than the democratic work style and experience of individual leaders.

Fourth, they are comprehensive and systematic. In terms of the relationship between institutional improvement and other aspects of Party building, the former is embodied in the latter ones, while the former is the guarantee for the latter ones. For example, to strengthen the Party's ideological and theoretical building, Marxists should improve the system of theoretical study; to develop inner-party democracy, the system of inner-party supervision should be improved; to strengthen the pool of qualified cadres, the cadre and personnel system should be improved; to strengthen the primary Party organizations, the system of activities for primary Party organizations should be improved; to improve the Party's style of work, the system that guarantees cadres are clean, honest and self-disciplined should be improved; to improve the Party's style of work and building clean government, the leadership responsibility system should be implemented. The institutional improvement covers every aspect of Party building, every sector of Party activities, and effects the whole parts of the Party. To a certain extent, it affects the overall situation and can propel Party building from all aspects. These institutions themselves are closely related to each other, forming an organic system.

8.2.2 Functions of Marxist Party Institutions

With the above characteristics, the institutions of the Party have particular functions which other tools do not possess of. To be specific, they have three functions.

First, the restraining function: Under a framework made up of various systems and mechanisms, the Party's institutions restrain every sector and every member of the Party under effective supervision and ensure normal, healthy and orderly life and work of the Party. In this way, they can effectively prevent and rectify all behaviors violating Party rules.

Second, protection function: As a series of positive, concrete systems and mechanisms, the Party's institutions protect Party members' democratic rights from being infringed and thus give full scope to Party members' initiative and creativity; thus they ensure that the Party's leadership and governance operations proceed smoothly and all the Party work progresses effectively.

Third, coordinating function: The Party's institutions help to define the relations between different aspects of the Party and thus enable correct handling of various contradictions within the Party, promoting a more harmonious inner-party relation. In this way, they make the whole Party unite in ideology and action and work hard to realize its tasks.

8.2.3 Types of Marxist Party Institutions

The institutions of the Party are diverse and can be divided into different types by different criteria.

In terms of the level of their function, there are basic and concrete institutions. Basic institutions refer to those playing a basic role in activities within the Party. Democratic-centralism is the basic organizational system and leadership system of the Marxist party, a fundamental system for activities within and outside the Party, and is the foundation and core of all the institutions of the Party. Concrete institutions refer to those playing a role in a certain spheres of activities within and outside the Party, such as the system of collective leadership, system of cadre selection and appointment, system for guaranteeing Party members' rights, system for managing Party members—those part of the floating population, system for maintaining close ties between Party members and the masses.

In terms of forms of their function, there are substantial and procedural institutions. Substantial institutions refer to those providing stipulations on the functions and powers, rights and obligations of the leading organs, organizations—including their members—at all levels. The constitution of the Party is an example. It provides stipulations on the functions and powers of the National Congress, Central Committee, Political Bureau of the Central Committee and its Standing Committee. Procedural institutions are those imposing the leading organs, organizations and their members of the Party—at all levels—how to perform their functions and duties and how to exercise their powers. Examples are the decision-making procedure and the election procedure.

In terms of the content, there are organizational, leadership, working, activity and supervision systems. The organizational system refers to organizational rules that Party organizations and members should follow in activities, including democratic-centralism, the cadre system, system for recruiting new members, system for educating and managing Party members, and system of activities at primary Party organization. The leadership system refers to rules that the leading organs and department of the Party should follow when exercising the Party's leadership, including the decision making rules of Party committees, working rules between Party committees and their functional departments, and rules governing the relations between Party committees and the government organs, armed forces and mass organizations. The working system refers to rules about the routine work of the Party, including the working methods and procedures of Party committees, their standing committees and functional departments. The activity system refers to rules of activities within the Party, including the system of political activities within the Party, system of democratic meetings for Party members and leading cadres, and system of regular activities for Party members. The supervision system refers to rules governing the supervision within and outside the Party, supervision system also includes: the system of collective leadership with individual responsibility, information sharing and reporting system on important matters, system under which leading cadres report in various ways on their work and their efforts to perform their duties honestly, system of persuasion and admonition, and system of supervision by public opinion.

Above I have tried to give a rough and relative categorization; naturally some functions are overlapped or interwoven, and sometimes it is hard to draw a clear boundary. Nevertheless such a categorization can help to understand the characteristics and functions of and relations among the Party's institutions and employ them efficiently.

8.3 Several Critical Relationships in Institutional Improvement

The Marxist Party's institutional improvement is a systematic project, involving every aspect of Party building. Therefore, the following relationships should be carefully studied.

8.3.1 Relationship between the Concrete and the Whole

Every institution is concrete, while connected with others, forms an organic complete structure. In this whole structure, different institutions supplement each other and promote each other, leaving no gap or loophole while on the other side causing few overlaps, and giving play to both the role of every individual institution and the composite function of the structure. Thus we need to plan and coordinate the institutional improvement efforts in an all-round way, thus ensure that basic and concrete institutions, substantial and procedural institutions supplement and match with each other, making the institutional structure more systematic.

8.3.2 Relationship between the Formulation and Application of Institutions

When formulating an institution, we should proceed from the reality, take into consideration all the subjective and objective conditions, make an in-depth research on the characteristics and laws of Party building under the new socialist economy, and work hard to make the institution more scientific and workable. As long as an institution is formulated, it is serious and we should resolutely implement it without relaxation. If an institution is isolated from current conditions—social, economic and political development; departs from the reality of Party building or is not understood or accepted by the majority of the Party membership, it can hardly find its place in the society or be implemented well. If an institution is good, but its implementation is interrupted by some man-induced factor, then this institution is not serious and cannot play a practical role. Therefore, the formulation and application of institutions are two aspects supplementing to each other; thus we should particularly overcome any tendency of neglecting the application. Moreover, we should do a good job in routine examination, intensify the efforts in investigating and handling violations of institutions, be strict in enforcing orders and bans, so as to safeguard the authoritativeness of the Party's institutions and make them norms of conduct for the whole Party.

8.3.3 Relationship between Ideological Education and Institutional Improvement

Both ideological education and institutional improvement are indispensable components of Party building; the two are closely connected and promote each other. Through ideological education the Party employs various educational ways to enhance the ideological and ethical standards and strengthen Party members' sense of Party spirit, so as to bring into play their initiative and creativity. Through institutional improvement the Party institutionalizes the traditions, rules and customs formed over the years and use such institutions to restrict its members. We should put equal stress on the two and never overemphasize one at the expense of the other. The reason is: every institution should be formulated and implemented by men; only by strengthening the education of Party members, particularly leading cadres on institutions, democracy and the legal system and making them more conscientious in acting according to institutions, can the Party have an ideological foundation for its institutional improvement. On the other hand, the achievements of ideological education are expressed in institutional improvement; thus only by strengthening institutional improvement, can we secure and make more achievements in ideological education.

8.3.4 Relationship between Inheritance and Innovation

The Party should strengthen the institutional improvement with a spirit of reform and a spirit of advancing with the times; should summarize its successful experiences while drawing on good methods of foreign countries; protect effective institutions and make bold innovations, repealing inapplicable institutions and formulating new, operable ones, particularly making those successful methods that have been proven and tested in practice into laws and regulations. In recent years, the Party has made significant progress in institutional improvement. By reforming, improving and innovating its institutions in practice, the Party is now opening up a new road in Party building based on institutional improvement rather than political movements practiced before.

For example, the CPC distributed in December 2003 the document titled "the Regulations on the Supervision within the Communist Party of China (for Trial Implementation)," designing ten institutions for inner-party supervision after summarizing previous experiences. The ten institutions can be divided into three types: the first are institutions that have been proven effective over the years, such as the system of collective leadership and individual responsibility, information sharing and reporting system on important matters, system of democratic meetings, system for evaluating letters—also visits—of the people, and system of supervision by public opinion; the second are institutions that have codified those successful methods and experiences which cover relatively specific spheres, such as the system under which leading cadres report in various ways on their work and their efforts to perform their duties honestly, system of inspection tours and system of persuasion and admonition; the third are institutions that have not been put into practice and still need further study, such as the system of inquiries, and system of recall or reshuffling. I think this document reflects both inheritance and innovation approach.

For another example, the Party has brought into being a set of institutions for inner-party activities over the years, such as the system of democratic meetings for leading party groups. In 1990, the CPC Central Committee had distributed the document titled "Several Regulations on Democratic Meetings of Leading Cadres from Party and State Organs at or above the County Level." In 1997, the Central Commission for Discipline Inspection of the CPC and the Organization Department of the CPC Central Committee had distributed the document titled "Opinions on Increasing the Quality of Democratic Meetings of Leading Cadres from Party and State Organs at or above the County Level." In 2000, these two Party organs had jointly distributed another document titled "Several Opinions on Improving Democratic Meetings of Leading Cadres from Party and State Organs at or above the County Level," The newest document had proposed specific requirements about the time of democratic meetings, a few important points before the meetings, serious criticism and self-criticism, giving play to the primary responsibility of secretaries of Party committees or leading groups that they should offer more guidance to such meetings. The newest document had also discussed over the implementation democratic meetings; commenting that they—at some organizations or organs—were of low quality and yielded few effects and that the system was not appropriately practiced. I think if the relationship between inheritance and innovation is accurately handled, we could be more successful in practicing the system of democratic meetings and at the same time increase their quality.

8.3.5 Relationship between the Party's Institutions and Democracy and the Legal System

The nature and position of the CPC as the ruling Party of China determine that the Party's institutional improvement depends largely on the improvement of democracy and the legal system of the country and at the same time determines and influences the process of the latter. The two are closely related and promote each other. The Party's institutions are made on the grounds of the Constitution and laws of China and on the other side the Constitution of the CPC is connected with concrete laws and regulations. Only with a good relationship between the two, normal performance of the Party's institutions can be protected and regulated. Thus we could combine the principles: running the Party according to institutions with ruling the country by law and also preventing that Party's institutional improvement is separately treated from the improvement of the state legal system. The two should also not replace each other.

To improve the Party's work style and build clean government, the Party has released many policies over the years. However, state laws are lesser than Party policies, and thus sometimes Party policies are employed to make up the absence of state laws, regretfully this practice to a certain extent weakens the rigidity of institutions. Since the 16th National Congress of the Party in 2002, the Central Committee has attached great importance to the improvement of institutions about combating corruption. In the meantime, the Central Commission for Discipline Inspection and the

Ministry of Supervision have worked with relevant organs and classified over 1,500 previous policies and regulations—they were all issued after the Reform policies were set, which were about improving the Party's work style, combating corruption and building clean government. The joint working group had abolished 115 old documents and formulated several new important regulations succeeding and extending the old ones. The three major ones among them are "the Regulations on the Supervision within the Communist Party of China (for Trial Implementation)", "Regulations of the Communist Party of China on Disciplinary Measures (for Trial Implementation)", and "the Regulations of the Communist Party of China on Guaranteeing Members' Rights (for Trial Implementation)." Others include: "the Provisions on Discipline Inspection Commissions Helping Party Committees Organize and Coordinate Anti-Corruption Work (for Trial Implementation)"; "the Interim Provisions on Inspection Tours of the Central Commission for Discipline Inspection of the CPC and the Organization Department of the CPC Central Committee"; "Opinions on Discipline Inspection and Supervisory Organs' Handling Cases According to Discipline and Laws"; "Several Provisions on Honest and Clean Work of Leaders of State-owned Enterprises (for Trial Implementation)"; and "the Regulation on Penalties and Sanctions against Illegal Fiscal Acts". Moreover, the Central Commission for Discipline Inspection and the Ministry of Supervision categorized regulations and institutions in a scientific way, and decided a working plan from 2004 to 2007 for institutional improvement in this regard. Along with the Party, the government had also issued a decree titled "the Implementation Regulation for the Law of the People's Republic of China on Administrative Supervision". On August 27, 2006, the Standing Committee of the Tenth National People's Congress deliberated on and approved at its 23rd meeting "the Law of the People's Republic of China on the Supervision of Standing Committees of People's Congresses at Different Levels". This Law has 48 articles under nine chapters, defining how standing committees of the people's congresses at different levels should exercise the function of supervision according to the Constitution and relevant laws and regulations.

The law was put into effect on July 1, 2007. It plays an important role in strengthening the supervision on organs of state power and institutionalizing such supervision operations. The Party's regulations and state laws and the Party's supervisory institutions and state supervisory system together make up an institutional framework for combating corruption and building clean government. I think all above constitute an exploration to find a new way for the improvement of the Party's institutions and on the other side improvement of democracy and the legal system of the state spontaneously.

8.4 How to Do the Institutionalization?

The purpose of the Party's institutional improvement is to set up systems and mechanisms for standardizing various relations within the Party, ensure regular Party activities, and facilitate the Party's leadership according to basic requirements of the Constitution of the Party. The major aim is to gradually lead Party building and Party work onto a standard, scientific and institutionalized course. At present, I think it is necessary to pay adequate attention to the following aspects in strengthening the Party's institutional improvement.

8.4.1 Several Fundamental Principles in Institutional Improvement

First, to strengthen the Party's institutional improvement, the efforts should be based on the Constitution of the Communist Party of China, which is the fundamental thing. A party's constitution is the most basic and highest code of its political conduct, a collective expression of its political attitude, form of organization, theoretical level and ability of organizing movements, and is indispensable for a Marxist party. The constitution of a proletarian party distinguishes it from other political parties, reflects its nature and general will, and is the most authoritative party regulation. Deng Xiaoping once pointed out, "Just as the country should have laws, the Party should have rules and regulations. The fundamental ones are embodied in the Party Constitution. Without rules and regulations in the Party, it would be hard to ensure that the laws of the state are enforced."[1] He had asked the whole Party to study the Party Constitution, conscientiously abide by it, effectively implement it and resolutely safeguard it. This shows that the Party Constitution enjoys a supreme status in the Party, is the most authoritative, stable and serious regulation of the Party, and is the general rules with which the Party builds itself, is strict with members and exercises self-discipline. The Party Constitution is carefully designed as the General Program part and eleven chapters, covering the Party's nature, purpose, program and guiding ideologies, general requirements of Party building, criteria for its membership, the organizational system, central organizations, local organizations, primary organizations, cadres, discipline, discipline inspection organs, leading Party members' groups, its relationship with the Communist Youth League of China, Party emblem and flag. To strengthen the Party's institutional improvement, the efforts should be based on the Party Constitution and not violate it and all Party organizations and members should act totally in accordance with it.

Second, to strengthen the Party's institutional improvement, efforts should be guided by the three principles as: seeking truth from facts, democracy and openness, and system and level. The Party's institutions should be the correct expression of objective laws. It means that, when making them, we should uphold the principle of seeking truth from facts, proceed from reality in everything we do, make thorough investigation and research, consult and demonstrate before action. And when practicing the institutions, we should carefully consider the local realities. The essence of the Party's institutional improvement is to institutionalize the principle of democratic-centralism; all the concrete institutions should be formulated on the basis of this principle, be detailed and practical. Thus, in the Party's institutional improvement, we should work hard to develop inner-party democracy, bring into play Party members' enthusiasm and initiative, guarantee their rights to be informed and their rights to participate in Party affairs, increase openness and transparency in Party affairs by democratic

---

[1] *Selected Works of Deng Xiaoping* (2nd edition), Volume 2, p.147.

ways of work and procedures. The Party's institutional improvement is a huge systematic project. We should advance this project bearing in mind the overall situation and system and also its different levels and layers, and take into consideration the connection between various institutions and the social environment, integrate them and form a complete system.

Third, to strengthen the Party's institutional improvement, the principle of being strict with Party members and strictly enforcing Party discipline is the key. Being strict with its members is a fine tradition of the Party, as well as a consistent principle. It guarantees that the Party's vanguard nature and purity are preserved, while its cohesion and fighting capacity are enhanced. "To govern the state well, we should first run the Party well; to run the Party well, we should be strict with Party members. As long as we do a good job in running the Party, our efforts in governing the state will be correct and effective."[1] This principle should be carried out in all aspects of Party building, including ideological education, recruitment of new members, activities within the Party, and enforcement of Party discipline. Among the four above, strict enforcement of Party discipline is a more important link. The promotion of Party discipline includes three aspects: establishment, observation and enforcement of Party discipline. During the establishment of Party discipline, we formulate norms of conduct for Party members, making them understand what they may do and what not. For the observation of Party discipline, we educate Party members to strengthen the sense of discipline and observe it more conscientiously. For the enforcement of Party discipline, we investigate and deal with any violation of Party discipline and safeguard the authority and seriousness of Party discipline. The Constitution of the Party provides explicit principles and policies for members violating Party discipline, and exactly defines and classifies the disciplinary measures and procedures. "The Regulations of the Communist Party of China on Disciplinary Measures", which was issued in December 2003, has 3 parts, 15 chapters, and 178 articles, totaling over 27,000 Chinese characters; that means approximately thirty A4 pages in English. It

[1] *Selected Works of Jiang Zemin*, Volume 2, p.496.

provides explicit stipulations on ten discipline offences and corresponding disciplinary measures; the ten offences are: acts violating political discipline, acts violating organizational and personnel discipline, acts violating the regulations of honesty and self-discipline, acts of corruption and bribery, acts undermining the order of the socialist market economy, acts violating the discipline in financial and economic affairs, negligence and dereliction of duty, acts infringing the rights of Party members or citizens, acts severely violating socialist morality, and acts impeding the socialist management system. The regulation paper covers all aspects of Party discipline and of Party members' social life with emphasis on four kinds of discipline: political discipline, organizational discipline, economic discipline and discipline in mass work. At present, some Party members have a weak sense of discipline; and some Party organizations enforce Party discipline too leniently, enabling some corrupt members to escape from legal sanctions. The seriousness of the Party discipline and authority of state laws are safeguarded only when Party members have the sense of "being disciplined and law-abiding; not being chaotic and lawless". And only when Party organizations and discipline inspection organs at all levels strictly enforce Party discipline, properly handle the relations between Party discipline, administrative discipline and the laws, and see to it that laws are observed and strictly enforced and that law breakers are brought to justice. Only when these were achieved, the Party's institutions will be sacrosanct and unleash their solid effect.

8.4.2 Self-Cultivation of Party Members

Party members' self-cultivation in institutions refers that they understand the importance of institutions and they possess consciousness and capacity of observing and safeguarding institutions. It also includes Party members' opinion of attitude toward and understanding of the Party's institutions, their consciousness of observing institutions and capability of acting according to institutions. It is the basis of and prerequisite to the Party's institutional improvement and adequate attention on this aspect is quite necessary. The circumstances of the CPC history has been: a country with remnants of the long feudal political culture and wars, repeated political movements and the highly centralized planned economy practice; and all through these circumstances the institutions and the legal system of the country were not perfect. As a result of this history we can say that the Party members have a weak sense of institutions and a weak ability of acting according to institutions and are rather used to acting according to the will of the leadership, which forms a hotbed and conditions for feudal patriarchal system and personality cult. Within the Party, there still exist the group behavior psychology, and an old mentality that "the law does not punish everybody" and guanxi psychology; some leading cadres are arbitrary in decision making and randomly violate rules and institutions; and there is usually a "hidden rule" inside some Party organizations, providing convenience for some people. All these interrupt and impede the Party's institutional improvement. A hard work is necessary to solve such problems.

To strengthen Party members' self-cultivation of institutions, first, we should educate them to have a stronger sense of institutions, democracy and the legal system, making Party members, particularly leading cadres, fully understand the importance of institutional improvement and be more conscious in observing and safeguarding institutions. Second, we should strengthen the training of Party members about knowledge of institutions, making them know the Party's institutions, their contents and requirements, and how to handle various relations and affairs of the Party according to them. Last but not least, we should intensify the investigation into any violation of institutions. Institutions should not be randomly violated; anyone who violates it, should be punished. By doing so, we can safeguard the authority of institutions, and help the members to have a correct value orientation and behave well. Only when every Party member has a firm sense of institutions and takes an active part in practice, can the Party's institutional improvement have a broad and solid foundation and a favorable environment.

8.4.3 Focuses in Institutional Improvement

The Party's institutional improvement covers a wide range, and it is an arduous tasks. Therefore, we should make breakthroughs in key sectors and develop the overall work, and gradually set up a system that is all-inclusive. At present, we should concentrate on the following aspects.

First, the Party's organizational system should be improved. Democratic-centralism is the fundamental organizational system and leadership system of the Party, and is the basis and core of all the Party institutions. Upholding and improving democratic-centralism should be the focus of the Party's institutional improvement. Leading bodies at all levels and their chief cadres should take the lead in practicing democratic-centralism, particularly the system of collective leadership and individual responsibility. To uphold and improve democratic-centralism, we should set up and improve a series of supportive systems. For example, we should formulate, improve and strictly apply the rules of procedure and decision-making mechanism within Party committees according to the principle of collective leadership, democratic-centralism, individual consultations and the principle of decisions in the meetings. We should formulate and carry out the system under which all major problems, including decision-making system on major issues such as: appointment or dismissal of cadres in important positions, and arrangement of important construction projects and deciding the use of a large amount of funds, these issues should undergo democratic discussion in Party committees and be decided by the collective. It is necessary to oppose arbitrary decision-making by an individual or a minority of people, and this should be prevented.

Second, leadership system of the Party should be improved. This system is an important guarantee for realizing the Party's leadership and governance. To improve this system, we have to improve the leadership mechanism and governance mechanism of the Party.

To improve the Party's leadership mechanism, the most important thing is to improve the system of Party congresses. Party congresses at different levels are the highest organ of power at their respective levels. We should establish their status of authority within the Party, and ensure that Party congress at different levels are held on schedule as required by the Constitution, they should effectively exercise functions and powers endowed by the Constitution and play their role as the highest organ of decision-making and supervision. Therefore, concerning the system of Party congresses, we should reform and improve the methods of nomination and election; establish a suggestion system for delegates and a mechanism for handling and replying delegates' proposals; strengthen the connection between delegates and Party members at the same organizations and enable delegates to listen to and report opinions and suggestions of Party members. Before a Party committee holds a meeting, it can solicit advice and opinions on the topic from delegates of the Party congress at the same level or invite some delegates to attend the meeting. We should implement the system of Party congresses with—a fixed term system—on a trial basis in more cities and counties, and actively explore ways to give play to the role of delegates when Party congresses are not in session. In the meantime, we should improve the relationships among Party congresses, Party committees and their standing committees, ensuring that Party committees and discipline inspection commissions at different levels are responsible to and fulfill responsibilities endowed by Party congresses at their respective levels; in this way, we can bring into being a system of decision making, implementation and supervision which are relatively independent from each other while forming an organic whole, and establish a scientific leadership mechanism under which responsibilities and powers are clearly defined, different organs cooperate with each other, and at the same time restrain each other, and this could be an effective method.

To improve the Party's governance mechanism, the most important thing is to combine the two needs: the need to uphold the Party's leadership; i.e. to ensure that the people are the masters of the country with the need to rule the country by law. To be more specific, we should improve the relationships between the ruling CPC and the National People's Congress, relationship between executive and judicial branches of the government, between the CPC and the non-Communist parties and mass organizations. Between them we should establish an interaction mechanism that runs well, correctly exercise the Party's political leadership, give play to the Party's role in assuming overall responsibility and coordinating all quarters concerned, and ensure the Party exercises the governing power in a scientific, democratic and law-abiding manner.

Third, the inner-party supervision system should be strengthened. The essence of inner-party supervision is that the Party conducts self-restraint and self-supervision according to the interests of the people and according to the requirements of being strict with Party members. The major content and the aim of inner-party supervision is that Party organizations and members correctly carry out the Party's line, principle and policies, correctly exercise the power entrusted to them by the people, and strictly abide by various institutions of democratic-centralism. To develop inner-party democracy and strengthen inner-party supervision, the core is to solve the institutionalization problem.

For example, we can establish and improve the system under which leading cadres report in various ways on their work. According to "the Regulations on the Supervision within the Communist Party of China (for Trial Implementation)" and "the Interim Regulations on Leading Cadres Reporting on Their Work and Probity", the Political Bureau of the CPC Central Committee should report its work to the Central Committee plenary meetings, and the Standing Committee of the Central Commission for Discipline Inspection of the CPC should report to the plenary meetings of the Commission; the standing committees of local Party committees should report to plenary meetings of their respective Party committees once a year. A leading body makes this report during its term and also one year before the expiration of the term, together with its democratic meetings. Before this report is given, the leading Party committee should solicit opinions from cadres and the masses about its members; and the chief official should send information back to the leader concerned. To set up the system for cadres to report on their work and probity, the key is to enable more cadres to make this report; discipline inspection organs and organization and personnel departments should intensify their supervision and guidance on this work.

Another example: we can set up and improve the system of inspection tours. It is a system under which the CPC Central Committee and Party committees of provinces, autonomous regions and municipalities directly under the Central Government supervise leading bodies and members of their subordinate Party organizations by means of special inspection organs and according to relevant regulations. This system was first established in the 1990s. In August 2003, the Central Commission for Discipline Inspection of the CPC and the Organization Department of the CPC Central Committee, approved by the CPC Central Committee and the State Council, set up special inspection organs and full-time inspectors. By the end of 2004, the inspection had covered one third of all the provinces, autonomous regions and municipalities directly under the Central Government. In 2005, more efforts were made on the inspection tours. The inspection tours at the central level had covered 10 provinces, autonomous regions and municipalities directly under the Central Government, 5 banks and 2 asset management companies under the central administration; while the inspection tours at the provincial level had covered 94 cities or districts and then extended to 210 counties at the lower level. Moreover, supervision in advance and concurrent supervisions were strengthened, which helped to overcome the defects of supervision by the same organ and solve the problem of "blind areas" in inner-party Supervision. At present, it is necessary to rationalize the relevant institutions further, improve the working system of inspection tours.

We should pay special attention to combining inner-party supervision with other kinds of supervision. At present, the supervision framework covers: inner-party supervision, supervision by people's congresses, supervision by special government organs (Hong Kong and Macao), supervision by judicial organs, supervision by the Chinese People's Political Consultative Conference, supervision by non-Communist Parties, and social supervision including media supervision and supervision by public opinion. We should give full scope to the role of various subjects of supervision and make them act in an interactive, concerted effort. In recent years, the National Audit Office of the People's Republic of China has tightened the auditing on central state organs and local governments, which is a highlight of the supervision work in China. In 1996, the State Council submitted to the Standing Committee of the National People's Congress a work report on the results of audit reform at the end of the year, though the report was not publicized. In 2003, General Auditor Li Jinhua of the National Audit Office made an audit report to the Standing Committee of the National People's Congress in three successive years, declaring the auditing problems to the public. Statistics show that from January to November 2005, altogether 91,000 organizations were audited, a total of over 29 billion Euro was found out to be involved in violation of the law and regulations, and a total of over 1.5 billion Euro was found out having been wasted. Through audit, a total amount of 1.7 billion Euros was returned to the state treasury and cut down in financial allocation or subsidies. More than 1,370 law-breaking cases were transferred to discipline inspection or judicial organs. Altogether 22,000 Party and government cadres accepted audit, and a total of 3.5 billion Euros was found out to be involved in violation of regulations and a total of 49 million Euros was discovered to be wasted. Through this "audit storm", people could see the role of special supervisory organs.

Fourth, institutions protecting Party members' rights should be implemented. A brief introduction was given on Party members' rights and the relationship between Party members' rights and duties and "Party members' rights" was added to the Party Constitution adopted at the 16th National Congress of the Party, and was made one of the tasks of discipline inspection organs of the Party. Based on the Party Constitution, the Regulations of the Communist Party of China on Guaranteeing Members' Rights provides detailed, explicit provisions about the measures for protecting Party members' rights and the accountabilities for encroachment of the rights, which is significant for developing inner-party democracy and enhancing the vitality of the Party. These in Party Constitution and the Regulations should be implemented, and measures for Party members to exercise their rights should be supported: such as, protecting their rights from encroachment, creating an environment for the discussion of different views within the Party, encouraging Party members to tell the truth and their innermost thoughts, respecting and protecting the legitimate rights of those who violate discipline.

Fifth, the system of transparency in Party affairs should be prompted. With the progress in the political civilization and the expansion of democracy at the grassroots level, institutions of keeping the public informed of matters, including government affairs, factory affairs, village affairs and school affairs, have been gradually established and improved. As the ruling party of China, the CPC should be at the forefront of the whole society and make more efforts to increase transparency in Party affairs. For example, we should keep Party members better informed of Party affairs and to provide them with more opportunities to participate in them, including important decisions, appointment of cadres and recruitment of new members. To be specific, we need to establish and improve inner-party information sharing and reporting systems and the system of soliciting opinions concerning major policy decisions; improve the rules and procedures for major policies decisions; establish and improve a system keeping Party members informed on recruitment of new members and election of model persons and a system of keeping Party members informed of Party affairs and a feedback system. By doing so, transparency in Party work will be more established.

In summary, the key for being strict with Party members is to establish a whole set of systems and mechanisms which are convenient, effective and binding. By establishing and improving basic and concrete institutions, an effective framework will be put in place under which governance acts are regulated by institutions and people are managed by institutions.

The Governance Capability and Art of Leadership

In the practice of Marxist parties, it has always been an important idea as well as a major topic to enhance their governance capability. In the new period of the new century, the goal of the Party is to build a moderately prosperous society in all respects and reach a new situation and level in building socialism with Chinese characteristics. The key to realize this objective is to enhance the Party's governance capability and improve its art of leadership and governance.

9.1 Governance Capability of the Ruling Party

In its report to the 16th National Congress, the CPC clearly raised the theme of "enhancing governance capability", the first time in the history of the Marxist Theory of Party Building. At the Second Plenary Session of the

16th Central Committee, General Secretary Hu Jintao had commented that the focus of the new, recent project of the Party building was to enhance the Party's governance capability. This idea was repeated on several occasions as the most important thing in Party building and concentrated efforts were necessary. At the Fourth Plenary Session of the 16th Central Committee, the Party had made a special decision on this issue, the first time since it came to power. Below, I would like to offer my ideas on why this issue is so highly valued in the Party at present.

9.1.1 Party's Governance and the Ruling Marxist Parties

After proletarian parties take power, the first thing they face is how to lead the people to develop socialist economy and social productive forces. In his practice of leading the first socialist country in the world, Lenin had explored and proposed a lot of valuable ideas about the building of a ruling party, including ideas of enhancing the governance capability. He had emphasized that a ruling party should give priority to economic construction and increase productivity, so as to defeat capitalism economically. Lenin had raised a famous slogan: "Learn, learn and learn again." He demanded that all party members should learn to manage economy, learn to manage economic work from experts outside the party, and Party should train its own experts.

In China, the three generations of the central collective leadership made unremitting efforts to enhance the governance capability of the CPC.

In March 1949, before taking state power after 28-year hard struggle, Mao Zedong had raised the question of shifting the focus of the Party's work. To adapt to the change, he had proposed that Party members should respectfully and conscientiously learn from all who knew; try to turn yourselves from outsiders into insiders; try to learn how to manage and build cities, and learn how to make economic, political, cultural and diplomatic struggles. In a reply to an argument that "the CPC could successfully seize state power but will not be able to run the state," Mao Zedong had pointed out that only the CPC was qualified and able to lead New China. At the Eighth National Congress in 1956, which was held at the beginning point of building socialism in all respects, Liu Shaoqi had pointed out that no Party member should be content with being a layman in those things he could not understand. "The Party calls on its cadres and members to study painstakingly, to master the things they do not understand in their works. The more we study, the better will we be able to lead."[1]

In the new period of Reform and Opening-up, the second generation of the central collective leadership, with Deng Xiaoping at the core, had pointed out that Marxists should "carry on the work of Party building on the basis of the Party's basic line and make the work serve the line, so as to build the Party into a militant Marxist party, a strong core of leadership leading the people in promoting socialist material progress and cultural and ideological progress". This was actually a higher requirement to enhance the Party's governance capability, with view to the aim and guiding ideology of Party building. He had stressed that to uphold the Party's leadership called for improving its leadership. I think, here, to improve the Party's leadership is in fact to improve its governance capability and art of leadership. Deng had especially demanded the whole Party to study harder in three aspects: economics, science and technology, and management.

After the Fourth Plenary Session of the 13th Central Committee, the third generation of the central collective leadership of the CPC, with Jiang Zemin at the core, had also put emphasis on enhancing the Party's vanguard nature, and decided to deepen the project of Party building. In this period the exploration was started to elevate the Party's governance capability into a systematic theory. Also concrete requirements were defined particularly for the leading cadres on how to enhance the Party's governance capability.

Since the 16th National Congress, the Central Committee of the CPC, with General Secretary Hu Jintao at the core, has given a priority to the improvement of the Party's governance capability, and has advocated that— in the last analysis—all aspects of Party building could be reduced to the enhancement of the Party's governance capability and ruling status. I think in the last three decades the Party has indeed achieved progress on this theme.

---

[1] *Selected Works of Liu Shaoqi*, Volume II, p.264.

9.1.2 Objective Needs of the Party's Governance Capability

For a Marxist party, to have a correct understanding of the spirit of the times and adapt to the trend of the times is a prerequisite to take more initiative or consolidate its ruling position. This is a necessity on the basis of domestic and international competition. The new historical conditions bring about good opportunities for the Party's governance but also severe challenges and tests.

First is the challenge brought by economic globalization. After the Second World War, economic globalization has become an irreversible trend for economic development; scientific and technological development is also much faster; imposing the economic ties among different countries ever closer. At present, the wave of economic globalization cannot be reversed, and it provides several new development opportunities for China. Moreover, economic globalization imposes the realization of a larger scale of social production of commodity economy. Any country participating in the global economic competition should abide by the objective law governing the market economy; for China, these may help to establish and improve the socialist market economic system faster and could achieve gains. Active participation in economic globalization can also help to narrow the economic and social gap between China and developed countries. However, the Party and state have to shoulder bigger international responsibilities and obligations or take bigger and more risks. After joining the World Trade Organization, China has agreed on adapting to common international practices; on the other hand realistically the Party could not be successful to adapt to the new international situation with the old way of economic governance corresponded to the former planned economy system. Around the world, there are more and more uncertain and unpredictable factors, such as oil price increase and dollar depreciation, which will inevitably have an impact on the economic development of China. The wave of globalization embodies risks and raises higher requirements for the Party. It is hard and complex to make good use of the "double-edged sword" of economic globalization, strive for greater space of development and remain invincible in the world economic system.

Second is the challenge brought by the multi-polar world political structure. After the collapse of the former Soviet Union and East Europe, the old structure was suddenly perished and various political forces had to split apart and re-arranged their positions, presenting a trend of multi-polarization in the world political pattern. This great change in international relations is generally better for world peace and stability. The Party can seize the opportunity of this relatively peaceful international environment to concentrate on economic development and enhance the overall national strength of China, and at the same time make use of the checks and balances among international political forces to bring into full play its wisdom and art of governance, improve China's international status and functions in the international community and win more international support. However, I should note clearly that no radical changes have taken place in the old, unfair and irrational international political and economic order; there are more and more negative factors affecting world peace and development, such as widening gap between the South and North and between the rich and poor; local war-like incidents caused by national, religious, territory, resource related conflicts rise one after another; various separatist forces, religious extremist forces and international terrorist forces are a challenge to the international community. And global problems such as environment, drugs and refugees are ever more conspicuous. In particular, Western countries are pressing—more and more—human right and democracy as "soft weapons" to "westernize," "split apart" and "weaken" socialist countries. The world in the early 21st century is not an idyllic era for mankind. Socialist countries are facing long-term, complex and tortuous struggles of infiltration and counter-infiltration, containment and counter-containment, evolution and counter-evolution. I think these new phenomena naturally raise higher requirements for the Party's governance capability.

Third is the challenge brought by the new revolution in science and technology. Science and technology progresses faster with each passing day; the rapid development of modern science and technology, represented by information science and life sciences, opens up new prospective for the development of productive forces. Only by seizing the opportunity of the new revolution, making strategic adjustment of economic structure and enhancing sci-tech content in productive forces, can a developing country bring into full play its advantage of late-development. On the other hand, the revolution in science and technology brings about new changes in people's mentalities, and if they could be transformed to opportunities, this may be an inexhaustible internal motivation for the Party to enhance its governance capability. To a certain extent, to adapt to the revolution depends on the quantity and quality of competent personnel. Therefore, how to solve the problem of attracting, keeping and training personnel and realizing great-leap-forward development in productive forces through developing science and technology is also a challenge for the Party's governance capability.

Fourth is the challenge brought by the new changes in domestic environment and in the Party itself. Over three decades since the Reform and opening-up policies were carried out, China has witnessed rapid development in its economy, remarkable increase in the people's living standards and a stable growth in its overall national strength; China is now in the best period of development and the booming socialism with Chinese characteristics has won the people's support. With the deepening of Reform and Opening-up and the development of socialist market economy, major and profound changes have taken place in domestic circumstances. During the institutional transition, the drawbacks of the old system, obstacles of conventional ideas and pressures and difficulties from all aspects manifest themselves one after another. The new sectors of the economy, new organizational forms, new ways of employment, benefit-based relationships and modes of distribution are diversifying; and many new remarkable trends appear in the fields of ideology and politics. Under such circumstances, the Party is confronted with many difficult problems: how to turn state-owned enterprises into modern corporations; how to realize public ownership in diversified forms; how to ensure both efficiency and quality in economic growth; how to coordinate economic development with social development; and how to give attention to both efficiency and fairness and avoid social polarization.

The Party has changed from a party that had led the people in their efforts for the state power to a party that has led the people in exercising the power and to a one which has long remained in power; also it has changed from a party that led national reconstruction under external blockade and a planned economy conditions to a party that is leading national development while the country is opening to the outside world and developing a socialist market economy. Such changes undoubtedly have brought about many new topics of Party building. Within the Party, there exist the contradiction between the significant growth in the membership and some Party members' poor sense of vanguard nature, and the contradiction between the succession of the older cadres by the new cadres and the shortage of high-caliber leading cadres; some primary Party organizations are feeble and lax; inner-party democracy is not perfect; the Party's leadership system and way of governance still have some drawbacks. All these problems do not conform to the situation and tasks that the Party is facing or the mission it shoulders, restrict the Party's governance capability and affect its performance. The times have raised for the Party "two major historical puzzles": how to enhance the Party's art of leadership and governance and how to raise the Party's capacity to resist corruption, prevent degeneration and withstand risks and also "three major tests" of how to remain in power for a long time, how to carry on the reform and opening-up and how to develop the socialist market economy. There has emerged an enormous challenge for the Party's governance capability to adapt to the needs of modernization and make the Party building work more modern, and to solve new various complicated contradictions and problems of the country and the Party.

9.1.3 Lessons of Former Soviet Union and East Europe

In the late 1980s and early 1990s, many big sized, long-standing parties in the world had successively lost the power of government. Communist parties of the former Soviet Union and East Europe were among them.

There were many reasons, and the most important one was that they had long remained in power; these communist parties finally lost the support of the people due to the rigid governance system, deteriorating governance capability and poor performance in governance. To be specific, they had lost the ideological leadership with their conservative ideas, lagging theories and unbalanced policies; they were unqualified for governance since they had failed to formulate correct strategies for development, which then resulted in decline in economic development and consequently little improvement in people's life. They could not bring their leadership into full play because they could not properly handle the relationship between the party and government and the highly centralized governance system had resulted in a fusion of party work with government work; they had lost the social foundation as some party members and cadres had divorced from the masses and some party and government leaders had practiced corruption; they had lost the influence and control over the ideological sphere as they had failed to properly lead and regulate mass media and guide a healthy public opinion; and they had lost vitality because they had ignored the improvement of democracy and the socialist legal system while arbitrary decision-making had prevailed. From one aspect, all these problems were actually questions of the party's governance capability, including the capability to make theoretical innovations, the capability to control the pattern of the economic and social development, the capability to make institutional innovations, the capability to control corruption, the capability to build an advanced socialist culture, and the capability to develop socialist democracy. Such bitter lessons should remind a Marxist party that it should attach great importance to the improvement of its governance capability.

In summary, enhancing the Party's governance capability constitutes "a major strategic theme with a bearing on the success of China's socialist cause, the future and destiny of the Chinese nation, the life and death of the Party, as well as the lasting stability and prosperity of the country.

9.2 Tasks for Enhancing Governance Capability

Generally speaking, a Marxist party's governance capability may include capability to carry out its political program, line, principle and policies—when in power—and rule the country and consolidate the post-revolutionary regime. Maybe part of this definition could be used for all kinds of ruling parties around the world. For the CPC, the governance capability refers to the ability to put forth and carry out correct theories, guidelines, principles, policies and tactics, play a leading role in the formulation and enforcement of the Constitution and laws, adopt a scientific system and mode of leadership, mobilize and organize the people to manage state and social affairs plus the economic and cultural undertakings in accordance with laws, effectively run the Party, state and army, and transform China into a modern socialist country. At its 16th National Congress, the CPC had required that Party committees and leading cadres at all levels should enhance their abilities to cope with the situation in a scientific way, keeping the market economy well under control, dealing with complicated situations, exercising state power according to law, and commanding the whole situation. At the Fourth Plenary Session of the 16th Central Committee, the CPC had adopted the document titled "the Decision of the Central Committee of the Communist Party of China on the Enhancement of the Party's Governance Capability", in which it required the whole Party to enhance the abilities of keeping the socialist market economy well in hand, developing socialist democracy, building an advanced socialist culture, building a harmonious socialist society, and coping with the international situation and affairs. I think, the set of requirements raised in the above two documents are supplementary, the former stressing the qualities and abilities of Party and government cadres at all levels while the latter stressing on the overall governance capability of the Party.

The enhancement of the Party's governance capability can also be considered as a campaign aiming to improve the Party's governance capability according to the general objectives and by strengthening all aspects of Party building and improving the Party's leadership system and working mechanisms. Below, I will offer general ideas on the tasks of this strategic campaign in five points.

9.2.1 Ability to Manage the Socialist Market Economy

Development is the key to the resolution of all major problems in China. To enhance the Party's governance capability, its capability of leading development is a key factor. At present, China in general can still be considered at the preliminary stage of establishing the socialist market economy, and there are still a series of deep-rooted problems occurring in the transition from the planned economy to market economy. Therefore, the primary task for the Party to enhance its governance capability is to give priority to development in governing the country and improve the Party's capability of running the socialist market economy.

On the one hand, it is necessary to strengthen and improve the Party's leadership over economic work, and enhance its ability of leading economic work. Many scholars term it as an art. The party should firmly attach to the strategic principle of seizing opportunities to accelerate development and persist in the central task of economic development, and meanwhile properly treat the major contradictions and conspicuous problems in economic operation and raise appropriate principles and policies to promote sustained, rapid, coordinated and healthy economic development. This is the new "Scientific Outlook on Development" that emphasizes putting people first and comprehensive, coordinated and sustainable development, I will study in later chapters of the book. The party should adhere to the direction of socialist market economic reform and always stand in the forefront of the times to lead and plan the reform; and at the same time take good control over the timing and tempo for releasing reform measures. To guarantee the initiative in opening to the outside world, it should properly combine "bringing in" with "going out" efforts in economic sphere and better utilize the domestic and international markets and resources, basing our feet mainly on domestic demand while expanding the international market, making full use of domestic capital while effectively utilizing foreign investments, relying and developing domestic human resources while introducing foreign talents. The Party should lead economic work based on the laws governing the socialist market economy, and constantly improve the institutions and ways for leading economic work in line with the requirements of the socialist market economy. In leading economic work, the Party should make overall plans, work out strategies and policies, push forward legislative work and create a favorable environment for all these efforts. This means Party committees should take the overall situation into consideration and concentrate their efforts on key issues.

On the other hand, the Party should solve major problems with a bearing on the overall situation of economic restructuring and difficult problems in developing market economy. I think major problems are: to maintain a sustained, fast and healthy development of the national economy; to properly handle the relationship between keeping public ownership as the main pillar of the economy and on the other side promoting the development of the non-public (private) sector; to correctly handle the relationship between keeping the socialist distribution system "according to work" as the main pillar of the distribution system and on the other side practicing a variety of other modes of distribution. To realize common prosperity of all the population and prevent excessively wide income gap among different regions and different groups of people although under current conditions that certain regions and people have become rich first. The Party should make breakthroughs on the solution of such problems.

9.2.2 Ability to Develop Socialist Democracy

For building a moderately prosperous society in all respects, an important condition is to develop socialist democracy and establish a socialist political civilization. Therefore, the second task for the Party to enhance its governance capability is to integrate the adherence to Party leadership and the people being the masters of the country with ruling the country by law and to improve its ability to develop socialist democracy. To be specific, under current concrete conditions socialist democratization includes four aspects: to lead, support and guarantee the people's status as masters of the country—as the essence of the Party's governance; secondly, to integrate the adherence to Party leadership and the people being the masters of the country with ruling the country by law—as the basic requirement; to resolutely stick to the path of political development which the Party and the people have chosen—as an important approach; and to exercise the governing power in a scientific, democratic and law-abiding manner—as the mode of government.

To lead, support and guarantee the people's status of masters of the country, the Party should develop people's democracy system, improve various systems of democracy, develop diverse new forms of democracy and promote the institutionalization, standardization and regularization of socialist democracy. To be more specific, improve the people's congress system—the fundamental system of China—support the people to exercise state power through people's congresses; support people's congresses and their standing committees to perform their duties according to law, particularly their functions of legislation and supervision; and improve the self-structure of people's congresses and maintain close ties between their deputies and the masses. The system should ensure that human rights are respected and guaranteed; expand channels for citizens to participate in political affairs in an orderly way; ensure that the people go in for democratic elections and decision-making processes, exercise democratic management and supervision according to law; and improve the system of keeping the public informed of matters being handled, such as government affairs, factory affairs and village affairs.

To properly integrate "the Party leadership and people being the masters of the country" principle with the principle to rule the country by law and virtue, it is mainly necessary to depend on the leadership by the Party as the fundamental guarantee that the people are the masters of the country and that the country is ruled by law, but the essential requirement of socialist democracy that the people are the masters of the country, and adhere to the basic principle of ruling the country by law should also be completely promoted. Since the most important thing is to adhere and improve the Party's leadership, it is necessary to reform and improve the Party's style of leadership and properly handle its relations with the people's congresses, government organs, the Chinese People's Political Consultative Conference and people's self-organizations based on the principle that the Party should only assume overall orienting functions. It is necessary to standardize the establishment of Party and government organs; improve the organizational structure of standing committees of Party committees; push more Party and government leaders to take posts in the other line; cut down the number of posts in leadership cadres; solve the problem of overlapping functions; and merge Party committees with government departments when they have same or similar functions.

To advance in the path of political development which the Party and the people have historically chosen, it is necessary to maintain and improve "the system of multi-party cooperation and political consultation under the CPC leadership". Between CPC and the other 8 different democratic parties, the historical principle of "long-term co-existence, mutual supervision, treating each other with all sincerity and sharing weal and woe" is continued for nearly 70 years and proved successful. It is necessary to develop more cooperation with these non-Communist parties, improve the system of consultation—long practiced with them—before making decisions on important issues, sincerely accept supervision from them, select and recommend more number of qualified non-Party cadres to leading government posts, thus give full play to the features and advantages of the China's own political parties' system. It is necessary to improve "the system of regional ethnic autonomy" to consolidate and enhance socialist ethnic relations of equality, solidarity and mutual assistance and it is necessary to promote common prosperity and progress for the 52 ethnic groups of China, and properly handle the work related to religions and believers, overseas Chinese, non-Party intellectuals, people from the non-public sectors of the economy and individuals from other strata of society, thus unite with all forces that can be united with, and consolidate the long practiced patriotic united front policy.

To exercise the governing power in a scientific, democratic and law-abiding manner should be the Party's basic philosophy and basic style of governance. To exercise the governing power in a scientific manner, the Party should take scientific theories as guidance and implement the decision-making processes, leadership systems and managerial systems on a more scientific basis by improving the decision-making mechanism, such as improving rules and procedures for major decisions, strengthening consultation and discussion, peer review, technical consultation and decision-making evaluation, and setting up diverse forms of the decision-making consultation mechanism and the information support system. To exercise the governing power in a democratic manner, the Party should stick to the principle of "trying to provide benefits for the public and doing the governing work for the people." To exercise the governing power in a law-abiding manner, the Party should play a leading role in legislative work and it should itself be an example of abiding laws and also ensure enforcement of the laws. It is necessary to ensure that the Party's views become the will of the state only through legal procedures, guaranteeing institutionally and legally that the Party's line, principles and policies are carried out and ensuring that such institutions and laws will be not changed with changes in the leadership or changes in the views or focus of attention of any Party leader. Party members, especially leading cadres, should firmly establish a sense of law, act within the scope of the Constitution and laws, and play an exemplary role in safeguarding the authority of the Constitution and laws. It is necessary to promote the reform of the judicial system under which judicial and procuratorial organs have properly defined powers and responsibilities. These organs should cooperate with and restrict each other, and work efficiently, so as to provide legal guarantee for fairness and justice in the society. Moreover, it is necessary to strengthen restraint and supervision over the exercise of power. For example, "the system of inspection tours" should be improved to tighten supervision over leading cadres and especially those holding the key posts; improve "the system of reporting on important matters", "the

system under which leading cadres report in various ways on their work",
"the system of democratic appraisal and the economic accountability auditing
system"; carry out "the systems of making inquiries on accountability and
removal according to law". It is necessary to strengthen leadership over
discipline inspection organs and improve the Party's discipline inspection
system; guarantee that special organs of people's congresses and governments
and judicial organs exercise the function of supervision and guarantee that
the Chinese People's Political Consultative Conference exercises democratic
supervision according to its charter. It is necessary to strengthen citizens'
supervision and guarantee citizens' right to report, complain and appeal. I
think when above policies are applied, the Party can ensure that the power
endowed by the people is indeed used for the benefit of the people.

9.2.3 Ability of Building an Advanced Socialist Culture

To promote socialist cultural and ideological progress and develop
advanced culture is an important part of the Party's basic program at the
primary stage of socialism. Therefore, the third task is to adhere to the
guiding status of Marxism in the sphere of ideological super-structure and
improve the Party's ability of building an advanced socialist culture.

First, it is critical to consolidate the common ideological base on which
the Party and the people unite and progress forward, press for theoretical
innovation, and try to make the Party's ideological and theoretical work more
creative, convincing and influential, offering answers to major theoretical
and current realistic problems. It is necessary to strengthen the structure of
Marxist theories on governance and the research on Marxism and build a
contingent of Marxist theoreticians, while fostering a social environment
favorable for theoretical innovation, pay special attention to training young
and middle-aged theoreticians and encourage them to work for the cause of
the Party and the people.

Second, it is critical to maintain an appropriate orientation in public
opinions sphere, enhance the capability of guiding public opinion, improve
the initiative in media work, and make media and publicity work more

attractive and effective. It is necessary to uphold the principle of the Party controlling the media, persuade the media to express the Party's views and at the same time reflect the people's desires and feelings, and apply the principle: "combining positive publicity with media's critical supervision". It is necessary to improve the information briefing system and develop the ability of news media to rapidly respond in case of major emergencies. Moreover, it is critical to pay great attention to the influence of the Internet and new media forms on public opinion, and strengthen the Internet management system and increase the contingent of online publicity personnel, thus making positive public opinion the main pillar of online media.

Third, it is important to upgrade the ideological and ethical standards as well as the scientific and cultural qualities of the people, strengthen ideological and political work, and give priority to developing education and science. It is necessary to strengthen education on ideals and beliefs, advocating the national spirit with patriotism as the core, the spirit of the times that focuses on reform and innovation and collectivism and socialist thought. It is necessary to push the campaign for improving civil morality, promote the people to apply the eight socialist maxims of honor and disgrace[1]. At the same time it is necessary to carry forward the traditional virtues of the Chinese nation, and advocate basic ethical values. We should encourage the advanced culture while showing proper consideration for the majority of the people, try to reach a common understanding while respecting differences, and solve both ideological and realistic problems, particularly focusing on the ideological problems of different social groups. In the sphere of adolescent education, it is necessary to combine the mass campaign for ideological and cultural progress with improving education network in school, family and society all playing their part and cooperating

---

[1] Love the country; do it no harm. Serve the people; never betray them. Follow science; discard superstition. Be diligent; not indolent. Be united, help each other; make no gains at other's expense. Be honest and trustworthy; do not sacrifice ethics for profit. Be disciplined and law-abiding; not chaotic and lawless. Live plainly, work hard; do not wallow in luxuries and pleasures.

with each other. Bearing in mind the aim of enhancing the scientific and cultural qualities of the entire people, it is necessary to deepen the reforms in educational system and scientific and technological system, give full play to the basic and guiding role of education and science and education in the modernization drive, carry out the Party's policy for education, advocate the scientific spirit, and disseminate scientific knowledge.

Last but not least, it is necessary to enhance the general strength and international influence of the Chinese culture by actively pushing forward the cultural restructuring and liberating and developing productivity in the cultural industries. To support the requirements of the socialist market economy, we should, in accordance with the socialist ideological and cultural tenets, eliminate structural blockages that have hampered cultural development and improve the system of markets for cultural products. In addition, we need to make more and better research on the strategies for cultural development, work out plans for cultural development and cultural restructuring as soon as possible, and build up a contingent of cultural workers.

9.2.4 Ability of Building a Harmonious Socialist Society

In its report to the 16th National Congress, the CPC had declared that it would work to build a moderately prosperous society—with higher standards and developed in an all-round way—in which economy would be more developed, democracy improved, science and education advanced, culture more prosperous, society more harmonious and the texture of life for the people upgraded. At the Fourth Plenary Session of the 16th Central Committee, the CPC had chosen a new phrase "developing harmonious socialist society" as part of its modernization strategy. Thus a fourth concept was added to former three: the development of the socialist market economy, socialist democracy and advanced socialist culture. It means that the modernization drive covers four aspects: material progress, political progress, ideological and cultural progress, and social progress. At the Sixth Plenary Session of the 16th Central Committee, the CPC had approved "the Decision of the Central Committee of the Communist Party of China on Several Major Issues Concerning the Building of a Harmonious Socialist Society" in which more concrete tasks and goals were defined. The ideological design of the document was based on Scientific Outlook on Development. I would like to summarize the basic ideas and definitions in this recent document.

First, a harmonious socialist society should manifest a creative and innovative vitality. In order to create an atmosphere in which the will of creation and innovation respected; the principles of respecting labor, knowledge, competent personnel and creativity should be promoted.

Second, a harmonious socialist society should be a society in which interests and relations among different parties (strata) should be effectively coordinated. "During the process of building socialism, we should take the fundamental interests of the overwhelming majority of the people as the starting point and goal of the formulation and implementation of policies, in order to properly reflect and care the interests of the people belonging to different strata. "In the meantime, we should strengthen our capabilities of handling contradictions among the people; make good use of political, legal, economic and administrative measures and education, consultation, meditation and other means; improve the working mechanism for handling contradictions among the people and establish and improve a coordination system of social interests; and deal with issues of great concern to the people promptly. Moreover, we need to establish and improve a coordination system of social interests, and guide the masses to express their interest-related concerns and solve interest-related contradictions by reasonable and lawful means, so as to safeguard social stability and unity. The Party should adhere to the principle of relying on the working class wholeheartedly, bring into full play the role of the working class and farmers as basic forces in pushing forward economic and social development, and encourage and support people of other social strata to actively contribute to economic and social development. The Party should protect the development vitality of developed regions, competitive industries and groups who have become rich before others, while paying great attention to and concern about underdeveloped areas, less competitive industries and people in harder circumstances. The Party should work hard to bring into being a fine social trend that people work in unity and close cooperation and care for the needy and those with extreme difficulties, and an interpersonal environment characterized by equality, friendliness and harmony.

Third, a harmonious socialist society should be a society in which the social management system is constantly innovated and improved. As the sectors of the economy, organizational forms, ways of employment, interest-based relationships and modes of distribution are diversifying. We should make in-depth research on the laws of social management; improve the social management structure and relevant policies, laws and regulations; re-allocate resources of social management; and set up and improve a structure of social management comprising Party committee leadership, government responsibility, non-governmental support and public participation. In the meantime, Party organizations and members at the grassroots level should play an active role in serving the masses and rallying public support; autonomous organizations in urban communities and village administrative bodies should play a role in coordinating the interest relationships, resolving contradictions, clearing up worries and problems; mass organizations, trade organizations and social intermediaries should play a role in offering services, reflecting people's appeals and regulating behaviors. All these should be integrated into a concerted effort in social management and social services. On this basis, the social security system consisting of social insurance, assistance and welfare and charity should be promoted. In the meantime the Party and government's management and supervision on all kinds of social organizations should be enhanced.

Last but not least, a harmonious socialist society should be a stable and orderly society. Social stability is a social as well as political issue; it bears not only on the people's good and prosperous life, but on the stability and unity of the country and society. We should uphold the principle that maintaining stability is of top priority, carry out a job responsibility system protecting social stability, and actively explore new ways to prevent and solve social contradictions. On the one hand, we should set up a mechanism to collect and analyze public opinion and maintain effective channels for reporting social conditions and public opinion, so that the people can fully express their opinions and we can solve the problems of great concern to the people in a timely and rational manner. On the other hand, taking into consideration the impact of current negative factors on social stability, we should set up and improve an early warning system related to disturbances to social stability, establish an emergency response mechanism with multiple functions, quick response and high efficiency, and enhance the abilities of preserving public security. Finally, we should give play to the role of judicial organs in punishing criminal offenses, resolving contradictions and safeguarding stability, strengthen and improve the working mechanism for maintaining law and order by comprehensive measures, and crack down on criminal activities lawfully, so as to protect the people's lives and property.

I think "the building of a harmonious socialist society" will depend on concerted efforts of the Party and the society. The Party's mass line should be applied and the mass work should be perfected. Now, some new leaders are not good at the mass work; some cadres who have been in leading positions for a long time have a faint mass viewpoint, and seldom go deep among the masses to listen to their voice or help them with their hardships; the Party's mass work is weak in some areas and departments, affecting the relations between the Party and the masses and between the cadres and the masses. These phenomena have aroused strong public resentment. The Party should pay high attention to this new situation. It is necessary to strengthen publicity and education about the mass viewpoint of Marxism and the Party's mass line. Leading cadres at all levels should go down to the grassroots units, concentrate on hotspot and difficult problems that the masses are concerned about, and do mass work well by persuading, setting examples and providing services, so as to give full scope to the initiative of the people.

In summary, the document had proposed a new evaluation on the changes in the society, and had advised to make more efforts to deal with and resolve contradictions, maximize factors conducive to harmony while minimizing those factors harmful to harmony. Social harmony was defined: a society in which all strata of people are well positioned, do their best, live in harmony and share the benefits.

9.2.5 Ability to Cope with the International Issues

Over the years since the Reform and Opening-up policies were carried out, China's international status has been growing and exchanges with the international community have been expanding. The Party should take into account the interdependence between domestic and foreign affairs and try to create a favorable international and neighboring environment for China's modernization drive. Therefore, for the Party, the fifth task for it to enhance the governance capability is to adhere to the independent foreign policy of peace and constantly improve its ability of coping with the volatile international situation and affairs.

The current world is varied, complicated and quite volatile. By observing and analyzing problems with Marxist theories and from a historical and overall angle, we can understand the profound changes taking place around the world and their features. The party should keep up with the trend of the times, take both domestic and international situations into consideration, give judicious guidance according to circumstances and draw on advantages and avoid disadvantages, and thus seize opportunities and create better conditions to develop China.

Second, the Party should carry out the country's foreign policy and gain the leverage in handling international affairs; that means proceeding from fundamental interests of the Chinese people and the common interests of the people across the world, and oppose hegemony politics, power politics and terrorism. In the past, the CPC had worked out a series of correct principles and policies in foreign affairs, such as the Five Principles of Peaceful Coexistence and Five Principles for inter-party Relations. China should resolutely carry out the independent foreign policy of peace, adhere to the road of peaceful development and never seek hegemony. It is necessary to handle properly and differentiate the relations with big countries, neighboring countries and developing countries, actively participate in multi-lateral foreign activities, play an active role in the United Nations and other major international organizations, and develop friendly, reciprocal cooperative relations with countries across the world according to the Five Principles of Peaceful Coexistence and other universally recognized rules of international relations. In handling international affairs, it is necessary to evaluate and cope with the situation cool-headedly, adhere to the principle of mutual respect and seek common ground while shelving differences.

Third, the Party, as a separate subject, should enhance the ability of making exchanges with the international community. As the ruling party of a big, developing country, the CPC is playing a more and more important role in the international arena. The Party should make an overall analysis of and properly cope with the opportunities and challenges from the outside, and try to turn challenges into opportunities. It should get familiar with and make good use of international rules and common practice and take an active part in the negotiation and decision-making of international affairs and rules, trying to fully express China's views. Moreover, it is necessary to welcome the positive attention that the international community pays to China, strengthen and improve foreign publicity, actively conduct cultural exchanges with other countries and regions, and work hard to create a positive international opinion environment favorable for China's development.

Last but not least, it is necessary to safeguard the sovereignty and security of China. The complex geopolitical environment and numerous contradictions and conflicts cropping up in economic globalization bring threats to the state security of China. Therefore, in face of the new situation characterized by the interweaving of traditional and non-traditional threats to security, it is necessary to increase the sense of state security, improve the strategy of state security, and spare no time to establish a highly efficient work mechanism, so as to maintain state security in politics, economy, culture and information. The armed forces make up an important pillar of state security. It is critical to oppose interferences in Hong Kong and Macao affairs and cross-straits affairs (Taiwan) by outside forces, firmly oppose and stop any interference in cross-straits affairs by outside forces, resolutely oppose and crush any conspiracy or activity aimed at separating Taiwan from China and safeguard state sovereignty and territorial integrity.

In summary, the enhancement of the Party's governance capability covers economy, politics, culture, society, diplomacy, state sovereignty and security spheres. The ability of developing socialist democracy is an inevitable requirement of building socialist political civilization. The ability of building an advanced socialist culture is an inevitable requirement of promoting ideological and cultural progress. The ability of building a harmonious socialist society is an inevitable requirement of consolidating the social foundation of the Party's governance. The ability of coping with the international situation and affairs is an inevitable requirement of safeguarding state sovereignty and security and realizing the complete reunification of the motherland.

9.3 How to Enhance the Party's Governance Capability?

The enhancement of the Party's governance capability is a systematic project, involving both the Party as a whole and individual Party members and cadres, both Party organizations at all levels and the Party's leadership system. It is necessary to base the efforts on the current realities while looking ahead to the future, focus on key points while promoting the work in all respects, and constantly study new situations, solve new problems, set up new institutions and acquire new abilities.

9.3.1 Summarizing the Experience of Governance

The Party has accumulated rich experience of governance in the long practice of leading the people to run the country; it is indeed a valuable asset. In recent years, the Party's top leaders have summarized the experience on different occasions. For example, Jiang Zemin summarized these experience into 11 points at a celebration of the 20th anniversary of the

Third Plenary Session of the 11th Central Committee of the Party, three points at the Meeting Celebrating the 80th Anniversary of the Founding of the Communist Party of China, 10 basic points in the report to the 16th National Congress in 2002, and six points at the Fourth Plenary Session of the 16th Central Committee of the Party. These summaries of the Party's experience in governance are also important guiding principles for enhancing its governance capability.

The difficulty of governance lies in the understanding of its laws. The laws on governance refer to the intrinsic relations among the essence, content, conditions, style and other factors of governance, and basic principles that a ruling party should uphold in controlling and exercising state power. Thus, we should base the enhancement of the Party's governance capability according to the objective laws on governance. On the one hand, it is necessary to study the laws on governance with its relations; i.e. the laws on development of human society, the laws on building socialism. To be specific, naturally it is necessary to give top priority to the development of productive forces according to the basic law that relations of production and the superstructure should be adapted to the development of productive forces. On the other hand, it is critical to draw on the experience of governance in the world history and all over the world, and in particular learn some lessons from the collapse of the former Soviet Union and East Europe.

9.3.2 Party's Governance Capability in Party Building

The enhancement of the Party's governance capability is closely connected with all aspects of Party building. They are not isolated from each other. The enhancement of the Party's governance capability is embodied in all aspects of Party building. The enhancement of the Party's governance capability is also closely connected with the strengthening of its vanguard nature. The two have different emphases, but are intrinsically unitary. On the one hand, as the ruling Party, the CPC can enhance its governance capability and consolidate its governing status only by preserving its vanguard nature, which is the foundation of Party building. On the other hand, it is possible to find out and test whether a Marxist party is progressive from its governance capability and performance. Therefore, strengthening the Party's vanguard nature is the foundation of the enhancement of the Party's governance capability, which is the key to the former.

At present, to strengthen the Party's governance capability, it is necessary to follow the guidance of Party's ideological systems up to today, carry out the Party's basic line, program and experience, and work hard to combine the endeavors to strengthen the Party's governance capability with those to strengthen its vanguard nature in all aspects of Party building, with maintaining the flesh-and-blood ties with the masses as the core, building a high-caliber contingent of cadres as the key, improving the Party's leadership system and work mechanism as the focus, and strengthening primary Party organizations and membership as the foundation. To be specific, we should enhance the Party's capability of theoretical innovation to preserve and develop its vanguard nature in ideological and theoretical development.

To a certain extent, the enhancement of the Party's overall governance capability depends on that of Party members and leading cadres' qualities and abilities. Under the new historical conditions, all Party members, particularly leading cadres, should recognize the importance of their work from the perspective of the Party's governance, combine their work with the realization of the objective of communism and the consolidation of the Party's governing status, study more diligently and work harder, so as to better reflect the Party's governing philosophy and enhance its governance capability.

9.3.3 The Party System and the Style of Governance

After carefully studying the current conditions of the enhancement of the Party's governance capability and analyzing major factors obstructing it, we will find out that the Party's system and style of governance are also two important factors affecting the Party's governance capability. The style of governance covers all the institutions, approaches and methods that a party uses in governance. The style of governance that a party adopts mainly depends on its governing philosophy, conditions for governance and historical and cultural traditions; it also involves the relationship between a ruling party and state power. The CPC is an organic whole established on the basis of democratic-centralism, which determines that it should firmly hold the unitary leadership in the style of governance, allowing no other party to share the leadership; it also exercises governance on state activities, which can never be diluted in excuse of separation of the Party and government. Since this approach accords with the characteristics of proletarian parties, we should uphold the principle of the Party's unitary and collective leadership, adhere to its leadership politically, ideologically and organizationally, and practice the Party's leadership in all aspects and at all levels.

We have made some expositions on this problem when talking about enhancing the ability of developing socialist democracy, and improving the people's congress system and the system of multi-party cooperation and political consultation under the leadership of the CPC. Here, I will expound mainly on the issue of political restructuring. Political systems are various concrete systems set up on the basis of the fundamental political system of a country. The current political systems of China were bred in the years of revolutionary wars, took shape in the period of socialist transformation, and developed in the long period of planned economy. They inevitably have some shortcomings and drawbacks, such as concentration of power, lack of distinction between the functions of the Party and those of the government and between those of the government and those of enterprises, and overstaffing in government organs. Over the years, the Party has made a lot of efforts in reforming and improving the institutions of governance and has made remarkable progress. However, the political systems—we have inherited—cannot meet the needs of the new tasks, preventing the Party from bringing into full play its governance capability. Therefore, it is necessary to push forward political restructuring step by step along with economic restructuring, and gradually set up a set of mechanisms of governance that can meet the requirements of modernization, including mechanisms for the granting and acceptance of power, mechanisms for the exercise of power and mechanisms for the supervision of power. By doing so, it can be possible that the people mandate the power to organs concerned in accordance with law, the Party and government exercise the power in accordance with law and the people can supervise the exercise of power in accordance with law. All the Party and government activities should be incorporated into laws and legal procedures, the relationship between the Party and government should be more scientific, standardized and institutionalized according to laws.

In summary, all the Party members should work hard to enable the Party to remain a Marxist party that is built for public interest and exercises state power for the people, a party that exercises state power in a scientific, democratic and law-abiding manner, a party that is realistic, pragmatic and committed to reform and innovation, a party that is hardworking, efficient, upright and clean. In the final analysis, a ruling Marxist party that always represents the development trend of China's advanced productive forces, the orientation of China's advanced culture and the fundamental interests of the overwhelming majority of the Chinese people, preserves its vanguard nature, is able to withstand the test of trials and tribulations, and leads the Chinese people of all ethnic groups to realize national prosperity and rejuvenation, social harmony and people's well-being.

Chapter 10

The Program and Political Line of a Marxist Party and the CPC Practice

A party's program embodies the party's nature in the form of goal or objective, one of the major marks distinguishing one party from another. Different from changeable election programs and short-living governance programs of the bourgeoisie, the programs of a Marxist party for any stage are relatively stable and in particular consistence with its maximum program. And different from disguised or partial programs of some other political organizations of the working class, the programs of a Marxist party are public and cover its objectives in all sectors including politics, economy and culture. A Marxist party has a lofty ideal and undertakes a high practice. To realize its program, a Marxist formulates a line for each special stage in accordance with realities.

10.1 A Party's Program Is Its Public Banner

A program refers to concise statements of the objectives and tasks of a political entity, such as a country, political party or group. A party's program is its public banner, through which people can grasp the party's current level of movement. People can choose a party with the same or similar political pursuit and join it, and then strive with comrades to realize the party's program; or show sympathy for the party and support and sponsor it as an outsider. Generally speaking, bourgeois parties have two kinds of programs. One is election program, which usually sets fundamental goals about issues people are concerned about in a certain period produced by certain investigations. During the election campaign, the party will adjust its emphasis in accordance with the trend when promoting its election program, so as to win more support from voters. The other is its administrative program. As long as the party wins the election and takes power, its administrative program will generally be quite different from the election program. The reason is that the administrative program targets all the citizens instead of its own voters, who are just part of the population. Thus it is more inclusive than the election program, as the ruling party should naturally adopt some contents of its rival candidates' election programs, which may happen to be contrary to its own election program. Certainly, both the election program and administrative program of bourgeois parties are concentrated reflections of the interests and values of the bourgeoisie, no matter how they are labeled representing voters or citizens' interests. Instead, the program of Marxist parties is a concentrated expression of the political doctrine and goals of the proletariat.

10.1.1 Theoretical Development on the Program of Marxist Parties

Founders of Marxist parties all attached great importance to the improvement of the party program in the long period of revolutionary practice, and we advise to term it as the theory of improving the program of

Marxist parties.

Major contents are as follows:

First are basic characteristics of the party program. Founders of Marxist parties maintained that the program of any proletarian party should be public and the party should publicize its viewpoints instead of concealing them. "But a program is after all a banner planted in public, and the outside world judges the party by it."[1] Since proletarian parties take scientific socialism as their basis, they should be indisputable on the ideological and theoretical basis (part) of the party program, if party members could not reach consensus on this fundamental problem, it will mean that the party's nature, vanguard, ideal and pursuit could be randomly or arbitrarily changed and a Marxist party can not exist. The party program is a measure reflecting the level and the maturity of the Party movement, because it is a concentrated expression of the party's standpoint, political views, ideological basis, and principle of organization, strategies and all other aspects. Therefore, by drawing up a program of principles, "one sets up before the whole world landmarks by which it measures the level of the Party movement."[2]

Second is the importance of improving the party program. For the program of proletarian parties it is significant to maintain one mind among all party members and uniting them to strive for the common ideal and goals. "Without a program a party cannot be an integral political organism capable of pursuing its line whatever turn events may take. Without a tactical line based on an appraisal of the current political situation and providing explicit answers to the 'vexed problems' of our times, we might have a circle of theoreticians, but not a functioning political entity."[3] The program of proletarian parties can call upon the people, unite the class, and bring into being a revolutionary army composed of millions, which will strive for the interests of the overwhelming majority of the people.

[1] *Marx & Engels Selected Works* (2nd edition), Volume 3, pp.325-326. Beijing: People's Press, 1995.

[2] *Ibid.*, p.296.

[3] *Collected Works of Vladimir Lenin* (2nd Chinese edition), Volume 20, p.357. Beijing: People's Press, 1989.

Third are the principles for improving the party program. First, the party program should adhere to the basic principles of scientific socialism and proletariat. As Marx and Engels had suggested, since the program is "a banner planted in public," proletarian parties should show in this banner their views about basic questions of the human society: it is an inexorable law in the progress of human society that capitalism will perish and socialism will succeed the former. The party program should adhere to the immediate goal of overthrowing the rule of the bourgeoisie and establishing the rule of the proletariat, and the maximum goal of realizing communism; the party program should adhere to the principles of class struggle and the dictatorship of the proletariat; the party program should adhere to the principles of alliance of workers and peasants and proletarian internationalism. Second, the party program should follow the principle of combining theory with practice. According to Marx and Engels, the party program is the collective reflection of the party's ideological theories and its role is to guide practical activities; on the premise of adhering to the principle of scientific socialism, its specific contents change to adapt to the environment so as to fit in with different conditions for struggle; in this way, the party will be able to have wider class basis and social basis and become an "action party" that struggles for its immediate goal. Third, when formulating its program, a party should resolutely adhere to principles while be flexible in strategies. It shall never give up the ultimate goal for immediate interests; neither should it put undue emphasis on the ultimate goal neglecting the current nature of revolution. Moreover, the revolution will be divided into different stages, and consequently a Marxist party should not neglect the current ideological reality of its party members and the masses and also should when necessary adjust its strategies timely or make necessary compromises.

Fourth is the significance of the party program in practice. The founders of Marxist parties paid more attention to this aspect in addition to the improvement of the party's theoretical program. Both Marx and Engels had believed that the party program should be combined with reality, and it could have a value only when it could guide the practice. If a program is alienated from reality and cannot be employed to guide practice, it will bear no worth. In the meantime, a proposed program and lines and the strategies under former's guidance should be constantly tested, revised and improved in practice; in this way, it can better play its role of coordinating the whole party and lead the mass struggles. No program for a certain specific period should be regarded as a sacred doctrine which does not allow any changes.

10.1.2 Unity of the Maximum and Minimum Programs

When the founders of Marxist parties put forward the ultimate goal of realizing communism as the maximum program, they designed a realistic goal for every stage of proletarian revolution—a minimum program. For this reason, a true communist always believes in the necessity: the unity of the maximum and minimum programs.

In February 1848, Marx and Engels had drafted "The Manifesto of the Communist Party" for the first proletarian party in the world—the Communist League, in which they had clearly stated the contents of the maximum and minimum programs for communist parties. Regarding the maximum program of proletarian parties, "The Manifesto of the Communist Party" pointed out, "The distinguishing feature of Communism is not the abolition of property generally, but the abolition of bourgeois property." "The theory of the Communists may be summed up in a single sentence: Abolition of private property."[1] "In place of the old bourgeois society, with its classes and class antagonisms, we shall have an association, in which the free development of each is the condition for the free development of all."[2] Regarding the minimum program of proletarian parties, "The Manifesto of the Communist Party" had pointed out, "The immediate aim of the Communists is the same as that of all other proletarian parties: formation of the proletariat into a class, overthrow of the bourgeois supremacy, conquest of political power by the proletariat."[3]

---

[1] *Marx & Engels Selected Works* (2nd edition), Volume 1, p.286.

[2] *Ibid.*, p.294.

[3] *Ibid.*, p.285.

In April 1875, Marx had envisioned the stages of future social development in the "Critique of the Gotha Program of the German Social Democratic Party" pointing out that the social development would be divided into three stages after the proletariat took power: the transitional period from capitalist to communist society, the primary stage of communist society, and the advanced stage of communist society, and had stated the programs or objectives for each stage. "Between capitalist and communist society there lies the period of the revolutionary transformation of the one into the other. Corresponding to this is also a politically transitional period. "In a higher phase of communist society, after the enslaving subordination of the individual to the division of labor, and therewith also the antithesis between mental and physical labor has vanished; after labor has become not only a means of life but life's prime want; after the productive forces have also increased with the all-around development of the individual, and all the springs of co-operative wealth flow more abundantly—only then can the narrow horizon of bourgeois right be crossed in its entirety and society inscribe on its banners: From each according to his ability, to each according to his needs!"[1] But the first phase or "primary stage" of communist society, "not as it on its own foundations, but, on the contrary, just as it from capitalist society, which is thus in every respect, economically, morally, and intellectually, still stamped with the birthmarks of the old society from whose womb it emerges."[2] Therefore, this phase could only adopt the principle of distribution—from each according to his ability, to each according to his work.

In summary, the programs of a Marxist party are the objectives that the party puts forward based on the interests of the class and action lines to realize, in other words, the objectives and tasks of the party. The programs consist of maximum and minimum ones; the former one is a concise formulation of the ultimate objective and tasks of the party while the latter one is a concise statement of the immediate objective and tasks at a certain

---

[1] *Marx & Engels Selected Works* (2nd edition), Volume 1, pp.305-306.
[2] *Marx & Engels Selected Works* (2nd edition), Volume 1, p.304.

phase. The two are uniform in their ideological and theoretical bases and class nature, and both combine theory with practice. The maximum program is always instructive for the formation and implementation of the minimum one, while gradually realized through minimum programs at different phases.

10.1.3 Programs of the Communist Party of China

Since its founding, the CPC, being a Marxist party, had always taken "the realization of communism" as its maximum program. In July 1921, the Program of the Communist Party of China stated, "The program of our Party is as follows: first, overthrow the bourgeoisie with revolutionary army of the proletariat, and reestablish the state with the help of the working class until abolishing class differences; second, adopt dictatorship of the proletariat so as to achieve the purpose of class struggles: abolition of classes; third, abolish private property of the bourgeoisie and confiscate all the means of production, such as machines, land, factory buildings and semi-finished products, to make them subjective to society; and fourth, unite with the *Comintern (the Third International).*" The Constitution of the Communist Party of China approved in November 2002 had also emphasized those ideas in its General Program, "The realization of communism is the highest ideal and ultimate goal of the Party."

In the long processes of revolution, reconstruction and reform periods, the CPC had raised programs gearing to changing national conditions at different periods. During the new-democratic revolution, the CPC put forward its minimum program for the first time at its Second National Congress in 1922: to eliminate internal disorder, bring down warlords and safeguard domestic peace; overthrow imperialist oppression and achieve complete independence of the Chinese nation; unite China (including the three provinces in Northeast China) into a true democratic republic. And at its Seventh National Congress held in 1945, the CPC had further interpreted that its minimum program in the new-democratic revolution period included the formulation of "new-democratic state system"[1]. In addition to the minimum

---

[1] *Selected Works of Mao Zedong* (2nd edition), Volume 3, p.1056.

programs, the CPC had also designed corresponding economic, political and cultural programs for the new-democratic revolution. After New China was founded, the CPC had also raised programs or objectives in different periods: task to transform from a new-democratic to a socialist society and later a task for all-round socialist construction. But in some periods, especially in the Cultural Revolution, since the CPC had departed from its ideological line, its program building—activity and by content—also strayed away from general principles of Marxist parties, and hence the then minimum program—"to continue the revolution under the dictatorship of the proletariat" "grasping the class struggle as the guiding principle"—had caused serious losses to the CPC and its cause. In 1978, after the Third Plenary Session of the 11th Central Committee of the CPC was held, the CPC restored and promoted the ideological line of "seeking truth from facts"—the factual and realistic work style, and thus attained a more correct judgment and understanding of international, domestic and inner-Party conditions and designed the new basic program of building socialism with Chinese characteristics covering economy, politics, culture and other fields.

Concerning the relationship between the maximum and minimum programs, the CPC has always believed in the unity of the two. As the Party goes deeper into the laws governing its rule, laws on the building of socialism and the development of human society, the CPC has a stronger and stronger faith in the Marxist fundamental principle that human society will inevitably move towards communism and that "in the communist society, there will be abundant material wealth, and people will have a relatively excellent mental outlook and be able to develop themselves freely and in an all-round way." In the meantime, the CPC has advocated the idea that "communism can only be realized on the basis of a fully developed and highly advanced socialist society." And thus the Chinese communists "should set up a lofty communist ideal, fortify their conviction and spur themselves by holding to the lofty ideological and moral standards. More importantly, they should make unremitting efforts in a down-to-earth manner to realize the Party's basic program for the current stage and put their energy into each single piece of day-to-day work. To care about the immediate interests only while forgetting the lofty ideal will result in the loss of direction of progress. But to talk big about the lofty ideal without doing any practical work will get one divorced from reality."[1]

10.2 Political Line of the Marxist Party

The political line of a Marxist party refers to basic principles, position and action norms that the party formulates in a given period considering the maximum program as the fundamental principle and at the same time based on requirements of the minimum program in order to implement given tasks and realize objectives.

10.2.1 The Line, Principles and Policies

The line is the basic principle that people follow in the process of interpreting and transforming the world. The line of a Marxist party refers to basic policies that it formulates to implement tasks in a given period.

Principles are guiding rules that a Marxist party formulates in a given period to achieve certain objectives, and are attitudes and positions that the party adopts towards several major events or problems in accordance with its program. Principles include general and specific ones; the general principle is for the overall situation while specific principles are for some certain spheres, such as economy or art and literature. In general, a party only has one general principle but several specific ones in each period. Only when a Marxist party works out the general principle for a period in a timely and correct manner and then formulates specific principles on the basis of the general principles, can the party effectively realize its political leadership over the revolution, construction and reform tasks.

Policies are the bases and norms for action that a Marxist party formulates to implement certain tasks in a given period. Policies also include general and specific ones. All the actions that a Marxist party

---

[1] *Selected Works of Jiang Zemin*, Volume 3, p.293.

engages in are implementing some policies and serve its long-term strategic tasks. Only by adhering to correct ideological line and making scientific judgment of objective circumstances, can a party make correct policies. After making policies, a party should test them in practice and then adjust, revise, supplement and develop them in accordance with realities. The formulation and implementation of correct policies is an important guarantee for improving party building and facilitating the revolution, construction and reform toward success, as well as a major expression of the qualities of the party's leadership.

To formulate a correct line, a Marxist party should follow the correct principles. First, it should rest on basic requirements of scientific socialism; otherwise it will face errors of "direction". Second, it should combine the theory of scientific socialism with fundamental realities of the country. Theory will lose its value for application if not combined with realities, whereas practice will lose direction without the guidance of theory; only when combined, the two can work for the formulation of a practical and correct line. Third, a line should be tested again and again in practice and should be enriched and improved in practice so as to more intensively represent the fundamental interests and requirements of the working class and the broad masses of the people. Last but not least, the implementation of the correct line will depend on the Party's correct leadership, resolute enforcement of leading departments and cadres at all levels and the vanguard and exemplary role of Party members.

In short, the correct formulation and implementation of the Party line, principles and policies have a direct bearing on the Party's survival and development, and the success and failure of its cause.

10.2.2 The Political Line

A party's political line, also called general line or basic line, usually refers to general action policies and the basic approaches formulated in a given period to direct specific works in all spheres, in order to realize its minimum program. The political line of a Marxist party reflects the fundamental interests and requirements of the working class and the broad masses of the people; it expresses the vanguard nature of the party, and constitutes fundamental significance for the party building of the period, and plays a basic and comprehensive role in directing the party's cause.

When leading the Chinese people to struggle for revolution, construction and reform, the Party had combined the basic theories of Marxism with the concrete realities of the Chinese revolution, and brought into being a general line in each period on the basis of repeated practice in accordance with historical tasks in that period. In the new-democratic revolution period, the CPC formed a general line of "a new-democratic revolution led by the proletariat, for the people, opposing imperialism, feudalism and bureaucrat-capitalism." During the socialist revolution period, the CPC had formulated a general line for this transitional period: "gradually realize socialist industrialization and the socialist transformation of agriculture, handicraft industry and capitalist industry and commerce over rather a long period." And by the early stage of socialist construction in 1956, the CPC had formulated a general line as "go all out, aim high and achieve greater, faster, better and more economical results in building socialism." In the new stage of reform and opening-up, the CPC has raised a general line—basic line—for the primary stage of socialism which mainly includes "one central task and two basic points."

10.3 The Basic Line for the Primary Stage of Socialism

At the Third Plenary Session of the 11th Central Committee, the CPC had restored the positioning of the CPC's ideological line and guiding ideology—Mao Zedong Thought, providing new ideological and theoretical directions for the formulation of a political line in the new period. At the Fourth Plenary Session of the 11th Central Committee, the CPC put forward its general task in the new period: "Unite the people of all our ethnic groups and bring all positive forces into play so that we can work with one heart and one mind, go all out, aim high and achieve greater, faster, better and more economical results in building a modern, powerful socialist country."[1] This formulation was approved as the CPC's political line at the Fifth Plenary Session of its 11th Central Committee. And Deng Xiaoping had given a more concise definition, "In sum, the political line of the Party at the present stage is to work with one heart and one mind for our country's four modernizations."[2] In 1982, at its 12th National Congress, CPC established its general task in the new period: "Unite the people of all our ethnic groups, work hard and self-reliantly to modernize the country's industry, agriculture, national defense and science and technology step by step to turn China into a socialist country with a high level of culture and democracy."[3]

After the 12th CPC National Congress, China's socialist modernization entered a new epoch-making period, a new page was opened in the history of exploring the building of socialism with Chinese characteristics and the Party had attained a more profound understanding of the Chinese conditions. At the 13th CPC National Congress in 1987, the CPC could be able to formulate rather a complete and scientific definition of "the primary stage of socialism": "Our country is at the primary stage of socialism. This conclusion had two meanings. First, it affirmed that the Chinese society has already been a socialist one. We should adhere to and never depart from socialism. Second, the socialist society of our country is still at the primary stage. We should proceed from this reality and never skip this stage."[4] The primary stage of socialism in China is not necessarily the starting stage that any country would go through when entering socialism, but refers particularly to a special stage that China should go through when building socialism on the conditions of legged productive forces and underdeveloped commodity economy. It

---

[1] *Selected Important Documents since the Third Plenary Session of the 11th Central Committee of the Communist Party of China*, Volume 1, p.206. Beijing: People's Press, 1982.

[2] *Selected Works of Deng Xiaoping* (2nd edition), Volume 2, p.276.

[3] *Selected Important Documents since the 12th National Congress of the Communist Party of China*, Volume 1, p.13. Beijing: People's Press, 1986.

[4] *Selected Important Documents since the 13th National Congress of the Communist Party of China*, Volume 1, p.9. Beijing: People's Press, 1991.

was envisaged that this stage, starting from the 1950s when the socialist transformation of ownership of productive means was completed to a future period when socialist modernization will be achieved, would last for over 100 years. This awareness provides the grounds for the Party in formulating and carrying out correct line and policies.

With this awareness, the CPC put forward at its 13th National Congress, "The basic line of the Communist Party of China in the primary stage of socialism is to lead the people of all ethnic groups in a concerted, self-reliant and pioneering effort to transform China into a prosperous, strong, democratic, culturally advanced and harmonious modern socialist country by making economic development the central task while upholding the Four Cardinal Principles and the reform and opening-up policy."[1] This formulation reflected the CPC's basic line for the primary stage of socialism, which was summarized as: "one central task and two basic points."

The persistence in "taking economic development as the central task" is determined by the principal contradiction at the primary stage of socialism in China, as well as the fundamental tasks of socialism. The principle contradiction at the primary stage of socialism in China is one between the ever-growing material and cultural needs of the people and the low level of production—productive forces, which runs through the whole primary stage of socialism and penetrates, reflects every aspect of social life in China. This determines that the Party should take economic development as the central task, always make it the emphasis of the whole party and the country, and push the development of productive forces as one of the fundamental tasks. And it was suggested that the Party should not shift that emphasis—economic development—even if some achievements would be realized, much less "take the class struggle as the guiding principle." And except in the event of a massive foreign aggression, the Party should concentrate on that central task; allowing nothing to interfere with its fulfillment. And even if there will be a large-scale war, people should still develop the economy that the war needs and permits.

---

[1] *Selected Important Documents since the 13th National Congress of the Communist Party of China*, Volume 1, p.15. Beijing: People's Press, 1991

The Four Cardinal Principles embodies the notions as: to keep to the socialist road and to uphold the people's democratic dictatorship, leadership by the CPC, and Marxism-Leninism and Mao Zedong Thought.

These Principles were first advocated by Deng Xiaoping summarizing the experiences accumulated by the Party over a long time and a manifestation of the common will of the Chinese people; and they have also been included into the Constitution of the People's Republic of China. They constitute the foundation for building the country as well as the basic guarantee for the healthy progress of reform and opening-up and modernization. Among the Four Cardinal Principles, keeping to the socialist road highlights the fundamental direction for the country; upholding the people's democratic dictatorship is the fundamental guarantee for running the country; upholding the leadership by the CPC is the key to modernization and the core of the Four Cardinal Principles; and upholding Marxism-Leninism and Mao Zedong Thought is to hold higher the great banner of Chinese revolution and construction and adhere to correct guiding ideology of the Party and the Government. The Four Cardinal Principles are interdependent and interactive, guaranteeing socialist modernization from different aspects. Only by adhering to the Four Cardinal Principles, can socialist China remain invincible. To adhere to the Four Cardinal Principles, the CPC should combat bourgeois liberalism with a resolute stand, identify and clear away "left" or "right" interferences without delay, and do a good job in handling the relationship between reform, development and stability.

"Reform and opening-up policy" was a major decision concerning the future of China initiated in the Third Plenary Session of the 11th Central Committee of the CPC in 1978. The term "reform" here refers to a series of revolutionary changes, whose nature and objective is to radically change the economic system that had restrained the development of the productive forces. Meanwhile, reform also covers political system and other system changes to realize socialist modernization. In terms of emancipating and developing productive forces, the Reform policy is praised as the second revolution of China, possessing several aspects similar to the first revolution which transformed the old semi-colonial and semi-feudal China to a new socialist society. But different from the first revolution, the Reform cannot be equaled to a political revolution in which one class overthrows another, and not a rectification of the old economic system in minor details, but indeed offers a radical change in the old system. The assumptions behind the Reform have not negated or undermined the basic system of socialism that has been previously established in China, but rather have aimed to improve it.

Observing and comparing the stagnant and backward Chinese society and drawing a lesson from the past closed-door policy, the Party had made an evaluation and agreed to open China to the outside world. After the Third Plenary Session of the 11th Central Committee of the CPC was held, China gradually started to open its doors, and in succession established special economic zones, opened coastal cities to the outside world, made Hainan a province and set up a special economic zone there, and opened Pudong New Area in Shangai, border cities, cities along the Yangtze River, provincial cities and some cities with appropriate conditions to the outside world.

The Party had formulated a more complete basic line for the primary stage of socialism at its 13th National Congress, and followed this basic line, besides gained new understandings and made new progress in practice. Although some important changes had occurred in the international situation and domestic conditions, this basic line was not changed.

First, the Party has acknowledged that the primary stage of socialism would be a relatively long process. "China is now at the primary stage of socialism and will remain so for a long time to come. The primary stage of socialism is the initial stage of the long historical process of building socialism with Chinese characteristics."[1] That means the basic line should be resolutely followed all through this long period and carried out in an all-round sense.

Second, to implement the basic line, the Party should properly monitor the relationship between "one central task" (economic development) and "two basic points" (the Four Cardinal Principle and Reform and Opening-

---

[1] *Selected Works of Jiang Zemin*, Volume 3, p.293.

up policy). The two are interdependent and constitute an integral and unified whole. Economic development demands the Four Cardinal Principles as political direction and the Reform and Opening-up as a strong driving force; Reform and opening-up is to further emancipate and develop productive forces, and consolidate and develop the socialist system; and the Four Cardinal Principles guarantee that reform and opening-up and economic development proceed towards a correct direction.

10.4 The Basic Program for the Primary Stage of Socialism

Guided by the basic line, China has made great achievements in reform and opening-up and socialist modernization. In the mid- and late 1990s, the practice and theoretical exploration of building socialism with Chinese characteristics went deeper and the socialist market economic system was gradually established. In the face of several opportunities and challenges in the new century, the Party, based on Deng Xiaoping Theory and the basic line for the primary stage of socialism, made an explicit new formulation at the 15th national Congress agreed on the basic program for the primary stage of socialism: **to build a socialist economy, politics and culture with Chinese characteristics.** I would like **to present the reader main parts of this document:**

To build a socialist economy with Chinese characteristics means to develop market economy under socialist conditions and constantly emancipate and develop the productive forces. To achieve this objective, we should adhere to and improve the basic economic system with the public ownership playing a dominant role and at the same time diverse forms of economic sectors with other ownership structures should also be developed side by side. The socialist market economic system should be followed and improved; and we should ensure that the market forces play an essential role in the allocation of resources under the state's macro-economic regulation; adhere to and improve the basic distribution system with distribution according to work remaining as a dominant mode, and on the other hand allow some regions and some people getting rich earlier so that they can help others for common prosperity; and adhere to and improve the policy of opening-up, and take an active part in international economic cooperation and competition. With these practices, we will guarantee the sustained, rapid and healthy development of national economy and ensure that people share the economic prosperity.

—To build a socialist politics with Chinese characteristics means to run the state according to laws and promote socialist democracy under the leadership of the Party and on the basis of ensuring the people remaining the master of the country. To achieve this goal, we should adhere to and improve the people's democratic dictatorship led by the working class and based on the alliance of workers and peasants; uphold and improve the people's congress system, the system of multi-party cooperation and political consultation under the leadership of the CPC, and the system of regional ethnic autonomy; and promote democracy, improve the legal system and build a socialist country under the rule of law. With these practices, we will manage to create a dynamic political situation, in which the society is stable, the government is clean and efficient, and people of all the ethnic groups are unified and live in harmony.

—To build a socialist culture with Chinese characteristics means to develop national, scientific and popular socialist culture geared to the needs of modernization, of the world and of the future, under the guidance of Marxism and with the objective to train citizens with lofty ideals, integrity, knowledge and a strong sense of discipline. To achieve this, we should arm the whole party and educate the people with Deng Xiaoping Theory, and work hard to improve the ideology and moral integrity and educational, scientific and cultural attainments of the whole Chinese nation; persist in the orientation of serving the people and socialism and the principle of letting a hundred flowers blossom and a hundred schools of thought contend, so as to make academy and literature and art flourish. With these practices, we will build socialist spiritual civilization that is based on China's realities, carries forward the fine tradition of our national culture and absorbs the achievements of foreign cultures.[1]

The basic program has manifested a deeper understanding of the realities at the primary stage of socialism, an important part of Deng Xiaoping Theory, and an expansion of the basic line in the fields of economy, politics and culture. It was also an action program by which the CPC will lead the people to push forward the building of socialism with Chinese characteristics in the first half of the new century.

10.5 The Basic Principles for the Primary Stage of Socialism

After political disturbances in the 1980s, particularly the Tiananmen Square protests in 1989, the Party had a clearer understanding on how to treat the three relationships between: the speed of economic development, the momentum of reform and the stability of the general public order. In early 1994, the Central Committee, after holding repeated discussions and careful research, proposed a new principle for balancing reform, development and stability. At the celebration of the 20th anniversary of the Third Plenary Session of the 11th CPC Central Committee, Jiang Zemin had made a comment on the issue: "Facts prove that our Party's principle aiming to seize opportunities, deepen reform, open China wider to the outside world, promote development and maintain stability is right. We should always follow this principle, and make careful plans in the light of the overall situation and specific conditions of a given period; take into full consideration the momentum of reform, the speed of development and the stability of the general public order; press ahead with reform and development amidst social stability and promote long-term social stability through reform and development."[2]

---

[1] *Selected Important Documents since the 15th National Congress of the Communist Party of China*, Volume 1, pp.18-19. Beijing: People's Press, 2000.

[2] *Selected Works of Jiang Zemin*, Volume 3, pp.534-535.

I would like to offer an interpretation on this paragraph in the current situation:

First, "to seize opportunities" means to explore and seize objective advantages and accelerate socialist modernization. Opportunities are objective and could be too easily missed. Whether you can seize opportunities and make good use of them will have a great effect on the success and long-term aims. The idea assumes that China has great opportunities for development. First, in terms of international environment, peace and development have become the main themes of the present era; the pattern of the world is changing toward multi-polarization; and it is quite possible to maintain a peaceful international environment for a fairly long period of time. The Asia-Pacific region, where China is located, is becoming a place with relatively stable political atmosphere and enjoying a highly dynamic economic development. The scientific and technological revolution is forging ahead by leaps and bounds; a new round of adjustment of industrial structure is going on; and a great amount of idle financial fund is searching for new markets to invest. These are evaluated as new opportunities for China's economic development. Second, in terms of domestic conditions, since the founding of New China, particularly in the last two decades, a considerable overall national strength has been built up in China; the reform and opening-up have brought about favorable conditions for the modernization drive, created a higher domestic market demand and sources of funds, and people's enthusiasm for development has been greatly enhanced. That means domestic opportunities are also abundant.

Second, "to deepen reform" means to take reform as the motive force for propelling the efforts in all other spheres. In the field of economy, a new pattern of industrialization is envisaged and the strategy of "rejuvenating the country through science and education and sticking to sustainable development" is highlighted. To make the rural economy flourish, speed up urbanization, building a new socialist countryside; continue to carry out large-scale development in the western underdeveloped regions, rejuvenate northeast China and other old industrial bases in an all-round way, boost the development of the central region and support the eastern region in taking the lead in development are the main parts of that strategy. To bring about a coordinated development of regional economies; stick to and improve the basic economic system and deepen the reform of the state property management system; improve the modern market system and tighten and improve macro-economic control; deepen the reform of the income distribution system and improve the social security system; do a better job in opening up by "bringing in" and "going out"; and do everything possible to create more jobs and improve the people's lives are underlined as guiding aims. In the field of politics, to improve the system of socialist democracy is taken as the main strategy. To improve the socialist legal system; improve the Party's style of leadership and governance; improve the decision-making mechanisms; deepen administrative restructuring; promote the reform of the judicial system; deepen the reform of the cadre and personnel system; tighten the control and supervision over the use of power; and maintain social stability are the parts of political reform. In the field of culture, orientation to an advanced culture constitutes the strategy. To progress forward and cultivate the national spirit; promote cultural and ethical progress; develop education and science; develop cultural undertakings and the cultural industry; and continue to deepen cultural restructuring are evaluated as parts of the cultural strategy.

Third, to "open China wider to the outside world" is evaluated as a long-term commitment and opening to the outside world is set as a long-term basic state policy. That means, faced with the globalization trend in the economic, scientific and technological development, China should take an even more active stance in the world by improving the pattern of opening up in all directions, at all levels and in a wide range, developing an open economy, enhancing international competitiveness, optimizing the economic structure and improving the quality of the national economy. And China's entry into the WTO is assessed as an opportunity to participate in international economic and technological cooperation and competition on a broader scale, covering more spheres and achieving higher levels. To make the best use of international and domestic markets; optimize the allocation of resources; and expand the space for development; expand the trade in commodities and services, emphasize exports, attract more foreign direct investment and utilize it more effectively; try to bring in from overseas large numbers of professionals and other intellectual resources in various areas; and improve the environment for investment. All these are concrete parts and aims covered in the concept of opening to the outside world.

Fourth is the notion to "promote development." Development is valued as the fundamental principle; and the country should mainly rely on its development to solve all the problems. Development is evaluated as on overriding necessity in order to strengthen the compound national capacity of the country and improvement of the people's lives, consolidating and improving the socialist system and maintaining the social stability, in safeguarding state sovereignty and independence against all forms of hegemony and power politics, and elevating China to the level of advanced countries. Thus giving top priority to development and taking economic development as the central task is considered as a key solution.

Fifth aspect is to "maintain stability." Stability is underlined as a prerequisite to reform and development. In history, no country could be able to develop economy in chaos, or to undertake a successful reform in chaos. In the primary stage of socialism, it is of the utmost importance to balance reform, development and stability and to maintain a stable political environment and a positive public order. For this aim, the leadership by the Party, upholding the people's democratic dictatorship and the principle of promoting all aspects of social development is emphasized. Eliminating all factors jeopardizing stability, opposing bourgeois liberalism and guarding against the infiltrative, subversive and split activities of the international and domestic hostile forces are more concrete objectives. Here, I would like to comment that stability approach is quite dynamic, and this is reflected in the following formulation as: "promoting reform and development amid social and political stability and securing social and political stability through reform and development".

To sum up my comments, I would like to employ an analogy: reform, development, and stability are evaluated as three closely connected pawns on the chessboard of China's modernization in the primary stage of socialism; if each pawn is played correctly, the play will proceed to success; if any of the three is played improperly, the other two will face trouble and the play will face setbacks.

10.6 The New Idea: Scientific Outlook on Development

In the new century, the CPC has summarized the experience gained from socialist modernization practice and has also evaluated the modernization course of several other developing countries. Moreover, the Party has studied the most recent and the future development patterns in light of new features of social development. Hence, several new development concepts were developed as follows:

First, development requires concentrating on economic development. The history of China since modern times and that of other developing countries have proved that "the wealthy would speak louder than others, and who lags behind will be bullied." In the present world, a country without a strong economy will not be able to promote its national defense capabilities and national cohesion, and bear several consequences faced with advanced nations. In the last quarter of 20th century due to economic and social achievements, China's national strength has grown notably, people's lives have been greatly improved, and her status in the international community has risen. The idea suggests that though China is facing intense international competition and complicated domestic contradictions, as long as she practices the central task of economic development, the future will be more optimistic.

Second, a socialist society demands an all-round sense of development and progress. In exploring the prospects of communist society, founders of Marxism had concluded that it would be a free society developing and progressing in an all-round way in which free and all-round development of each individual would be the basis of it. Thus recently the Party has summarized this idea with a new formulation as: "to build China into a prosperous, democratic and civilized socialist country, attaching to the principle of promoting material progress and cultural and ethical progress with equal emphasis on both aspects." And several new notions were formulated in line with that idea as: "achieving sustainable development," "developing the country by relying on science and education," "ruling the country by law and by virtues"; all these ideas were quite systemized and termed as "the socialist outlook on development". At its 16th National Congress in 2002, the Party had officially set the goal of building a moderately prosperous society in all respects, defining the development objectives for the following two decades as: "a more developed economy, improved democracy, more advanced science and education, enriched culture, more harmonious society and upgraded life for the people."[1]. And it was underlined that objectives should cover material, political, cultural and ethical, and ecological aspects (Capability of sustainable development progresses.) Party building scholars generally agree that there are several new findings related to basic theories of Marxism in those new ideas.

Third, keep promoting the overall development of people. The essential requirement of Marxism regarding building a new socialist society is to keep promoting the overall development of people. It demands that in all the undertakings, in fact in every plan, the aim should not just be to meet the people's immediate material and cultural needs. Here I would like to offer the reader a comment from Jiang Zemin: "To advance an all-round development of men is the precondition for and the basis of boosting economic and cultural development and improving the material and cultural life of the people, and vice versa. The more comprehensively people develop, the more material and cultural wealth they will create for society and the better the people's life will be. Conversely, the more adequate the material and cultural life is, the better man will achieve his all-round development. The development of social productive forces, the economy and culture is a historical process of gradual

---

[1] *Selected Works of Jiang Zemin*, Volume 3, p.543.

and endless progress. All-round human development, too, is a historical process of gradual and endless progress. The two processes should interact with and promote each other forward."[1]

The Concept of People First:

Later, based on these understandings, the Party has formulated a brand new idea of "people-oriented scientific development" or "the principle of people first". I suggest it is indeed a part of Marxist party building since it is an extension of the older concept: "serving the people should be the Party's fundamental goal and to represent the fundamental interests of the overwhelming majority should be its main character". Putting the people first orients the Party to take the satisfaction of people's needs in all respects and the promotion of overall human development as the primary goal and motive power of development. Shortly it evaluates the improvement of people's living standards as the starting point. Thus, putting people first and achieving a comprehensive, coordinated and sustainable development are two basic contents of development integrating the subject and the object aspect.

All those recent ideas I have reflected above are the key theoretical aspects of "Scientific Outlook on Development" grand policy of the Party. The theoretical foundations of the Scientific Outlook on Development are an attempt to integrate the basic tenets of Marxist dialectical materialism and historical materialism with the current reality of the world and China.

It is generally assessed as a smooth inheritance and development of the previous policy of the Three Represents thought and extends the idea of Party (building)—the Party is built for the public and that it exercises state power for the people" in the aspect of its character.

The Scientific Outlook on Development is a policy or a system to guide development, and attempts to define new criteria the theme of development. The Scientific Outlook on Development also sets new qualities for the Party building and governmental building in the cadres' aspect and on evaluating cadres' performances. It suggests that cadres' good performances are for development, and for the people's benefits and they should be evaluated

---

[1] *Selected Works of Jiang Zemin*, Volume 3, p.295.

with a practical, comprehensive standpoint and from the perspective of the masses. Here the "comprehensive standpoint" means to consider both economic indicators and social, human development and environmental indices, both urban and rural development, both the current development and the sustainability of development, both the growth of economic aggregate and practical benefits of the people, both economic development and social stability, both present and potential achievements of cadres, and both cadres' efforts and objective conditions. To evaluate Party cadres with a practical standpoint means to attach importance to concrete work, handle concrete affairs in a down-to-earth manner and seek practical results; thus each cadre's performance should be able to withstand the test of practice and history. To evaluate Party cadres from the perspective of the masses means they should highly consider people's appeals, follow the principle of serving the people wholeheartedly, and take the realization of the people's interests as the ultimate goal to improve cadres' performances. The basic criterion to evaluate a cadre's—in the Party or the government—performance is whether the people support, agree to, are happy with and approve it.

Ideological Line of the Party

An advanced Marxist party must adopt and adhere to a correct ideological line so that it can maintain an energetic and positive state of mind, keep enhancing its creativity and stand forever in the forefront of the times.

For Chinese Marxists: "emancipating the mind, seeking truth from facts and keeping up with the times" are the centerpieces of dialectical and historical materialism. Here seeking generally means to study. In one sense these ideas are contained in the essence of the Party ideology and included in the Constitution of the Party—general program part—as: Marxism-Leninism, Mao Zedong Thought, Deng Xiaoping Theory and the important thought of Three Represents.

11.1 The Ideological Line and the Success in the Cause

The ideological line, also known as the "line of cognition," is a philosophical issue concerning the world outlook that guides Marxist as we come to know and change the world. The CPC's ideological line is the Marxist world outlook and methodology applied and exemplified in its actual work. It lays the groundwork for the Party to adopt and implement a correct political line. It also ensures that it achieves success in its cause from an ideological dimension.

11.1.1 The Ideological Line of a Proletarian Party

Marx and Engels were the founding fathers of the ideological line of proletarian parties. In the mid-1840s, they founded the philosophy of dialectical materialism based on a review of the experience in the proletarian struggle, providing proletarian parties with the world outlook and methodology to know and change the world. Dialectical materialism and historical materialism are the most fundamental features of the Marxist theory as well as the theoretical foundation of the scientific system of Marxism as a whole. They serve as a new, scientific world outlook for proletarian parties as they engage in the practice of knowing and changing the world.

In a sense, the history of the development of Marxism is a history of following objective laws, emancipating the mind through practice, keeping up with the times, exploring new frontiers, making innovations and making new theoretical achievements to serve the needs of the times. Any major achievement in the Marxist theory and any historical leap forward in the socialist practice result from theoretical innovation that integrates the basic tenets of Marxism with concrete practice. Marx and Engels had criticized utopian socialism, revealed the law of surplus value as well as the objective law that socialism is bound to replace capitalism, turned socialism from utopian thoughts to a science and founded Marxism. Their achievement was a result of the innovative efforts they made in keeping with the times. Based on a study of historical and current documents on nature, society and human thinking, Marxism reveals the basic laws in these fields. In particular, it brings to light the basic laws governing the development of human society, pointing out that socialism and communism represent the general direction for the development of human society. Marxists regard Marxism as a science because it seeks truth from facts and its basic tenets have been proven correct. It also requires that we approach and develop it in a down-to-earth manner. Engels had made a comment on the issue: Marxism is a "theory of evolution, not a dogma to be learned by heart and to be repeated mechanically." In fact, after Marxism was born, Marx and Engels had continued to improve and develop their theory in keeping with the development of practice by summarizing experience in workers' struggle and drawing on new achievements in the development of science.

In Russia, Lenin had studied the basic tenets of Marxism in light of the historical conditions at his time, while securing the role of Marxism in guiding the proletarian revolutionary movement. Instead of clinging to certain stereotypes of Marxism, he attached great importance to actual conditions. He integrated the basic tenets of Marxism with the Russia's practice, thereby applying and developing Marxism in a creative way. He had challenged the dogma that socialism can only triumph in most countries at the same time and put forward the theory that one country or several countries can achieve victory ahead of others. Under the guidance of this theory, Lenin led the Russians in winning the October Revolution and establishing the first socialist country in the world. At the same time, he moved Marxism into a new phase—Leninism. His achievement was a result of his innovative efforts in keeping with the times.

In China, the CPC—after a long exploration has developed—the ideological line of seeking truth from facts, emancipating the mind and keeping up with the times, since its founding more than 80 years ago as it leads the Chinese people of all ethnic groups in carrying out revolution, socialist construction and reform. Proceeding from China's reality, Mao Zedong integrated the basic tenets of Marxism-Leninism with the practice of the Chinese revolution. He was the first to put forward the strategy of encircling urban areas with rural areas and seizing state power by force. He had also created theory of new democracy and led the Chinese revolution to victory. Mao Zedong Thought is the culmination of the CPC's efforts to keep up with the times. In the new era of reform and opening-up, Deng Xiaoping put forward the theory of building socialism with Chinese characteristics as he focused on the basic theoretical questions of "what socialism is and how to build it," thereby guiding China's socialism into a new period of vigorous development. Deng Xiaoping Theory is another innovative achievement the CPC made under the principle of keeping up with the times. At the turn of the century, Comrade Jiang Zemin, standing in the forefront of the times, studied China's national conditions with a Marxist position, viewpoint and approach. He summed up experience in socialist revolution, construction and reform, both in China and in other countries, and he had especially focused on the experience and lessons in building the CPC as China's ruling party. He initiated the important thought of Three Represents, giving a further answer to the questions of "what socialism is and how to build it" as well as an innovative answer to the questions of "what kind of Party to build and how to build it." It is a powerful ideological tool with which the CPC can forever preserve its vigor and vitality. As another innovative development of Marxism, the important thought of Three Represents is the latest achievement under the principle of keeping up with the times.

For a mature political party, its ideological line is a reflection of its world outlook in its political practice. Classes, strata and social groups in different stages of history have different world outlooks due to such factors as social conditions, features of the times and class characters. The proletarian class emerged in an era of mechanized mass production. It takes Marxism, the greatest cultural achievement in human history, as its guiding ideology and the liberation of mankind as its task. This determines that its supreme organization, which is the proletarian party, is bound to take the Marxist world outlook, i.e. dialectical materialism and historical materialism, as the theoretical basis of its ideological line. The ideological line of a proletarian party is therefore developed as the party flexibly applies the basic tenets of dialectical materialism and historical materialism in its work. Just as Marx pointed out, "The question whether objective truth can be attributed to human thinking is not a question of theory but is a practical question."

11.1.2 Ideological Line Is the Theoretical Basis for Political and Organizational Lines

Engels had pointed out that theoretical thought is a historical product in every epoch. The development of the Party's ideological line is closely related to the epoch and environment the Party is in and the circumstances and tasks it faces. Since the CPC has developed its ideological line under the guidance of Marxism, the ideological line is a Marxist ideological line. The CPC, also changes the content and form of its ideological line, which is an integral part of Marxism, to keep with the times. Mao Zedong said: "Communists should set an example in being practical...For only by being practical can they fulfill the appointed tasks.[1]" Deng Xiaoping had underlined the importance of a correct ideological line from the perspective of rectifying the mistakes of the Cultural Revolution. "Our ideological line is important because it serves as the basis for working out our political line. Whether a correct political line can be implemented depends primarily on whether we have a correct ideological line." he said in 1979, "It is impossible to establish a correct political line—let alone carry it out—unless we clarify our ideological line and emancipate people's minds.[2]" In his speech commemorating the 20th anniversary of the Third Plenary Session of the 11th CPC Central Committee, Jiang Zemin had summarized major historical experience in reform and opening-up in the previous two decades in 11 points. The most important point was that the CPC must adhere to a Marxist ideological line. In his report to the 16th CPC National Congress, Jiang had emphasized efforts to "uphold Deng Xiaoping Theory as our guide and constantly bring forth theoretical innovation" which he underlined as the most important experience in building socialism with Chinese characteristics since the Fourth Plenary Session of the 13th CPC Central Committee.

History and reality have repeatedly shown that a correct ideological line is indispensable for the Party to survive and succeed in the cause it leads.

---

[1] *Selected Works of Mao Zedong* (2nd Chinese edition), Volume 2, p.522.

[2] *Selected Works of Deng Xiaoping* (2nd Chinese edition), Volume 2, p.191.

11.2 The Adoption and Development of the Ideological Line

The Party has developed an ideological line in its efforts to lead the China's revolution, and later in socialist construction and reform and opening-up. The line represents the integration of the Marxist theory of knowledge with China's reality.

11.2.1 The First Adoption and Development of the CPC's Ideological Line

In the history of the CPC, Mao Zedong was the first person to put forth the scientific concept of "ideological line." In the late 1920s and early 1930s, the CPC was inclined to dogmatize Marxism and hold sacred the Communist International's resolutions and the Russia's experience, which is wrong. In resolving major problems, it mechanically cited Marxist doctrines and blindly referred to the revolutionary experience of other countries and the Communist International's resolutions. As a result, the Chinese revolution suffered severe setbacks. In this context, Mao Zedong led the CPC in rectifying these erroneous practices, thereby freeing people's minds from the shackles of dogmatism and establishing the principle of "seeking truth from facts" as the CPC's ideological line.

Mao Zedong first used the concept of "ideological line" in a letter to Lin Biao on June 14, 1929. In the letter, Mao had analyzed some erroneous views in the Fourth Army of the Chinese Workers' and Peasants' Red Army and evaluated them as the "last struggle of the wrong ideological line in history."[1] In his article "Oppose Book Worship" (May 1930), he had once again clarified the issue of ideological line, raising the slogan: "No investigation, no right to speak." "Those comrades who are inflexible, conservative, formalistic and groundlessly optimistically think that the present tactics of struggle are perfect, that the 'book of documents' of the Party's Sixth National Congress guarantees lasting victory, and that one

[1] *Selected Works of Mao Zedong*, Volume 1, p.71. Beijing: People's Press, 1993.

can always reach victory merely by adhering to the established methods ....
These ideas are absolutely wrong and have nothing in common with the idea
that Communists should create favorable new situations through struggle;
they represent a purely conservative line."[1] He believed that "without
investigating the actual situation, there is bound to be an idealist appraisal of
class forces and an idealist guidance in work, resulting either in opportunism
or in putschism."[2]

After the Central Front of the Red Army had arrived in north Shaanxi
Province at the end of 1935 following the Long March, Mao had deliberated
and summed up the experience and lessons in the Chinese revolution in a
more comprehensive manner, while directing critics at some CPC members'
dogmatism and book worship. In his theoretically innovative essays "On
Practice" and "On Contradiction," he had summarized the experience
and lessons in the Chinese revolution from the perspective of the theory
of knowledge. He had enriched the Marxist theory of knowledge and
dialectics by celebrating the essence of Chinese philosophy. During the Yan'an
Rectification Movement after 1942, Mao had emphatically pointed out
that there was a conflict between Marxist style of study and anti-Marxist,
subjectivist style of study. He stressed for the first time that "seeking truth
from facts" should be the Marxist style of study that Chinese Communists
should adopt.

In May 1941, Mao had given a scientific definition of "seeking truth
from facts" in his report "Reform Our Study": "'Facts' are all the things
that exist objectively, 'truth' means their internal relations, that is, the laws
governing them, and 'to seek' means to study. We should proceed from the
actual conditions inside and outside the country, the province, county or
district, and derive from them, as our guide to action, laws which are inherent
in them and not imaginary, that is, we should find the internal relations of
the events occurring around us. And in order to do that, we must rely not on

---

[1] *Selected Works of Mao Zedong* (2nd Chinese edition), Volume 1, pp.115-116. Beijing: People's
Press, 1993.
[2] *Ibid.*, p.112.

subjective imagination, not on spontaneous enthusiasm, not on lifeless books, but on facts that exist objectively; we must appropriate the material in detail and, guided by the general principles of Marxism-Leninism, draw correct conclusions from it."[1] Mao had employed the Chinese phrase *shishi qiushi* (seeking truth from facts) in his own calligraphy for the Party School of the Central Committee of the CPC as its motto in December 1941.

Through the Yan'an Rectification Movement between 1941 and 1945, the CPC's understanding of the ideological line of seeking truth from facts had reached a new height. Veteran proletarian revolutionaries Liu Shaoqi, Zhou Enlai, Chen Yun and Zhang Wentian had also contributed to the adoption of this ideological line. It also represents the collective wisdom of the CPC.

Seeking truth from facts captures the essence of Marxism. Philosophy is the foundation of the scientific system of Marxism, with materialism and dialectics constituting its essence. In this sense, seeking truth from facts, which exemplifies the principle of materialism, embodies the basic spirit of Marxism.

Specifically, the ideological line of seeking truth from facts consists of the following two aspects:

The first is always proceeding from reality: According to the Marxist theory of knowledge, the relationship between objectivity and subjectivity is a reflection of the relationship between matter and mind in real life. It is necessary to gain a correct knowledge of the world before we can go on to change it in a proper way. To gain a correct knowledge of the world, we must proceed from reality. In upholding the ideological line of seeking truth from facts, we should first of all proceed from reality instead of books or subjective wishes. During the New Democratic Revolution, some dogmatist party members, despite their a strong command of basic Marxist tenets, tended to proceed from books and the Communist International's resolutions and decrees and mechanically replicate foreign experience as they tried to understand, research into and guide the Chinese revolution. To expose their

---

[1] *Selected Works of Mao Zedong* (2nd Chinese Edition), Volume 3, p.801.

falsehood, Mao Zedong said: "This subjectivist method which is contrary to science and Marxism-Leninism is a formidable enemy of the Communist Party, the working class, the people and the nation; it is a manifestation of impurity in Party spirit. A formidable enemy stands before us, and we must overthrow him. Only when subjectivism is overthrown can the truth of Marxism-Leninism prevail, can Party spirit be strengthened, can the revolution be victorious."[1]

The second is integrating theory with practice: To uphold the ideological line of seeking truth from facts, it is necessary to correctly handle the relationship between theory and practice. It is critical to integrate theory with practice and refrain from dogmatism and book worship. Marxism is a scientific truth that has emerged from and been proven by objective practice. It is bound to develop along with the development of practice and the advancement of the times. The most fundamental and important task in studying Marxism is to study its essence, basic positions, viewpoints and methods. During the Yan'an Rectification Movement from 1941 to 1945, Mao Zedong had pointed out that the purpose of studying Marxism is to put it into practice. He had called on Chinese Communists to use the arrow of Marxism to shoot the target of the Chinese revolution. Practice, as the subjective translated into the objective, is the only criterion for testing truth. The development and enrichment of theory should accord with the requirements of the contemporary times as well as social and historical conditions.

Under the guidance of the Marxist ideological line of seeking truth from facts, the first-generation CPC central leadership with Mao Zedong at the core had independently developed an approach to New Democratic Revolution with Chinese characteristics—encircling urban areas with rural areas and seizing state power by force—by proceeding from China's reality without being confined to existing Marxist theories and experience in the international communist movement. Based on this, Chinese Communists had made the first breakthrough in integrating the basic tenets of Marxism with

---

[1] *Selected Works of Mao Zedong* (2nd Chinese edition), Volume 3, p.800.

the Chinese revolution with Mao Zedong Thought being their theoretical achievement, thereby laying the ideological groundwork for the final victory of the New Democratic Revolution. From the founding of the People's Republic of China in 1949 to the mid-1950s, the first-generation of CPC leaders had continued to uphold the ideological line of seeking truth from facts. And they had adapted the CPC's lines, principles and policies to China's national conditions. In this way, they led the Chinese people in fulfilling the remaining tasks of the New Democratic Revolution. As a new practice in the history of the international communist movement, they creatively carried out the socialist transformation of the private ownership of the means of production in a peaceful way. On this basis, they had started the socialist construction centered on socialist industrialization.

11.2.2 The Re-establishment of the CPC's Ideological Line

Emancipating the mind and seeking truth from facts are major developments the CPC has introduced to the Marxist theory. They are also the historical and logical starting points for the great practice of reform and opening-up. When China brought the Cultural Revolution to an end 33 years ago, the CPC had faced two options: One was to persist in carrying out the lines, principles and policies of "taking class struggle as the central task;" and the other was to rectify past "leftist" mistakes and shift the focus of the CPC and the country to socialist modernization. At that time, some major CPC leaders had clung to "two whatevers" (we will resolutely uphold whatever policy decisions Chairman Mao made, and unswervingly follow whatever instructions Chairman Mao gave), advocating the rigid thinking pattern. Veteran proletarian revolutionaries with Deng Xiaoping as their representative were the first to realize that resolving the issue of the ideological line is an important prerequisite to clarifying all other issues and achieving the shift of the CPC's focus. At this point of time, Deng had stressed that Mao Zedong Thought was an integrated system and Mao's remarks should not be quoted out of context or distorted at will. Instead he had underlined and pointed to the work style Mao had always advocated: "the mass line and seeking truth from facts are of fundamental importance". With a theoretical and political courage, Deng had made every effort to create an atmosphere of emancipating the mind prevailing in the CPC and re-establish the Marxist ideological line of seeking truth from facts. In a letter to the CPC Central Committee in April 1977, he had made the following comment: "We must always guide our Party, armed forces and whole nation with correct, complete Mao Zedong Thought to advance the causes of the Party, socialism and the international communist movement victoriously."[1] Deng had supported—the heated debate of the day—on the criteria of truth, and commented that the philosophical article written in regard with this debate entitled "Practice Is the Only Criterion for Testing Truth" was Marxist. He had also noted that that debate, which was triggered by "two whatevers," was inevitable and worthwhile.[2]

With the support of Deng Xiaoping and other veteran proletarian revolutionaries, the debate on the criteria of truth was carried out in full swing and soon created a nationwide mind emancipation movement, laying the ideological and theoretical groundwork for the Third Plenary Session of the 11th CPC Central Committee. In December 1978, Deng had commented in a speech at the closing session of the Central Working Conference: "When everything has to be done by the book, when thinking turns rigid and blind faith is the fashion, it is impossible for a party or a nation to make progress. Its life will cease and that party or nation will perish."[3] "…the primary task is to emancipate our minds," "Only then can we, guided as we should be by Marxism-Leninism and Mao Zedong Thought, find correct solutions to the emerging as well as inherited problems, fruitfully reform those aspects of the relations of production and of the superstructure that do not correspond with the rapid development of our productive forces, and chart the specific course and formulate the specific policies, methods and measures needed to achieve

---

[1] *Selected Works of Deng Xiaoping* (2nd Chinese edition), Volume 2, p.39.

[2] Party Literature Research Center of the CPC Central Committee, *A Chronology of Deng Xiaoping's Thought (1975-1997)*, pp.72-73. Beijing: Central Party Literature Press, 1998.

[3] *Selected Works of Deng Xiaoping* (2nd Chinese edition), Volume 2, p.143.

the four modernizations under our actual conditions."[1] The Third Plenary Session of the CPC Central Committee was convened in December 1978 with this speech as the guiding ideology. It had marked the reestablishment of the Marxist ideological line of emancipating the mind and seeking truth from facts in the Party.

As an advocate of the ideological line of emancipating the mind and seeking truth from facts and the chief architect of China's reform and opening-up and modernization programs, Deng had scientifically re-defined the concept of liberating the mind: "It means that, guided by Marxism, we should break the fetters of habit, subjectivism and prejudice, and study new situations and solve new problems."[2] "Emancipating our minds means making our thinking conform to reality—making the subjective conform to the objective—and that means seeking truth from facts."[3]

Emancipating the mind and seeking truth from facts are inherently consistent. Deng had underlined the dialectical relationship between the two concepts. He had pointed out that emancipating the mind means to seek truth from facts and to study new situations and solve new problems under the guidance of Marxism. In this sense, there is an internal relationship between them: Only when Marxists emancipate their minds can they seek truth from facts; and only when Marxists seek truth from facts can they truly emancipate their minds. We must seek truth from facts on the basis of emancipating our minds. Only in this way can we do well in seeking truth from facts. The CPC Constitution which was adopted at the 12th CPC National Congress has summarized the CPC's ideological line as follows: "to proceed from reality in handling all matters, to integrate theory with practice, to seek truth from facts, and to verify and develop the truth through practice."[4]

The re-establishment of the ideological line of emancipating the mind and seeking truth from facts has facilitated efforts to rectify the mistakes in the Cultural Revolution and promoted the vigorous development of reform

---

[1] *Selected Works of Deng Xiaoping* (2nd Chinese edition), Volume 2, p.141.

[2] *Ibid.*, p.279.

[3] *Ibid.*, p.364.

[4] *Selected Important Documents since the 12th CPC National Congress (Part I)*, p.67.

and opening-up and modernization programs. Under the guidance of this ideological line, the Party has created a new path termed as socialism with Chinese characteristics. And, remarkable progress was made in China's reform and opening-up and social development. The second-generation of the CPC central leadership with Deng Xiaoping at the core has persisted in emancipating the mind and seeking truth from facts in a bid to seek an answer to the fundamental questions of "what is socialism and how to build it." By inheriting from predecessors and making innovations, the Party had developed the lines, principles and policies on socialism with Chinese characteristics concerning the essence, development stages, driving force, fundamental tasks, external conditions, political guarantees, strategic steps, supporter base and leadership of socialism as well as the principle of "one country, two systems." It for the first time came up with a systematic solution to the basic question of how to build, consolidate and develop socialism in China, a country that is still economically and culturally underdeveloped. It can easily be observed that the Party has been adhering to the ideological line since the very beginning of reform and opening-up.

11.2.3 Further Improvements in the Ideological Line Since 1989

At the beginning of the 21st century, China has moved into a new development stage of building a moderately prosperous society in all respects and accelerating socialist modernization. It is generally accepted that the CPC faces serious challenges from at home and abroad and from both within and outside the Party.

On June 19, 1992, Jiang Zemin—in his speech at the Party School of the CPC Central Committee—had commented: "as we pursue development and reform we must persevere in emancipating our minds, a magic instrument that helps us maintain vigor and vitality in our thinking and work[1]."

Jiang had reiterated that keeping up with the times is the most

---

[1] Jiang Zemin, "Speech at a Training Session for Provincial and Ministerial Cadres at the Party School of the CPC Central Committee," *People's Daily*, June 20, 1992.

important theoretical feature of Marxism. In his report to the 16th CPC National Congress in November 2002, he had precisely defined the concept as follows: "Upholding the Party's ideological line, emancipating the mind, seeking truth from facts and keeping up with the times are decisive factors for our Party to retain its progressiveness and enhance its creativity. Keeping up with the times means that all the theory and work of the Party must conform to the times, follow the law of development and display great creativity."[1] At the Congress, the Party had decided to inscribe "persisting in emancipating the mind, seeking truth from facts and keeping up with the times" into its Constitution as one of the four basic requirements that must be fulfilled in Party building. I think this move manifests that the Party has deepened its understanding on the issue of ideological line by combining the inherent relationship between keeping up with the times on the one hand and emancipating the mind and seeking truth from facts on the other hand. This new approach has further improved the Party's ideological line by employing a contemporary meaning to the line. It had major implications for guiding Marxists in upholding the Party's ideological line in a more comprehensive approach and promoting the development of the causes of the Party and the state.

Preserving the mental state of keeping up with the times is essential to continued progress in socialist modernization. The world today is undergoing significant and profound changes. China's reform, opening-up and modernization programs are forging ahead. The people's great practice is developing. All these give rise to endless new situations and new problems. To achieve new progress in China's modernization under these complicated domestic and international circumstances, the Party should sum up new experience with Marxist political and theoretical courage, broaden its theoretical vision and develop new concepts. It should come up with new ideas for development, make new breakthroughs in reform, break new ground in opening-up and take new moves in all fields of endeavor in accordance with the requirements of the 16th CPC National Congress.

---

[1] *Selected Works of Jiang Zemin*, Volume 3, p.537.

Preserving the mental state of keeping up with the times is a source of the Party's vitality and creativity. Reviewing the Party history of more than 80 years, we can reach a simple yet enlightening conclusion: One of the most important reasons why the Party has grown stronger and achieved one victory after another is that it always maintains the mental state of keeping up with the times, a vigorous revolutionary spirit and strong vitality and creativity. And because it always keeps up with the times, the Party could forge ahead through practice while making theoretical innovations. I would like to give a quotation from Jiang Zemin on this point: "In emancipating the mind and seeking truth from facts, the most important thing is to resolutely rectify the past principles and policies inconsistent with the reality in the primary stage of socialism and dogmatic understanding of the principles of Marxism and socialism while upholding the basic system of socialism," .... "We should free ourselves from the shackles of these erroneous policies and thoughts so that our theory, lines, principles and policies truly conform to the requirements of development in the primary stage of socialism and the basic tenets of Marxism and socialism."[1]

Since the 16th CPC National Congress, the Central Committee with Comrade Hu Jintao as the general secretary has emphasized the principle and work style of being realistic and pragmatic. In his important speech at the Third Plenary Session of the Central Commission for Discipline Inspection in January 2004, Hu underlined the importance and urgency of remaining realistic and pragmatic in light of the new situation and tasks facing the Party: "Staying realistic and pragmatic is a scientific principle in conformity with dialectical materialism and historical materialism. It is at the core of the CPC's ideological line. It is also a fine tradition of the CPC as well as a political character that all CPC members should have. It is the source of the CPC's vitality and key to the robust development of the causes of the CPC and the people."[2] Hu had further stressed: "The key to celebrating the spirit of

---

[1] *Selected Works of Jiang Zemin*, Volume 2, p.251.

[2] *A Collection of Important Documents Since the 16th CPC National Congress (Part I)*, pp.723-725, Beijing: Central Party Literature Press, 2005.

remaining realistic and pragmatic in the whole Party lies in guiding all Party members in gaining a realistic understanding of China's national conditions in the primary stage of socialism and pursuing the pragmatic task of being devoted to hard work over a long time; in gaining a realistic understanding of the laws governing socialist development and the development of human society and pursuing the pragmatic task of doing a good job in promoting development—the top priority of the Party in governing and rejuvenating the country; in gaining a realistic understanding of the people's position and role in history and pursuing the pragmatic task of developing the people's fundamental interests; and in gaining a realistic understanding of the rules for the CPC to govern the country and pursuing the pragmatic task of comprehensively strengthening and improving Party building."[1] I think his remarks have linked the CPC's ideological line with the goal of building a moderately prosperous society in all respects, making it more relevant today.

To sum up, the three generations of the CPC's central leadership have formed, officially adopted, enriched and developed a Marxist ideological line in their long-term practice of the Party. The Party's understanding of the ideological line has gone through three stages. The stages are inherently consistent, with each stage inheriting from the previous stage. They also exhibit distinctive features because of continued innovation. Mao Zedong established the ideological line of seeking truth from facts. Deng Xiaoping restored and developed the ideological line of emancipating the mind and seeking truth from facts. Jiang Zemin defined the ideological line as emancipating the mind, seeking truth from facts and keeping up with the times. Hu Jintao has recently advocated the principle of remaining realistic and pragmatic. All these are evidence that we should enrich and develop theories keeping with the advancing times.

11.3 Basic Content of the Party's Ideological Line

Below, I would like to further comment on the basic content of the

---

[1] *A Collection of Important Documents Since the 16ᵗʰ CPC National Congress (Part I)*, pp.728-729, Beijing: Central Party Literature Press, 2005.

Party's ideological line. To support the ideological line, we should have a correct understanding of its essence.

11.3.1 Unity between Emancipating the Mind, Seeking Truth from Facts and Keeping up With the Times

Emancipating the mind, seeking truth from facts and keeping up with the times, which are connected with, influence and promote one another. Together, they form the complete ideological line of the CPC. Emancipating the mind stresses the fact that the subject's knowledge develops in keeping with the development of the object, as opposed to rigid thinking and dogmatism. Seeking truth from facts stresses the identity between the subject and the object, as opposed to subjectivism and book worship. Keeping up with the times stresses the contemporariness and openness of the subject's knowledge, as opposed to attempts of sticking to convention and reject innovation.

Keeping up with the times means that objective things as well as people's knowledge of them advances with the course of time and with the changes of the times. In other words, the Marxist theory and practice under their guidance should conform to the times, follow the law of development, display great creativity and keep making innovations. Contemporariness is the hallmark of keeping up with the times. Following the law of development is its most fundamental requirement. Creativity is its most vivid demonstration. Keeping up with the times is the Party's basic attitude toward its theories, its cause and the Party itself. It is a reflection of Marxist values and the Marxist view on history in the CPC's activities, highlighting the CPC's essential features of following the course of history, grasping historical trends and always standing in the forefront of the times.

There is an inherent unity between keeping up with the times, emancipating the mind and seeking truth from facts.

Seeking truth from facts is the starting point and aim of emancipating the mind and keeping up with the times. The essence of emancipating the mind and keeping up with the times is seeking truth from facts. Efforts to emancipate the mind and keep up with the times should be based on the principle and aim of seeking truth from facts. Only if we take seeking truth from facts as the starting point and as the aim can we give value to the efforts to emancipate our mind and keep up with the times. Without seeking truth from facts, attempts to emancipate the mind and keeping up with the times will lead to errors in theory and be harmful in practice.

Emancipating the mind is the inherent requirement and inevitable result of seeking truth from facts and keeping up with the times. Only if we emancipate our minds can we seek truth from facts and keep up with the times in the real sense. As we pursue socialist modernization, only if we emancipate our minds and continue to adapt the basic tenets of Marxism to China's practice can we seek truth from facts and keep up with the times under new circumstances, thereby making fresh progress in building socialism with Chinese characteristics.

Keeping up with the times is the prerequisite and guarantee for seeking truth from facts and emancipating the mind. Keeping up with the times is a deepening and development of emancipating the mind. They constitute the complete methodology with which we know and change the world. Both keeping up with the times and emancipating the mind aim to seek truth from facts, reveal objective laws more effectively and enable us to keep knowing and changing the world. Keeping up with the times requires that we should have a correct understanding of the features of the times, feel the pulses of the society and grasp historical trends. In this way, our ideas and actions will exhibit contemporary features, be innovative and conform to the rapidly changing reality.

To sum up, the dialectical unity of emancipating the mind, seeking truth from facts and keeping up with the times is crucial to the great cause of building socialism. The essence of building socialism with Chinese characteristics is proceeding from China's national conditions and integrating the basic tenets of Marxism with China's socialist development.

11.3.2 The Unity of Marxist Positions, Views and Methodology

The ideological line summarizes the theoretical content, essential features and social functions of Marxist philosophy. Marxist philosophy is the foundation of the entire Marxist theoretical system. The ideological line of seeking truth from facts is the essence of Marxist philosophy and represents a comprehensive application of the basic views of dialectical materialism and historical materialism.

Seeking truth from facts, which exemplifies the unity of materialism and dialectics, is the kernel of Marxist philosophy. Marxist philosophy is an organic combination of materialism and dialectics. Seeking truth from facts fully demonstrates this prominent feature. First of all, it recognizes the objective existence of things; their movement, changes and development; and the objective laws governing them. It demands that we proceed from objective facts and understand the world as it is. "Facts" are the combinations of phenomena and essence. In an effort to grasp the essence and laws of things, we should give full play to our initiative and carry out in-depth research by using dialectical thinking methods such as induction and deduction, analysis and synthesis, and abstraction and concretion. The theoretical principle of seeking truth from facts reflects the organic combination and unity of the views of materialism and dialectics.

Seeking truth from facts embodies the basic principles of the theory of knowledge of dialectical materialism, the basic view that practice is the foundation of knowledge and the basic process of human cognition. It indicates the correct path to knowing and changing the world. It underlines the decisive role of practice in cognition, takes practice as the foundation, proceeds from facts and upholds the dialectical materialist line of cognition—from things to sense perceptions and ideas. In this process, we obtain knowledge of the essence and laws of things, which represents a leap from practice to knowledge. We then verify the knowledge in our practice: If the knowledge is correct, we will use it as a guide to action. If it is wrong, we will correct it. This is a leap from knowledge to practice. The two leaps are both realized as we seek truth from facts. Seeking truth from facts is not to be completed in one stroke. We need to repeat the process for several times and even endlessly. Seeking truth from facts is therefore consistent with the endless process of practice, knowledge, again practice, and again knowledge.

Seeking truth from facts embodies the basic views of historical materialism and the unity of dialectical materialism and historical materialism. It acknowledges that the ways of material production lays the very groundwork for the existence and development of society and basic social contradictions promote the advancement of human society. It demands that Marxists should gain a strong command of the objective laws governing social development. It also embodies the mass line of historical materialism. For Marxists, the process of proceeding from facts and seeking truth from facts is a process of proceeding from the interests of the masses, respecting their position as masters of the country and their creativity and handling matters according to their wishes. Without a materialist view on history, we cannot gain a correct understanding of seeking truth from facts, let alone do well in it.

Seeking truth from facts means to adhere to the unity of Marxist positions, views and methodology. It also means to hold the positions of the proletariat and the masses, hold to the Party spirit and class character of the proletariat and the worldview and methodology of dialectical materialism and historical materialism.

11.4 Ideological Line in the Reform and Opening-up and Modernization

The establishment, enrichment and innovation in the Party ideology have created a new phase in the development of Marxism. Following the Party's ideological line is the key to applying the important thought of Three Represents in an all-round way. It is a powerful force driving China's reform and opening-up program and social progress. It is also a decisive factor in preserving the CPC's advanced nature, creativity and vigor and vitality. The

CPC has been committed to emancipating its mind and seeking truth from facts in rectifying the mistakes of the Cultural Revolution and carrying out comprehensive reforms in the past more than 20 years. In this way, it has resolved major issues concerning the future and fate of the Party and the state and found the path to building socialism with Chinese characteristics. However, China still has a long way to go to promote its socialist cause. I think we have yet to gain a clear understanding of the laws governing socialist economic, political and cultural development.

First, we must proceed from the realities of China's Reform and Opening-up and Modernization and take what we are doing as the central task. We should focus efforts to emancipate our minds and seek truth from facts on meeting current needs. At present, Reform and Opening-up and Modernization are Party's most pressing task, which bears on the fate of the Party and the state. As we emancipate our minds and seek truth from facts in these fields, we should do away with the influence of traditional concepts, keep "leftist" or rightist thinking from hindering the Party's central task and prevent regression in Reform and Opening-up policy. We should proceed from reality, uphold the Party's basic line in the primary stage of socialism and on the other hand resolve specific problems while focusing on the Party's central task.

Second, we should concentrate on the application of Marxism. Marxism provides not only a method for us to understand and analyze problems but also an ideological tool for us to know and change the world. It is our firm principle that we must take Marxism as the theoretical foundation and the guiding ideology as we emancipate our minds and seek truth from facts. Today, we cannot carry Marxism forward unless we study the scientific system and essence of Marxism in light of the practical problems in reform and opening-up and modernization and apply it creatively in our new practice.

Third, we should look at practical problems from a theoretical perspective. Practice should be guided by theory. Without theory, practice will become a blind action. Since Reform and Opening-up began, we have encountered many new problems. The Party has solved these new problems in the spirit of proceeding from reality. At the same time, it has considered these practical problems from a theoretical perspective and from the viewpoint of the Marxist theoretical system. In this way, it has creatively developed Marxism on a series of major issues such as the theory of the primary stage of socialism and on the nature of socialism. Deng Xiaoping Theory is an achievement of adapting Marxism to China's realities and the features of the times as China explores ways to build socialism with Chinese characteristics.

Fourth, we should focus attention on new practice and new developments. Since new things keep emerging, we face an arduous task of understanding new laws on a deeper level and in a broader scope. We have accumulated a lot of successful experience in the Reform and Opening-up for more than 20 years. However, new problems emerge as we solve old ones. Old experience may not necessarily be applicable to new situations. We must further deepen Reform and respond to the new situations with flexible economic, political and cultural policies. In the face of new problems, we should continue to emancipate our minds, seek truth from facts, conform to the trend of the times and take the initiative in analyzing new situations and solving new problems.

Fifth, we should have the courage to make bold explorations and at the same time stay realistic and pragmatic. To keep making progress in proceeding from reality, emancipating our minds and seeking truth from facts, we should demonstrate courage in two ways: First, we must have the courage to make theoretical explorations. We should be brave enough to break the shackles of old concepts and subjective prejudices, reach new conclusions in conformity with reality and make new theoretical summarizations of new practices. Second, we must have the courage to make practical explorations. Practice is full of vitality. We should explore ways to solve new problems in the spirit of reform and innovation. For example, our approach to ideological and political work was developed under uniform social and economic conditions. But now these conditions have changed; so how can we make innovations in our ideological and political work at a time when people have diverse ways of working and living conditions and when the information and Internet technology enjoys explosive development? We must be bold in finding an answer to this question in practice. Practical explorations lay the groundwork for theoretical explorations, while theoretical explorations summarize and upgrade practical explorations.

Sixth, we must respect the people's creations in their practice. The people are the major participants in social practice. The aim and outcome of socialism is to realize the people's common interests and the fundamental and long-term interests of the overwhelming majority of the people. We use practice as the criterion for verifying truth. By practice, we generally mean the practice of building socialism, which is the practice of the people. Respecting the people's practice therefore is consistent with the principle that practice is the sole criterion for testing truth. Since the Party is the faithful representative of the common interests and long-term interests of the overwhelming majority of the Chinese people. Needless to say, whether its policies are correct should be tested in the people's practice.

In conclusion, the three-step evolution of the Party's ideological line from "seeking truth from facts" to "emancipating the mind and seeking truth from facts" and to "emancipating the mind, seeking truth from facts and keeping up with times" reflects the consistency of the line as well as the CPC's advanced nature that enables it to always stand in the forefront of the times.

Chapter 12

Ideological and Theoretical Development of the Marxist Party

A Marxist party's guiding ideology is the ideological and theoretical system guiding all the party's activities. An advanced Marxist party cannot develop without the guidance of scientific theories. Underlining the party's ideological and theoretical development is an outstanding feature and ideological and political advantage of a proletarian party. In an effort to preserve and develop the advanced nature of the Party, Marxists should give top priority to its ideological and theoretical development to enhance all Party members' theoretical competence and promote the development of its guiding ideology in keeping up with the times.

12.1 Ideological and Theoretical Development

Proletarian parties came into being as they combined Marxism with workers' movement. Scientific theories serve as the ideological foundation for their emergence and development. Their advanced nature is, first of all, closely linked to the advanced nature of their guiding ideology. The ideological and theoretical development of the Party therefore occupies an important place and plays a unique role in the entire project of the Marxist party building.

12.1.1 Marxist Principle for the Party Building

The greatest contribution of Marx and Engels lies in the fact that they founded Marxism by drawing on the fine achievements of human civilizations. They put forward a system of scientific theories, including dialectical materialism, historical materialism, the theory of surplus value and scientific socialism. They had devoted their lives to creating scientific theories, leaving behind works totaling volumes of works. Their theories had laid the theoretical foundation for the founding and development of proletarian parties in different countries and served as a powerful ideological guide for the proletariat's pursuit of emancipation. Marx and Engels had attached great importance to the role of theory as a guide. They had called for imbuing proletarian parties and the masses with scientific theories. According to Marx, "The weapon of criticism cannot, of course, replace criticism of the weapons, material force must be overthrown by material force; but theory also becomes a material force as soon as it has gripped the masses."[1]

Engels had also commented that "a major advantage of the Communist Party is that it takes a new scientific view as its theoretical foundation[2]. At the end of the 19th century and the beginning of the 20th century, Lenin had integrated the basic tenets of Marxism with Russia's reality and put forward the theory and strategies for proletarian revolution and proletarian

---

[1] *Marx & Engels Selected Works* (2nd Chinese edition), Volume 1, p.9.
[2] *Marx & Engels Selected Works* (2nd Chinese edition), Volume 2, pp.39-40.

dictatorship by taking into account the new features in the era of "imperialism and proletarian revolution". Thus, he had enriched and developed Marxism. He had always attached a great value on the important role of theory. He had criticized the dominant wrong concepts such as "Narodnism" and later the "Russian economist trend" in Russia, and thus unified the thoughts of the party with scientific theories, and created a new-type proletarian party different from the opportunist groups in the Second International.

12.1.2 Emphasizing Ideological and Theoretical Development

Revolutionary theory is a decisive factor for the Party's advanced nature. In 1902, Lenin had discussed the critical importance of revolutionary theory for a revolutionary party in *What Is to Be Done?*—A book which had laid the groundwork for the ideological and theoretical development of proletarian parties. His comments had included: "Without revolutionary theory there can be no revolutionary movement," ... "The role of vanguard fighter can be fulfilled only by a party that is guided by the most advanced theory."[1] These remarks are frequently quoted as a maxim on strengthening proletarian parties' ideological and theoretical development. In December 1989, shortly after he became the general secretary of the CPC Central Committee, Comrade Jiang Zemin had also commented on this issue during a seminar on the theory of Party building at the Party School of the CPC Central Committee: "A Marxist party that is not armed with advanced theories cannot be an advanced party. A Communist that is not armed with advanced theories cannot play the role of a vanguard fighter. Those who refuse to arm their brains with advanced theories cannot have the true Party spirit and therefore are not qualified to be ranked among the vanguards of the working class"[2] ... "We must keep up with the times and continue to enrich and develop Marxism. If we cling to old conventions and stop making progress, we will fall behind and our Party will risk losing its advanced nature and

---

[1] *Selected Works of Vladimir Lenin* (3rd Chinese edition), Volume 1, pp.311-312. Beijing: People's Press, 1995.

[2] *Selected Works of Jiang Zemin*, Volume 1, p.95.

leadership".[1] Only by taking the scientific theory of Marxism as the guide and adhering to Marxist worldview and methodology, can proletarian parties get a clear understanding of the trends and laws of the development of human society, clarify their historical mission, devise programs, lines, principles and policies conforming to objective reality and the interests of the working class and the people and lead the people in achieving victories in revolution and national development. Only if they strengthen ideological and theoretical development can they enhance the theoretical and ideological competence of their members, overcome the influence of non-proletarian ideas and preserve and develop their advanced nature.

12.1.3 All-Round Development of a Marxist Party

Party building mainly involves the Party's ideological, political and organizational development as well as the improvement of its work style. The Party's ideological development is closely related to and serves as the foundation, prerequisite and guarantee for its development on other fronts. Despite their different forms, mistakes in the Party history, such as Chen Duxiu's right-leaning opportunism, the "Left" mistakes of Qu Qiubai, Li Lisan and Wang Ming, and Mao Zedong's erroneous decision to launch the Cultural Revolution in his late years, could all be attributed to errors in the Party's ideological line: The detachment of theory from practice had led to errors in the Party's political line. The CPC's progress in political development since the Third Plenary Session of its 11th Central Committee should first of all be attributed to its efforts to rectify its ideological line and adopt correct theories. In its organizational development, the Party must establish a common ideological foundation to uphold democratic-centralism and safeguard its solidarity and unity. I think the Party has achieved unity in thinking, solidarity in organization and consistency in action precisely because of the rectified ideological line and theories: Deng Xiaoping Theory and the important thought of Three Represents. One of the direct causes of the Communist Party of the Soviet Union's collapse was that Mikhail

---

[1] *Selected Works of Jiang Zemin*, Volume 3, p.335.

Gorbachev had disavowed the guiding position of Marxism and pushed for "diversification in thinking", thereby depriving the party of its spiritual guide. The confusion in thinking had finally resulted in the party's organizational dissolution. In improving its work style, a Marxist party should strengthen the ideological and theoretical education of its members, especially leading cadres, so that they have a firm belief, a correct outlook on the world, life and values and an enhanced sense of the Party spirit. To sum up, achievements in the Party's ideological and theoretical development can greatly contribute to its all-round development and the overall improvement in Party building.

12.1.4 Successful Experiences of the CPC

Since its founding, the CPC had taken Marxism-Leninism as the theoretical foundation of its guiding ideology. Because of China's unique national conditions, the CPC's development environment, major tasks and work approach were different from proletarian parties in developed European countries. How to establish a Marxist party with a wide popular support in a country with few industrial workers but a large number of farmers and members of petty bourgeoisie was a new challenge facing the Party. The first generation of the collective central leadership of the CPC, with Mao Zedong at the core, had put forward the important principle of attaching primary importance to the Party's ideological development in their long-term practice of Party building. When he led the revolutionary base works in Jinggang Mountains, Mao had underlined the proletariat's ideological leadership. He had personally worked in the drafting of the Resolution of the Gutian Conference, stressing that Communists should conquer non-proletarian ideas with proletarian thinking. In Yan'an, Mao had underlined the principle that Party members should join the Party not only organizationally but also ideologically. He also launched the great Rectification Campaign in 1941 to educate the whole Party about Marxism-Leninism. In his report on the amendment to the CPC Constitution at the Seventh CPC National Congress in 1945, Liu Shaoqi had made it clear that attaching primary importance to the Party's ideological development as well as organizational development and putting ideological education and ideological leadership at the top of the Party's leadership agenda were important features of Mao Zedong's correct approach to Party building. It should be noted that emphasizing the Party's ideological development is an innovative development of the Marxist theory on Party building in China's unique national conditions and also the CPC's conditions. In the past 80 years and more, the CPC has focused on ideological and theoretical education at every critical juncture, thereby ensuring that the Party continues to make progress in its cause. Attaching great value to building, strengthening and prospering the Party by its ideological characteristics is the CPC's basic experience in preserving and developing its advanced nature and achieving success.

12.1.5 Party Building under New Circumstances

Under new historical circumstances, the Party faces a complex international situation and arduous tasks at home. It has to sum up its rich practical experience, solve many major problems and explore many unknown spheres. All this makes it imperative that the CPC should become theoretically more mature. Maturity in theoretical thinking is an important symbol of the Party's maturity and Marxist theories are essential for the Party's leadership. For both the Party and its cadres, theoretical maturity is the basis for political maturity. If Marxists do not study, conduct research and gain mastery of Marxism in earnest, they will be unable to differentiate the right from wrong. If they unarm themselves ideologically, they will lose the direction and commit serious mistakes. In the face of the severe pressure and impacts from the drastic changes in Eastern Europe, the disintegration of the Soviet Union and Western hostile forces' attempts to Westernize and split China was a serious challenge. On the other hand, the negative influence from the diversification of economic elements in Chinese society and the new pattern of economic interests, social life, the way society is organized and the new forms of employment, pose even a greater need of correct theoretical guidance and a strong spiritual guide based on correct theories. In particular, as China keeps deepening the reforms, expanding opening-up, adjusting people's interests, Party members, scholars and the general public have been exploring a great number of hot issues that have to be addressed, such as how to view new emerging social strata and how to bridge the gap between the rich and the poor. If they cannot come up with answers to these questions from a theoretical perspective, people will become confused and less confident about socialism and communism. I think, under new historical circumstances, the Party shoulders an even heavier task in pursuing ideological and theoretical development.

12.2 New Tasks in Ideological and Theoretical Development

Under new circumstances, I think the Party faces the following major tasks in ideological and theoretical development: strengthening efforts to carry out theoretical study, publicity, research and innovation; upholding the guiding position of Marxism in the ideological sphere; guiding diverse thinking patterns in society with advanced theories and culture; consolidating the common ideological basis for the whole Party and people across the country to work together in unity; strengthening and improving the Party's work in ideological and political spheres; striving to improve the ideological and moral standards of the Party and the nation; and promoting the people's all-round development.

12.2.1 Education on Scientific Theories

In China, the most fundamental task in promoting the Party's ideological and theoretical development is to educate all Party members with Marxism-Leninism, Mao Zedong Thought, Deng Xiaoping Theory and the important thought of Three Represents and to improve the whole Party's mastery of the Marxist theory. Since the Fourth Plenary Session of the 13th CPC National Committee in 1989, the Central Committee has taken a series of important measures in this regard. For example, it edited and published the third volume of *Selected Works of Deng Xiaoping*. It published the revised first and second volumes of *Selected Works of Deng Xiaoping*. It republished the first to the fourth volumes of *Selected Works of Mao Zedong*. It published the re-translated versions of *Marx & Engels Selected Works*, *Selected Works of Vladimir Lenin* and *Collected Works of Vladimir Lenin*. It has realized the re-translation and re-publication of *Marx & Engels Collected Works*. It has recently edited and published three volumes of *Selected Works of Jiang Zemin*. The CPC has also launched a campaign to educate its members about the Party's basic theories and basic line as well as basic knowledge of the Party. It has called on its members to study Marxist theories and the CPC Constitution. It has initiated an educational campaign that stresses theoretical study, political awareness and integrity among leading cadres. In addition, it has launched a campaign to educate all Party members about the important thought of Three Represents. All these initiatives have played an important role in unifying the thinking of the whole Party and ensuring the correct direction of China's reform and opening up.

I think, to do a good job in arming the whole Party with scientific theories, we should attach paramount importance to studying and implementing the important thought of Three Represents in earnest. The third generation of the collective central leadership of the CPC, with Comrade Jiang Zemin at the core, had created the important thought of Three Represents by pooling the whole Party's wisdom. The important thought of Three Represents is based on a scientific judgment of the current international situation, a scientific understanding of the developments and changes in China today and a scientific analysis of the Party's conditions. As a system of scientific theories, it puts forward a series of interrelated new ideas, concepts and arguments in the following aspects: reform, development and stability, domestic and foreign policies, national defense, and the governance of the Party, the state and the armed forces. It gives further theoretical answers to the questions of what socialism is and how to build it and creative answers to the questions of what kind of Party to build and how to build it. The Party Constitution adopted at the 16th CPC National Congress in 2002 had included the idea that the important thought of Three Represents as a guiding ideology that the Party must uphold for a long time together with Marxism-Leninism, Mao Zedong Thought and Deng Xiaoping Theory. The Constitution has defined the implementation of the Three Represents as the foundation for building the Party, the cornerstone for its governance and the source of its strength. In June 2003, the CPC Central Committee has issued a notice titled as: "Outline on Studying the Important Thought of Three Represents." In his important remarks at a seminar a month later, General Secretary Hu Jintao had clarified the historical significance, scientific content and essential features of the important thought of Three Represents, calling on the Party to bring about a new upsurge in studying and implementing that thought.

To do well in studying and implementing the important thought of Three Represents, we should first of all improve our understanding of the important thought of Three Represents. We should reach a new understanding of the circumstances under which it was put forward as well as its practical basis, scientific content, essential features and its historical meaning. General Secretary Hu Jintao has offered a new approach on this study: "The important thought of Three Represents is sinicized Marxism for the 21st century and a fundamental principle guiding the whole Party and people across China in their pursuit of the development goals and grand prospects in the new century and new stage."[1] This new statement represents the CPC's latest understanding of the historical significance of the important thought of Three Represents. It indicates that in the new century and new stage, belief in the important thought of Three Represents means belief in Marxism, and adherence to the important thought of Three Represents means adherence to Marxism. The important thought of Three Represents provides an ideological foundation and spiritual guide for the whole Party and people across China.

To do well in studying and implementing the important thought of Three Represents, we should integrate theory with practice and make new progress in fulfilling the fundamental requirements of the important thought of Three Represents and persist in observing Three Represents. Integrating theory

[1] *Selected Important Documents since the 16th CPC National Congress*, Part I, pp.366-367.

with practice is a basic principle of Marxism and a fine style of study that Chinese Communists have fostered since the period of revolutionary wars. To develop this style of study under new historical circumstances, we should try to achieve the "three links" proposed by General Secretary Hu Jintao: linking studying theory with guiding practice, linking changing the objective world with changing the subjective world and linking applying the theories with developing them. In particular, we should study, understand, believe in and apply the important thought of Three Represents in good faith. Studying the important thought in good faith means that we should not study it in a superficial manner but concentrate on gaining a comprehensive mastery of the scientific system of the important thought of Three Represents.

At present, to do well in arming the Party with scientific theories, we should give prominence to studying the Scientific Outlook on Development. Since the 16th CPC National Congress, General Secretary Hu Jintao has put forward "the Scientific Outlook on Development" under the guidance of Deng Xiaoping Theory and the important thought of Three Represents. The Scientific Outlook on Development proposes that we should put people first to achieve comprehensive, balanced and sustainable development. We should balance and combine: urban and rural development, development among regions, between economic and social development, relations between man and nature, and domestic development and opening to the outside world to promote a sound and a rapid economic and social development. The Scientific Outlook on Development offers answers to a series of fundamental questions including "what development is and why and how to achieve development." As a complete ideological system, it is a continuation and development of Deng Xiaoping Theory and the important thought of Three Represents as well as a guiding ideology for China's socialist development. We should educate the Party with the Scientific Outlook on Development, help Party members and cadres acquire a deep understanding of the background in which it was put forward, the implications it will have for guiding practice as well as its scientific content and use it to unify the Party's thinking. We should implement the Scientific Outlook on Development in all areas of our work, seize opportunities to pursue development, change our concepts on development, make innovations on the model of development and improve the quality of development.

12.2.2 Promoting Theoretical Innovation in the Party

To promote the Party's ideological and theoretical development, it is necessary to focus on new practices and new developments and keep promoting theoretical innovation. Marxism is a continuation and development of mankind's fine cultural heritage. As the most scientific worldview and methodology, it has summarized natural and social sciences at a supreme level. It had originated in practice and guides practice. It has been repeatedly tested by practice and keeps developing in practice. I think the history of Marxism is a history of innovation. It is through innovation that Marxism shows long-term vitality.

At a time when China was engaged in building socialism in an all-round way after 1956, Mao Zedong had suggested that members of CPC committees at all levels read Marxist classics, including the Soviet Union's *Textbook on Political Economy*, to gain a better understanding of basic Marxist economic theories and recognize and rectify the erroneous trends at that time. He had personally organized a study group to take the lead in doing this research. In his remarks on the *Textbook on Political Economy* published in Hangzhou, Shanghai and Guangzhou from December 1959 to February 1960, Mao had commented: "It is of primary importance that Party members should read Marxist classics and abide by basic Marxist principles. But Communist parties and intellectual communities in all countries need to create new theories, write new works and create their own theoreticians to meet current political needs, and excessive dependence on classics won't do.[1]

In the new era of Reform and Opening-up, Deng Xiaoping had made another breakthrough in Marxism by adapting it to the features of the times and China's reality. While meeting with Mikhail Gorbachev, Chairman of the

---

[1] *Collected Works of Mao Zedong*, Volume 8, p.109. Beijing: People's Press, 1999.

Presidium of the Supreme Soviet of the U.S.S.R. and General Secretary of the Communist Party of the Soviet Union in May 1989, Deng had summed up the historical experience of both the CPC and the Communist Party of the Soviet Union: "Nobody was clear about exactly what changes had taken place over the century since Marx's death or about how to understand and develop Marxism in light of those changes. We cannot expect Marx to provide ready answers to questions that arise a hundred or several hundred years after his death, nor can we ask Lenin to give answers to questions that arise fifty or a hundred years after his death. A true Marxist-Leninist must understand, carry on and develop Marxism-Leninism in light of the current situation."[1] ... "The world changes every day, and modern science and technology in particular develop rapidly. A year today is the equivalent of several decades, a century or even a longer period in ancient times. Anyone who fails to carry Marxism forward with new thinking and a new viewpoint is not a true Marxist."[2]

Since the beginning of the new century, new situations and problems have kept emerging. In the face of the opportunities and challenges, Comrade Jiang Zemin had stressed that innovation is essential to a nation's progress. Jiang had clarified the concept of theoretical innovation on different occasions. In his report to the 14th CPC National Congress, he had made the following comment: "We should not cling to the dogmatic understanding of certain Marxist principles and works, unscientific or twisted perceptions of socialism or incorrect ideas that transcend the primary stage of socialism". In his report to the 15th CPC National Congress, he had commented: "While centering on the practical problems in the Reform, Opening up and the Modernization drive and on the things we are doing, we must emphasize the application of the Marxist theory, the theoretical study of practical problems, and new practice and new development. We should adhere to and develop Marxism through practice while taking into account our new historical tasks". And in another comment: "We must conscientiously free our minds from the shackles of the outdated notions, practices and systems, from the erroneous

---

[1] *Selected Works of Deng Xiaoping* (1ˢᵗ Chinese edition), Volume 3, p.291.

[2] *Ibid.*, pp.291-292.

and dogmatic interpretations of Marxism and from the fetters of subjectivism and metaphysics".

I think to promote theoretical innovation, we must properly handle the relationship between continuation and development. In other words, we must develop theory while adhering to it and adhere to theory while developing it. I believe that Marxism-Leninism, Mao Zedong Thought, Deng Xiaoping Theory and the important thought of Three Represents are in the same line and advocate the basic positions, views and methods of Marxism or basic Marxist principles. We should hold this line so that we can pass them further to next generations. At the same time, Marxism is a pragmatic, open and developing science. In Marxism, there is no ultimate truth. We should not regard it as something unchangeable or too sacred to be amended. Instead, we should amend obsolete views and conclusions in keeping with the changed situation and enrich and develop Marxism with new experience and views to create a new realm in Marxist theory.

To promote theoretical innovation, it is necessary to focus on doing research and solving practical problems in contemporary China, especially major theoretical and practical problems in social development that call for immediate solution. At a seminar on the important thought of Three Represents, General Secretary Hu Jintao had raised 14 interesting how-to questions: "How to do a good job in promoting development, which is the top priority of the Party in governing and rejuvenating the country; how to improve the basic economic system in which public ownership is dominant and different economic sectors develop side by side; how to establish an improved socialist market economy; how to keep to the new path of industrialization and balance economic and social development in urban and rural areas; how to expand employment and re-employment; how to deepen reform of the income distribution system and improve the social security system; how to participate in international economic and technological cooperation and competition in a larger scope, in a wider range and at a higher level; how to prompt entire society to embrace an enlightened approach to development that results in expanded production, a better life and sound ecological and environmental conditions; how to better integrate the Party's leadership, the people's position as masters of the country and the rule of law; how to mobilize all positive factors in a most extensive and thorough manner to inject fresh impetus to the great rejuvenation of the Chinese nation; how to strengthen the guiding position of Marxism in the ideological field under new historical circumstances; how to celebrate and cultivate a national spirit; how to reform and improve the Party's leadership and governance styles; how to comprehensively carry forward the great new undertaking to build the Party". All these are major theoretical and practical questions that need to be answered as China improves and develops its socialist system. I think these questions chart a plan for the CPC's theoretical innovation. And the important thought of Three Represents is an example of adhering to and developing Marxism. It is not only the basic guideline for us to promote theoretical innovation but also a new starting point for us to deepen theoretical research. There is no end to practice or innovation. All the Party members, especially those working on theoretical studies, should continue to promote theoretical innovation and make new discoveries, innovations under the guidance of the important thought of Three Represents.

Here I would like to note that in April 2004, the Central Committee has decided to initiate the Project to Study and Develop Marxist Theory. The project aims organize—during the next 10 years—a large number of scholars for developing the academic system and a series of new textbooks that comprehensively reflect the latest Marxist theoretical achievements in China. The project also aims to prosper philosophy and social sciences studies, thus enhance the creativity, convincingness of the CPC's ideological and theoretical work and foster a group of new Marxist theoreticians in China.

12.2.3 The Ideological and Political Work of the Party

Ideological and political work refers to the ideological education carried out by Marxist parties in an effort to achieve their historical mission. Focusing on the Communist ideology, it takes addressing people's class positions, political views, moral standards, ideological awareness and thinking patterns as specific objectives. Its part inside the Party partially represents the efforts to promote the Party's ideological development. Outside the Party, it falls into the scope of the Party's ideological leadership.

All parties carry out ideological and political work in different ways. Proletarian parties, in particular, attach great importance to ideological and political work. Marx and Engels had proposed the concept of "propaganda" when they created the Communist League in 1847. In 1903, Lenin put forward the two concepts of "political propaganda" and "political education," calling those engaged in these efforts "political educationists" and "political propagandists." Stalin had used the terms "ideological work" and "ideological and political work" in 1934. While continuing to use these other concepts, the CPC had also highlighted the terms "political work" and "ideological education." Giving priority to ideological and political work is a fine tradition and political advantage of the Marxist Party. During the Agrarian Revolutionary War (1927-1937), Zhou Enlai underlined the importance of political work in the Red Army by describing it as "a political life-blood" and "life-line." In the editor's notes to *Socialist Upsurge in China's Countryside*, a book he had personally edited in 1955, Mao Zedong had made a comment on the issue: "Political work is the life-blood of all economic work. This is particularly true at a time when the social and economic system is undergoing fundamental change."[1] This was the most important theoretical statement about political and ideological work the Party had made since it had assumed power. It clarifies the relationship between ideological and political work and works on other fronts. During the Cultural Revolution, Lin Biao and members of the Gang of Four exaggerated the role of politics, while advocating that men's willpower is omnipotent. They put ideological and political work before everything else and tried to use political work to replace and exert influence on work on all the other fronts, and in fact these attempts had severely jeopardized the Party's ideological and political work.

Is ideological and political work still the lifeblood of work on all fronts in the new era of reform, opening up and socialist modernization? "The

---

[1] *Collected Works of Mao Zedong*, Volume 6, p.449. Beijing: People's Press, 1999.

Resolution on Several Historical Issues of the CPC since the Founding of the People's Republic of China" adopted at the Sixth Plenary Session of the 11th CPC Central Committee in June 1981 had given a positive answer to this question by affirming that ideological and political work is the lifeblood of economic work and work on all other fronts. The above document had also noted that the principle of ideological and political work was an important part of Mao Zedong's original theoretical contribution to the development of Marxism-Leninism in China.

Since the Fourth Plenary Session of the 13th CPC Central Committee in 1989, Comrade Jiang Zemin has repeatedly stressed that the CPC should make its ideological and political work more modern, focused, pragmatic, proactive, creative and convincing to address problems such as improper content, poor coverage, lack of focus, obsolete methods and failure to meet the new situation and new tasks. To this end, the Central Committee had adopted two resolutions on promoting socialist ideological and cultural development in 1986 and 1996 respectively. In 1999, the document titled: "Several Opinions on Strengthening and Improving the Ideological and Political Work of the CPC Central Committee" was adopted. "The Outline on Citizens' Moral Development" was adopted in 2001. "The Outline on Strengthening the Ideological and Political Work Concerning College Students" was adopted in 2004. These documents had aimed at strengthening the Party's leadership in the ideological and political work, exploring the laws governing the ideological and political work under new circumstances, proposing "more effective methods, approaches, systems and mechanisms and making ideological and political work more convincing, popular, appealing and cohesive".

To improve the ideological and political work, it is necessary improve its content and methods. I think for a long time, the Party's ideological and political work has exhibited excessive political and ideological features. The Party had focused on political propaganda instead of mental guidance in terms of content. In terms of methods, it had tended to impose ideas on others, leading to the resistance of some people. To address these problems, it is necessary to make the ideological and political work more systematic and scientific in content with a focus on education in patriotism, collectivism, socialism, current affairs and state policies, democracy and rule of law, ethics and revolutionary traditions. It is necessary to provide people with all-round guidance including ideological, theoretical and cultural dimensions and also social values and norms. It is necessary to change spoon feeding approach with an interactive approach and develop a broader perspective. It is critical to utilize the Internet to expand coverage, and improve efficiency. The Party should also distinguish different levels in that work, linking education with management and solve ideological problems while addressing practical problems.

12.3 Inner-Party Ideological Struggles

Given the environment in which Marxist parties came into being and develop themselves, inner-party contradictions and struggles exist objectively no matter people like them or not. Engels had made a comment on that: "workers' parties in any major country can only develop through internal struggle, which is consistent with the dialectical laws governing development in general."[1] ... "Opposition and struggle between ideas of different kinds constantly occur within the Party."

Mao Zedong, in his article "On Contradiction" had made an evaluation on this issue: "If there were no contradictions in the Party and no ideological struggles to resolve them, the Party's life would come to an end."[2] Contradictions exist in everything, and the CPC's activities are no exception. They can be observed in the Party since its founding. Proletarian parties grow strong just as they resolve their internal contradictions. Liu Shaoqi had analyzed the necessity, root causes and nature of inner-party struggles as well as the principles and methods of correctly carrying out inner-party struggles in "On Inner-Party Struggles," which was one of his masterpieces on Party

[1] *Marx & Engels Selected Works* (2nd Chinese edition), Volume 4, p.651.
[2] *Selected Works of Mao Zedong* (2nd Chinese edition), Volume 1, p.306.

building. I think this article is still applicable to the Party building project of today.

I think, today some members have long been fearful of inner-party struggles due to the influence of the political movements in the past. There is no doubt that the Party has learned many bitter lessons in carrying out inner-party struggles. This, however, should not become a reason for denying their importance. Of course, it is necessary to develop harmonious relations in the Party and promote social harmony together with inner-party harmony, but harmony should be based on common ideals. It is necessary to pursue harmony while taking the Party spirit and equity and justice as the prerequisite instead of seeking rapport without observing principles or making no distinction between the beautiful and the ugly and between right and wrong. Marxists should not consider inner-party harmony and unity and inner-party struggles as contradictory goals. Today, the tendency toward liberalism and an offend-nobody approach is still haunting the Party. The 11 types of liberalism which Mao Zedong had criticized in his article "Combat Liberalism" exist to varying degrees, such as indulging in irresponsible discussions in private and spreading unconfirmed information, even political rumors, at will; putting personal interests and freedom first, unwilling to undertake tasks assigned by the Party; not following the Party's resolutions; being obsessed with developing inter-personal relations, building narrow group type connections, working contacts and forming cliques; and not daring to criticize or fight against harmful trends, letting them alone and criticizing as little as possible while knowing perfectly well what is wrong. These problems have given rise to a decadent work style in the Party, robbed the Party of strict discipline and have weakened its combat effectiveness. They run counter to the requirements of an advanced Marxist party. As a ruling party, the Party should not blindly negate the necessity of inner-party struggles. It should gain a correct understanding of the nature of inner-party contradictions, handle inner-party contradictions and contradictions among the people in an appropriate manner and safeguard the Party's solidarity and unity.

In nature, inner-party contradictions are conflicts and contradictions between ideas. Struggles to resolve these contradictions are essentially ideological struggles. Therefore it is necessary to adopt a correct approach to carrying out inner-party struggles. During the Yan'an Rectification Movement, Mao Zedong had put a formulation as: "unity-criticism-unity" and the principles of "learning from past mistakes to avoid future ones" and "curing the sickness to save the patient." He had also created a way to resolve inner-party contradictions and problems through large-scale educational campaigns. Under new historical circumstances, it is critical to draw on this experience to shape harmonious relations in the Party. I suggest more attention to the following issues:

First, it is necessary to clearly distinguish inner-party struggles with the external struggles. Mao Zedong had suggested that inner-party struggles were "a reflection within the Party, of those contradictions between classes and between the new and the old in society."[1] For a long time, we had enjoyed to cite these remarks to explain the relationship between inner-party struggles and struggles outside the Party. As a result, naturally we had equated inner-party struggles with struggles outside the Party, putting normal Party life in jeopardy. It should also note that Mao was correct when he made those remarks at a time when China was fighting the War of Resistance against Japanese Aggression. However, the Party did not need interpret them simplistically and use them inappropriately after the CPC had gained state power, just because the large-scale and torrential class struggles had come to an end. That was because there were no inevitable connections between inner-party struggles and the class struggle in society. The Party did not need to apply the methods of class struggles in inner-party struggles. Instead, it would be much better to conduct inner-party struggles in an organized manner under unified leadership in accordance with the Party Constitution and its regulations. In particular, it could be better to promote democratic-centralism and abide by the norms governing inner-party political life. I think these ideas are still relevant for today.

[1] *Selected Works of Mao Zedong* (2nd Chinese edition), Volume 1, p.306.

Second, the term "struggle between two lines" is no more appropriate. In the past, under the influence of "Left" mistakes, the Party had made erroneous judgments about inner-party struggles and inappropriately used such terms as "struggle between two lines" and "'error of Party line." The excessive inner-party struggles had given great harm to Party comrades. Therefore, Deng Xiaoping, shortly after the Cultural Revolution, had made an important comment: "In the past the formulations 'struggle between two lines' and 'error of Party line' were used inaccurately, indiscriminately and too often... So far as inner-Party struggles are concerned, we should judge their nature and the errors involved in each case on their own merits. We should make their content clear and, in principle, should no longer present them as 'struggles between two lines.'"[1] I think, Deng's above remarks had played a crucial role in helping to rectify the mistakes of the Cultural Revolution and also offered a new guidance for correctly conducting inner-party struggles. Today, it could be possible to discuss on the "Party line" but it is necessary to refrain from mentioning "struggle between two lines." It could be possible to talk about problems in the Party over principle issues but not accuse others as committing errors of Party line.

Third, it is necessary to correctly handle the relationship between inner-party education and inner-party struggles. Liu Shaoqi had pointed out that the purpose of inner-party struggles is to educate the Party and Party members who had committed mistakes. "Inner-party struggles are an indispensible part of inner-party education, while inner-party education is a kind of moderate inner-party struggle. Struggle and education are inseparable, with struggle being a kind of education and education being a kind of struggle, and it is wrong to separate them mechanically.[2] Unlike the vehement inner-party struggles in the past, inner-party struggles today are mainly designed to arouse the initiative of Party members through education from a positive perspective. The recent nationwide campaign to preserve the advanced nature of the Party members has been a new effort to address contradictions in

---

[1] *Selected Works of Deng Xiaoping* (2nd Chinese edition), Volume 2, pp.307-308.

[2] *Selected Works of Liu Shaoqi*, Volume 1, p.193.

the Party through education. One of the lessons of that campaign could be that it is necessary to give priority to education from a positive perspective and with a self-education notion, adopt an open attitude toward education, give full play to the role of democracy and keep to the Party's mass line. Party building scholars generally agree that the campaign had opened new perspectives.

Fourth, it is necessary to carry out appropriate criticism and self-criticism. Criticism and self-criticism are one of the three fine work styles the Party has developed in its long-term practice. They summarize the Party's experience in correctly conducting inner-party struggles. I think in today's inner-party life, self-criticism is rather easy, while it is difficult to criticize others. What we lack now is precisely criticism against others. Of course, it is not proper to interpret criticism as opposing each other categorically. A heart-to-heart talk or a reminder is also a kind of criticism. We should conduct criticism in a comprehensive, objective, calm and appropriate manner. Democratic meetings of leading bodies, which have been proven effective over the years, as well as the heart-to-heart talks which have been widely adopted in "the campaign to preserve the advanced nature of the Party members", are good ways to carry out criticism and self-criticism and could also work in future.

Draft Rules of the Communist League-1847

The Communist League

Draft Rules of the Communist League [332]

Working Men of All Countries, Unite!

Written: June 1847

Source: MECW Volume 6, p. 585

First published: Gründungs dokumente des Bundes der Kommunisten (Juni bis September 1847), Hamburg, 1969

SECTION I   THE LEAGUE

Art. 1. The League aims at the emancipation of humanity by spreading the theory of the community of property and its speediest possible practical introduction.

Art. 2. The League is divided into communities and circles; at its head stands the Central Authority as the executive organ.

Art. 3. Anyone who wishes to join the League is required:

a. to conduct himself in manly fashion;
b. never to have committed a dishonourable action;
c. to recognise the principles of the League;
d. to have acknowledged means of subsistence;
e. not to belong to any political or national association;
f. to be unanimously admitted into a community, and
g. to give his word of honour to work loyally and to observe secrecy.

Art. 4. All League members are equal and brothers, and as such owe each other assistance in every situation.

Art. 5. All members bear League names.

SECTION II   THE COMMUNITY

Art. 6. A community consists of at least three and at most twelve members. Increase above that number will be prevented by division.

Art. 7. Every community elects a chairman and a deputy chairman. The chairman presides over meetings, while the deputy chairman holds the funds, into which the contributions of the members are paid.

Art. 8. The members of communities shall earnestly endeavour to increase the League by attracting capable men, and always seek to work in such a way that principles and not persons are taken as guide.

Art. 9. Admission of new members is effected by the chairman of the community and the member who has introduced the applicant to the League.

Art. 10. The communities do not know each other and bear distinctive names which they choose themselves.

SECTION III   THE CIRCLE

Art. 11. A circle comprises at least two and at most ten communities.

Art. 12. The chairmen and deputy chairmen of the communities form the circle authority. They elect a president from among themselves.

Art. 13. The circle authority is the executive organ for all the communities of the circle.

Art. 14. Isolated communities should either join an already existing circle authority or form a new circle with other isolated communities.

SECTION IV   THE CENTRAL AUTHORITY

Art. 15. The Central Authority is the executive organ of the whole League.

Art. 16. It consists of at least five members and is elected by the circle authority of the place where it is to have its seat.

SECTION V   THE CONGRESS

Art. 17. The Congress is the legislative authority of the League.

Art. 18. Every circle sends one delegate.

Art. 19. A Congress is held every year in August. The Central Authority has the right in important cases to call an extraordinary congress.

Art. 20. The Congress in office decides the place where the Central Authority is to have its seat for the current year.

Art. 21. All legislative decisions of the Congress are submitted to the communities for acceptance or rejection.

Art. 22. As the executive organ of the League, the Central Authority is responsible to the Congress for its conduct of its office and therefore has a seat in it, but no deciding vote.

SECTION VI   GENERAL REGULATIONS

Art. 23. Anyone who acts dishonourably to the principles of the League is, according to the circumstances, (removed) either removed or expelled. Expulsion precludes re-admission.

Art. 24. Members who commit offences are judged by the (supreme) circle authority, which also sees to the execution of the verdict.

Art. 25. Every community should keep the strictest watch over those who have been removed or expelled; further, it should observe closely any suspect individuals in its locality and report at once to the circle authority anything they may do to the detriment of the League, whereupon the circle authority should take the necessary measures to safeguard the League.

Art. 26. The communities and circle authorities and also the Central Authority shall meet at least once a fortnight.

Art. 27. The communities pay weekly or monthly contributions, the amount of which is determined by the respective circle authorities. These contributions will be used to spread the principles of the community of property and to pay for postage.

Art. 28. The circle authorities should render account of expenditures and income to their communities every six months.

Art. 29. The members of the circle authorities and of the Central Authority are elected for one year and should then either be confirmed anew in their office or replaced by others.

Art. 30. The elections take place in every September. The electors can, moreover, recall their officers at any time should they not be satisfied with their conduct of their office.

Art. 31. The circle authorities have to see to it that there is material in their communities for useful and necessary discussions. The Central Authority, on the other hand, should make it its duty to send to all circle authorities such questions whose discussion is important for our principle.

Art. 32. Every circle authority and failing that the community, even every League member, should, if standing alone, maintain regular correspondence with the Central Authority or a circle authority.

Art. 33. Every League member who wishes to change his residence should first inform his chairman.

Art. 34. Every circle authority is free to take any measures which it considers advisable for the security of the circle and its efficient work. These measures should, however, not be contrary to the general Rules.

Art. 35. All proposals for changes in the Rules should be sent to the Central

Authority and submitted by it to the Congress for decision.

SECTION VII   ADMISSION

Art. 36. After the Rules have been read to him, the applicant is asked by the two League members mentioned in Art. 9 to reply to the following five questions. If he replies "Yes", he is asked to give his word of honour, and is declared a League member.

These five questions are:

a. Are you convinced of the truth of the principles of the community of property?
b. Do you think a strong League is necessary for the realisation of these principles as soon as possible, and do you wish to join such a League?
c. Do you promise always to work by word and deed for spreading and the practical realisation of the principles of the community of property?
d. Do you promise to observe secrecy about the existence and all affairs of the League?
e. Do you promise to comply with the decisions of the League?

Then give us on this your word of honour as guarantee!

In the name and by the order of the Congress

Heide [Wilhelm Wolff]
Secretary

Karl Schill [Karl Schapper]
President

London, June 9, 1847

The Duties of Primary Organizations from the Constitution Adopted at the 16th Party Congress in 2002

Article 31. The primary Party organizations are militant bastions of the Party in the basic units of society, where all the Party's work proceeds and they serve as the foundation of its fighting capacity. Their main tasks are:

(1) To disseminate and carry out the Party's line, principles and policies, the decisions of the Central Committee of the Party and other higher Party organizations, and their own decisions; to give full play to the exemplary,

vanguard role of Party members, and to unite and organize the cadres and the rank and file inside and outside the Party to fulfill the tasks of their own units.

(2) To organize Party members to conscientiously study Marxism-Leninism, Mao Zedong Thought, Deng Xiaoping Theory, the important thought of Three Represents, the Party's line, principles, policies and decisions, acquire essential knowledge concerning the Party and obtain general, scientific and professional knowledge.

(3) To educate and supervise Party members, raise the overall quality of the Party membership, cultivate their Party spirit, ensure their regular participation in the activities of the Party organizations, make criticism and self-criticism, maintain and observe Party discipline, see that Party members truly fulfill their duties and protect their rights from encroachment.

(4) To maintain close ties with the masses, constantly seek their criticisms and opinions regarding Party members and the Party's work, safeguard the legitimate rights and interests of the masses and do effective ideological and political work among them.

(5) To give full scope to the initiative and creativeness of Party members and the masses and to discover, nurture and recommend fine, talented people from among Party members and the masses and encourage them to contribute their skills and learning to the reform, opening up and the socialist modernization drive.

(6) To educate and train the activists who apply for Party membership, attend to the routine work concerning the recruitment of new members and attach great importance to recruiting Party members from among those in the forefront of production and work and from among young people.

(7) To see to it that Party and non-Party cadres strictly observe the law

and administrative discipline and the financial and economic statutes and personnel regulations of the state and that none of them infringe on the interests of the state, the collective or the masses.

(8) To encourage Party members and the masses to conscientiously resist unhealthy practices and wage resolute struggles against all illegal and criminal activities.

Printed in P. R. C. by order of Canut-Berlin.

www.ingramcontent.com/pod-product-compliance
Lightning Source LLC
Chambersburg PA
CBHW051710020426
42333CB00014B/922